The Vikings
Part I

Professor Kenneth W. Harl

THE TEACHING COMPANY ®

PUBLISHED BY:

THE TEACHING COMPANY
4151 Lafayette Center Drive, Suite 100
Chantilly, Virginia 20151-1232
1-800-TEACH-12
Fax—703-378-3819
www.teach12.com

ISBN 1-59803-071-X

Kenneth W. Harl, Ph.D.
Professor of Classical and Byzantine History, Tulane University

Kenneth W. Harl is Professor of Classical and Byzantine History at Tulane University in New Orleans, where he has been teaching since 1978. He earned his Bachelor's degree from Trinity College and went on to earn his Master's and Ph.D. from Yale University.

Dr. Harl specializes in the Mediterranean civilizations of Greece, Rome, and Byzantium and in the ancient Near East. He has published numerous articles and is the author of *Civic Coins and Civic Politics of the Roman East, A.D. 180–275* and *Coinage in the Roman Economy, 300 B.C. to 700 A.D.* He is a scholar on ancient coins and the archaeology of Asia Minor (modern Turkey). He has served on the Editorial Board of the *American Journal of Archaeology* and is currently is on the Editorial Board of the *American Journal of Numismatics*.

Professor Harl's skill and dedication as an instructor are attested by his many teaching awards. He has earned Tulane's annual Student Award in Excellence nine times. He is also the recipient of Baylor University's nationwide Robert Foster Cherry Award for Great Teachers.

Table of Contents

The Vikings
Part I

The Vikings

Scope:

The Vikings have long conjured up images either of ruthless pirates ravaging the coasts of Europe or of heroic pagan warriors dedicated to Odin, god of ecstasy, poetry, and battle. These images, well attested in the medieval sources, are only part of the story of the impact of the Scandinavians on early medieval civilization. The first 12 lectures of this course deal with the evolution of a distinct civilization in Scandinavia (Denmark, Norway, and Sweden) on the eve of the Viking Age (790–1100). In 790, Scandinavians still worshiped the ancient Germanic gods and, thus, were divided from their kin in Germany or the former Roman provinces of Gaul and Britain who had adopted Christianity and Roman institutions. Breakthroughs in shipbuilding and the emergence of a warrior ethos celebrated in Eddaic and later skaldic verse turned Scandinavians from merchants into Vikings at the end of the 8th century.

The second set of 12 lectures deals with the course and impact of the Viking raids between the late 8th through the early 11th centuries. Danish and Norwegian raiders profoundly altered the political balance of Western Europe. Danes conquered and settled eastern and northern England, a region known as the *Danelaw*. They compelled King Alfred the Great of Wessex (r. 870–899) and his successors to forge an effective monarchy. In France, Vikings under Rollo embraced Christianity and settled the fief of Normandy in 911, thereby founding one of the most formidable feudal states of Europe. Norwegian Vikings settled in the main towns of Ireland and braved the North Atlantic, settling the Faeroes, Iceland, and Greenland, as well as an ephemeral colony at L'Anse aux Meadows, Newfoundland. In Eastern Europe, Swedes developed a major trade route from the Baltic to the Caspian, laying the foundations for the Russian principalities.

The last 12 lectures explain the passing of the Viking Age. Over two centuries of overseas raids, trade, and settlement altered Scandinavian civilization. Scandinavians accepted Christianity and gained the high culture of Latin Christendom. Christian Danish and Norwegian kings in the 10th century first harnessed the Viking spirit to establish monarchies. Cnut the Great (r. 1014–1035), king of

Denmark, England, and Norway, briefly turned the North Sea into a Scandinavian lake. His institutions and example inspired the formation of Christian kingdoms in Scandinavia and turned Vikings into Crusaders. Yet perhaps the most enduring of achievements of the Viking Age were the sagas and verse of Iceland that immortalized pagan heroes and Christian kings, Norse gods and indomitable settlers of the remote island.

Lecture One

The Vikings in Medieval History

Scope:

The term *Viking*, originally used for a pirate who lurked in a cove (*vik*), came to designate the Scandinavians overseas engaged in war, commerce, and settlement in 790–1100. In popular imagination, the Vikings are cast as tall Nordic warriors, sporting horned helmets and wielding axes, who descended in longships to wreck havoc upon the civilized peoples of Western Europe, the Byzantine Empire, and the Islamic world. Such perceptions are based on the hostile reports of monks, so often the victims of Viking raids, who penned the medieval chronicles. Since the Reformation, Vikings have been idealized as noble Germanic savages untouched by corrupt civilization—an image based on stereotypes created by Roman authors. In recent decades, revisionist scholars have minimized the destructiveness and, thus, the importance of the Vikings. Yet for more than 300 years, Scandinavians excelled in shipbuilding and dominated the sea and river lanes of Europe with their longships and commercial vessels (*knarr*). Their attacks on Western Europe dictated the future of feudal Europe. They braved the Atlantic Ocean to plant settlements in Iceland, Greenland, and Vinland. In Eastern Europe, Scandinavians, known as *Rus*, extended the range of their commerce and created Orthodox Russia in the 11th century. Without the Vikings, the course of medieval European civilization would have been far different.

Outline

I. The Vikings had a far-ranging impact on medieval history, but before we begin to look at that history, it may be useful to look at some of the stereotypes about Vikings with which most of us are familiar.

    A. The term *Viking* conjures up one's worst nightmare of a Nordic warrior, sporting a horned helmet, slashing with a two-headed axe, and descending upon monks and peasants from longships.

    B. The word *Viking* comes from Norse *vik*, meaning a cove or a small fjord, a place where pirates could lurk and prey upon merchant ships. The term was extended to apply to any Scandinavians living between roughly 790 and 1100 who were engaged in raiding or conquering overseas kingdoms or in establishing settlements, such as in Iceland.

C. But, the term should be used only to designate Scandinavians overseas, especially as raiders or attackers of Christian kingdoms; later, as merchants and colonizers; and eventually, as kings.

D. *Viking* was just one of several names by which Scandinavian raiders were known overseas.

    1. Frankish chronicles often referred to these raiders as *Northmen*, from which derives the name *Normans*. A common prayer in the 9th century was "Oh Lord, deliver us from the fury of the Northmen."

    2. In England, where Danes were prominent, the Vikings were usually referred to as *Danes*.

    3. The term *Norman* was used for those Scandinavians who settled in Normandy in northern France.

    4. The Scandinavians from Russia were known as the *Rus* or *Varangians*, meaning "men of the pledge." This term designated Swedes and other Scandinavians who came to serve in the Byzantine armies.

II. We have an enormous amount of information about the Vikings; unfortunately, most of it comes, at least in the early period, from their opponents.

A. We must balance the monastic chronicles and hostile reports of the Vikings' victims against archaeology and the chronicles of the Scandinavians themselves in later generations, when they converted to Christianity.

B. This course, then, looks at three very different sets of evidence: the contemporary literary records, written by Christians and some Muslims, who see the Vikings as foes; the work that has been done in archaeology, including the recovery of Viking ships and fortifications; and the sagas and poetry written in Norse in the 13th–15th centuries but reporting events that took place in the 9th century and earlier.

C. As mentioned, stereotypes color our notions of the Vikings to this day and were, perhaps, even more powerful in the 19th century.

1. For example, the operatic cycle of *Der Ring der Nibelungen*, composed by Richard Wagner in 1848–1874, is based on the Norse version of the legend of the Volsungs, the earliest set of heroes known in Scandinavian literature.
2. The heroic and idealized image of the Vikings was also captured in paintings epitomizing the primeval barbarian, untouched by civilization.
3. Unfortunately, this image was later combined with German political theories at the end of the 19th century, resulting in the Aryan ideology of the early 20th century. Some of these myths and legends were invoked by the Nazi regime in ways that would have stunned most Viking kings and warriors of the Middle Ages.

D. Modern scholarship since World War II has taken a new look at the Vikings. A great deal of work has been done in archaeology and in understanding both the Scandinavian and Western European sources.

1. Some scholars have shown a revisionist tendency in this work. Professor Peter Sawyer, for example, in his seminal history of the Vikings, tends to downgrade the size and monetary rewards of the raids. This, in turn, has led to revisions in our understanding of the impact and importance of the Vikings in Europe.
2. Revisionist scholars have also stressed the continuity between the Viking Age and earlier periods. Agricultural change, for instance, is almost nonexistent. The pattern of agriculture seen in Scandinavia in the Viking Age is very much the same as that seen 700 years earlier.
3. Several good studies have also stressed the importance of trade; the Scandinavians were probably more often engaged in trade than in raiding or attacking.
4. Some of this scholarship may have gone a bit too far, however. It tends to downgrade the significance of the Scandinavian impact in medieval Europe by stressing social and economic patterns—more "ordinary" developments—over political and military matters, which are, by definition, "extraordinary."

III. Given the nature of our sources, this course will take a broad perspective in looking at the age of the Vikings.

    A. For the first third of the course, we will look at three related subjects.

        1. The first of these is the importance of the people, geography, and early culture in Scandinavia, going back to the Bronze Age, particularly the period between 1550 and 1100 B.C. (often known as the Northern Bronze Age). In this period, many of the cultural foundations of later Viking Age Scandinavia are laid. We will come to understand the extraordinary continuity and the ancient quality of Scandinavian civilization at the time of the Viking Age.

        2. We shall also stress the importance of the ancient Scandinavian religion and its heroic, martial ethos. As a result of the survival of manuscripts in Iceland, we have the best evidence for a pre-Christian religion in medieval Europe from Scandinavia. We will look particularly at two works: the *Poetic Edda*, a collection of poems that may date back to the 9th century, and the *Prose Edda*, written by Snorri Sturluson (1179–1242), an Icelandic chieftain, which records many well-known Scandinavian myths.

        3. The last topic in the first part of the course will be the breakthroughs in shipbuilding and warfare that are an integral part of the Scandinavian background.

    B. In the second third of the course, we shall look at the Viking impact on the wider medieval world.

        1. The Vikings' impact on the Carolingian Empire, what was essentially Western Christendom in the 9th century, was profound. It revealed the weaknesses of the empire of Charlemagne and lead to the emergence of feudal states.

        2. The Vikings also had a great impact on England; we shall look in particular at the movements and attacks of the Great Army from 865–878.

        3. We shall also examine the far reaches of Viking activity, in Ireland and Russia. Remarkably, the experiences of Norwegians in Ireland and Swedes in Russia were quite comparable in many ways, although the results of these experiences were quite different.

4. As we close the second part of the course, we shall look at the most daunting and impressive of all the Viking achievements—their tackling of the North Atlantic. The Vikings were the first people to sail beyond the sight of land, and the settlement of Iceland by the Norwegians during the period 870–930 represents the first European colonial endeavor.

C. The last third of this course will shift back to the Scandinavian homeland and assess this experience in the wider medieval world for the Vikings themselves. Here, we shall look at two important developments.

1. First, we shall examine the creation of the classic Scandinavian kingdoms. At the start of the Viking Age, Norway, Denmark, and Sweden did not exist as we understand them today; the region was politically divided. By the end of the Viking Age, the kingdoms of Norway, Denmark, and Sweden had come into existence as a direct outcome of the Viking experience.

   a. The overseas ventures of the Vikings in the 9th and 10th centuries netted an enormous amount of booty and wealth and led to the creation of ever-more professional armies and better ships.

   b. Using this wealth and these fleets, sea kings imposed their control over chosen regions and set up territorial kingdoms. We see this first in Norway with King Harald Finehair (r. 880–930). Less than a generation later, the same is achieved in Denmark by Gorm the Old (r. c. 936–958), who created a kingdom in Jutland.

2. The emergence of these territorial kingdoms went hand-in-hand with the second important development—the reception of Christianity, which helped end the Viking Age. We shall look at the slow Christianizing of the society, which saw the substitution of the ancient martial ethos with the acceptance of Christian doctrines and the establishment of Christian institutions.

3. The Scandinavian Christian kings after 1100 reinvented the earlier martial ethos as a crusading mission. Our final

two lectures in this course will look at Scandinavia in the immediate aftermath of the Viking Age and show how these Christian kingdoms redefined themselves in attempting to redirect their energies toward the Crusades.

Further Reading:

John Haywood. *The Penguin Historical Atlas of the Vikings*. New York: Penguin Books, 1995.

Peter Sawyer. *The Oxford History of the Vikings*. Oxford: Oxford University Press, 1998.

Questions to Consider:

1. What accounted for the stereotypical images of the Vikings since the Middle Ages? How did these perceptions influence interpretations of the historical importance of the Vikings? How have these perceptions had wider ramifications in Western history?

2. How has the nature of the sources, both literary texts and archaeology, influenced our understanding of the Vikings? What are the value and limitations of these sources? What accounts for the current scholarly debate on the significance of the Viking Age?

Lecture One—Transcript

The Vikings in Medieval History

My name is Kenneth Harl and I teach ancient and Byzantine and early Medieval history at Tulane University in New Orleans, and I'll be guiding you through a 36-lecture course on the Vikings. This course is really an excellent way to introduce the early Middle Ages as well as medieval Scandinavia because the Vikings have a very far-ranging impact on early medieval history, and in some instances, medieval history is almost inconceivable without them. But before we get into that and the structure of this class, I think it's useful to think about some of the stereotypes about Vikings which most of us are familiar with. They usually are stereotypes that are popularized in novel and film, and they're with us, and I think they're going to endure a long time. A Viking is usually used to designate one's worst nightmare of a Nordic warrior, sporting a horned helmet, slashing with the two-headed ax, descending upon unsuspecting monks and peasants from long ships. Believe me, we'll have a fair amount of Viking pillage and attacks in Western Europe and in Russia, but this is a stereotype.

And it's important to stress that even the Scandinavians in the Middles Ages used the term Viking for a very specific occupation. The best explanation is that the word comes from Norse *vik,* meaning a cove or a small fjord. It would be a place where pirates would lurk and they could prey upon merchant ships, and so, to go a Viking, or to go out Viking, was essentially a way of saying I was going out on a pirate raid. The term then gets extended to cover any Scandinavians between roughly 790–1100 who either go on raids or are trading or conquering overseas kingdoms or even engaged in settlements, such as Iceland, which we speak of the Viking age settlement.

It's fair to say that Scandinavia from 790–1100 experienced what we call the Viking age. You can talk of Scandinavian civilization and the Viking age. On the other hand, the term Viking really should be used to designate Scandinavians overseas, especially as raiders, attackers of Christian kingdoms, and then later as merchants as well as colonizers and eventually as kings, such as King Cnut of Denmark, who conquers England in 1014–1016. So we need to keep that designation in mind. The other important thing we have to keep in mind is that Scandinavians were known by a number of names overseas. Viking was just one of several. Frankish Chronicles, that is, the monks who would be writing today in what is Western Europe, France, the lowlands, West Germany, often just vaguely referred to them as Northmen or Normani, from which we get the word Normans—that is well known in the prayers that are repeated in the 9th century, "Oh, lord, deliver us from the fury of the North Men," a common prayer as a result of Viking raids.

In England, where Danes were prominent, usually the Vikings were simply referred to as Danes. The term Norman is used for those Scandinavians who settled in Normandy in northern France. Those Scandinavians from Sweden who operated in Russia are very often known as the Rus, a word of obscure origin—there are several explanations for it—or Varangians, which means men of the pledge. That's a term used to designate especially Swedes and other Scandinavians who come to serve in the Byzantine armies, that is, their men who take an oath and fight as a retinue to the Byzantine emperor. But all of these terms are referring to the same people. They are the Scandinavians from this period in the early Middle Ages who are popularly known as the Vikings.

We have an enormous amount of information about the Vikings; unfortunately, most of it comes, at least in the early phases, from their opponents. So we're constantly filtering these monastic chronicles and hostile reports of their victims, and we're balancing that against archeology and then what the Scandinavians tell about themselves in later generations when they've converted to Christianity. Part of the theme of this course is going to be looking at really three very different sets of evidence: the contemporary literary records which are written by largely Christians; some Muslim accounts, who see the Vikings as hostile, as their worst nightmare, that stereotypical barbarian; and in the case of the Western Europeans, they're drawing on a very, very old Roman tradition of seeing Northern barbarians that way. Then we're looking at all of the work that's been done in archeology—recovery of ships, for instance, Viking settlements, and fortifications. There's really been some significant work that's been done in, say, Iceland on the early settlement patterns. Then, finally we will be looking a great deal at the sagas and the poetry written in Norse, most of these from manuscripts from the 13th, 14th, 15th centuries but reporting events going back into the 9th century and earlier. And those present some of their own problems as well. We have these three very distinct set of sources.

As for the stereotypes, I think it's important to dwell on them for a moment because they really do color our notions about the Vikings, and I've taught courses at Tulane with the Vikings prominently figured there. And many of my students always think of this commercial of a Visa card where someone doesn't pay and all of these barbarians come surging in. Most people identify them as Vikings. I think they're actually Huns, but that's slightly flashed. And many of my students come up to me and say, "Is that what happened to an English king in the 9th century when he didn't pay his debts? He was descended upon by a group of Vikings?" I assure them it didn't quite work that way. The stereotype is there, and it's very powerful. It leads to cartoons. It leads to various heroic sagas, novels, other types of genres. It was extremely powerful in the 19th century. The 19th century fixed a number of our notions about the Vikings. Richard Wagner's cycle of the *Ring*, for instance, is based on the Norse version of The Legend of the Volsungs, and we'll be talking about the Volsungs later in this course, which is the earliest set of heroes known in Scandinavian literature. And there's a later German version of it in the *Nibelungen,* but Wagner went to the Norse tradition, even though he himself was a German, and really immortalized this conception of the gods, their final destruction—in Norse that would be *Ragnarök*, in German *Gotterdammerung*—and created this very heroic image. It was also captured in contemporary paintings, and anyone who's gone to some of the palaces of Mad Ludwig of Bavaria can get a very good idea of the types of very heroic and idealized painting of the Valkyries and Sigurd who slayed the dragon.

All of these notions of almost the primeval barbarian who's untouched by civilization, these notions are also very old. They go back to Reformation, when Scandinavians and Germans were shaking off the control of the Roman Catholic Church and very often pointed to the Vikings and the Scandinavians as their original ancestors. You have this very, very powerful heroic notion that is really capsulized in the 19th-century music and literature. It then unfortunately gets matched up with some German political ideology at the end of the 19th century and, presto, you have your Aryan ideology of the 20th century, the Second World War, in which some of these myths and legends were invoked by the Nazi regime in ways that I think would really stun most Viking kings and warriors of the Middle Ages. They couldn't imagine how these images would get misused.

Modern scholarship since the Second World War has really taken a new look at the Vikings, and there has been a great deal of work done on not only the archeology but understanding the sources, both the Scandinavian as well as the Western European sources. There has been a tendency among some scholars to revise their opinion. Some of these notions have gone a bit extreme. Professor Peter Sawyer has pioneered some of these arguments in a really seminal work that came out about 30 years ago on the age of the Vikings, and he tends to downgrade the importance of the raids, the size of the raids, the amount of money that might have been taken in plunder or Danegeld, which is essentially a Viking payoff. The Vikings essentially fine the Frankish king in silver and that's called Danegeld, payment of money to the Danes—it's also paid in England—and these numbers have been reassessed. This has led to revisions about the importance and impact of the Vikings, how much of a destructive impact they had. It's often noted that Western Europe at the time of the 8th and 9th centuries was a pretty violent place, and the Vikings were just part of the general landscape of mayhem that characterized most of medieval Europe.

There has also been a tendency in the revisionist scholarship to stress the continuity between the Viking age and the earlier periods as well as the later periods. For instance, agricultural change is almost nonexistent, as the pattern of agriculture you saw in Scandinavia in the Viking age is very much the same you would have seen 700 years earlier, and this has also led to an effort to stress the continuity, the fact that many people in Scandinavia were not engaged in the Viking raids. Several very, very good studies have stressed the importance of trade; you really can't have piracy without trade. One of the notions would be that the Vikings, or the Scandinavians, to be more accurate, were probably more often engaged in trade rather than raiding or attacking. Again, you have to qualify what the monastic chronicles tell you. There has been an effort to understand the Scandinavians within their own archeological context as well as their raw culture that we can reconstruct. Now some of these opinions have gone a bit too far in my opinion; they've tended to downgrade the importance of the Scandinavian impact in medieval

Europe. And that is because you are stressing social and economic patterns, more ordinary developments, and you tend to put on the sidelines matters such as military and political which, by definition, are always extraordinary. One of our efforts in this course will be to balance those two perspectives, to try to bring in what all the new archeology tells us, the new understanding of what life was like in Scandinavia in the Viking age against the record of the Viking attacks, take into account that many of these again are from hostile sources, but nonetheless these attacks were of a major order and had a very, very significant impact throughout most of Western Europe, particularly in the 9th and 10th century. And that is part of our task to balance that.

That gets us to the organization of this course and what I plan to do. Because of the nature of the sources and what I wish to achieve in this class, we're going to take a somewhat broader perspective of one might think of the age of the Vikings. The first third of this class we're going to look at three related subjects. One is the importance of people, geography, and early culture in Scandinavia going back into the Bronze Age, particularly the period between 1550–1100 B.C., very often known as the Northern Bronze Age, where really many of the cultural foundations of later Viking age Scandinavia are laid.

What is extraordinary is to understand the continuity and the ancient quality of Scandinavian civilization at the time of the Viking age. It was by no means new and the Scandinavian gods had been worshipped in one form or another for well over 1,000 years before the Viking age began. Also, in this first part I want to stress very much the importance of the ancient Scandinavian religion as well as its heroic ethos. This requires us to look at what the Scandinavians themselves thought about it. We have in Scandinavia the best evidence for a pre-Christian religion anywhere in medieval Europe, that is, because of the extraordinary survival of manuscripts in Iceland, above all, two works I'll refer to repeatedly. One is the *Poetic Edda*, which is a series of manuscripts that collect poems which may go back to the 9th and 10th century—it is disputed—and these are poems, some of them, are gnomic poems. There's the wonderful Voluspa of a seeress, prophetess, a *völva* in Old Norse, who tells of the origins of the world and its destruction. These poems give us an insight into the heroes and gods of the pagan past. Only in

Iceland and Scandinavia has this type of information survived, and it's because of the peculiar nature of the conversion of Scandinavia to Christianity, particularly the conversion of Iceland, which was by, in effect, an act of parliament and was not accompanied by the kind of zealous destruction that you would get in other parts of medieval Europe.

The second important work is a work in prose by Snorri Sturluson who lived between 1179 and 1242, an Icelandic chieftain of rather dubious reputation. He gets assassinated in these really bizarre politics of the early 13th century. He is a prolific writer, an incredibly witty author, and he wrote a work called the *Prose Edda,* which comes in three parts. And the first part, in particular, which is really set as a conversation between the legendary King of Sweden and these three mysterious figures, records many of the myths that were apparently well known in Scandinavia. This literature, to be sure, at the end of the Viking age and just after the Viking age has to be qualified. It's written by Scandinavians who were Christians; it's written in the Latin alphabet. Nonetheless, it gives us a window into the gods and the religion of these people and it corresponds extraordinarily well with what we're told in classical sources, that is, Greek sources, Roman sources of the Roman Empire, as well as what medieval sources tell us and as well as what the archeology tells us. We're in an exceptional position to look at the importance of these pagan cults and how they shaped the Scandinavians in the Viking age.

Finally, the breakthroughs in shipbuilding and warfare are part of that Scandinavian background. That is what we will look at in the first third of this course: The cultural background, the geography landscape, the religion, and the achievements in shipbuilding and warfare that made the Viking age possible.

The second third of this course we're going to shift and look at the Viking impact on the wider medieval world, and here we will really range quite widely; and, if nothing else, the scope of Viking activities is nothing short of staggering. Their impact on the Carolingian Empire—arguably, really Western Christendom in the 9th century was essentially the Carolingian Empire—was extremely profound. It would reveal the weaknesses of the emperor Charlemagne. It would lead to the emergence of feudal states. Most of the feudal states of northern Europe, actually the states that went on Crusade in the 11th and 12th century, can be traced back to lords who emerged during the Viking age who could fight off Viking attacks, consolidate their area where the monarchy had failed.

The Viking attacks really have a very important role in propelling the development of what we would call feudal Europe. They also had a profound impact on England—we'll be spending two lectures there—especially the attacks of the great army from 865 – 878, and the movements of that Viking army, which were primarily Danes, really force us to re-evaluate our notions about their being mindless barbarians who simply attack and plunder. The scale of movements, the logistics, their understanding of the political situation in England which they exploit very adroitly—they are able to play off the competing English kingdoms—within a matter of 15 years they overthrow three English kingdoms and virtually bring King Alfred to his knees. It really is an extraordinary story in and of itself. The Viking impact in England really does make the Kingdom of England possible. The settlement of Danes in England is on a very large scale. We'll be looking at that as well. We'll also be examining their impact on Ireland and Russia, that is, in the east and the west, the far ends of Viking activity, and remarkably those two experiences, one of Norwegians in Ireland and Swedes in Russia, are really quite comparable in many ways. We will see that the results will be quite different. In Ireland, it does not lead to any political unity. In Russia, it leads to the creation of this orthodox kingdom around Kiev which becomes the basis of the Russian state, but in their initial stages Norwegians and Swedes were essentially after the same thing. They were engaged in the slave trade. They were engaged in raiding. They set up in ports, or in the case of Russia fortified market towns, on rivers to develop trade routes. So that both in Russia and Ireland you'll see a very, very, similar pattern in the way the Scandinavians operated overseas.

And, finally, in this second third of the course we must look at perhaps the most daunting and impressive of all of the Viking achievements, and that is their tackling of the North Atlantic. These are the first people who sail outside of the sight of land. The discovery of the North Atlantic islands, the Shetlands, the Faeroes, Iceland, Greenland, and ultimately their brief venture into Vinland, really has fired everyone's imagination. Most Americans, at least, immediately recognize the names Eric the Red, really responsible for what I always think was the first land fraud in Western European history—he settled Greenland by giving it the name Greenland—and why the Icelanders followed him, they were really desperate for free land, the ones that went along with him—and his son, Leif the Lucky, who is credited with the discovery of North America. This is really an extraordinary venture. In the overall scheme of things, Greenland was a pretty remote settlement, and the Scandinavians had a very, very vague notion of what Vinland is. It's essentially Newfoundland. They didn't really understand they had found a new continent, but the settlement of Iceland is a remarkable achievement. Iceland, just below the Arctic Circle, was settled largely by Norwegians between 870 and 930. In Iceland, and to some extent you would have seen this in Greenland and Vinland also, is really the first European colonial settlement or the first frontier society that Europeans set up outside the core of European civilization. Iceland is extremely well illuminated for us by its family sagas and its other documents. It's also important to us because Iceland is where most of this literature will survive, and it's one of the great achievements of the Viking age that Iceland was settled the way it was.

The last third of this course is then going to shift back to the Scandinavian homeland and try to assess what that experience in the second third of the course, meant for the homeland. There we'll look at two very important themes, and these themes will actually take us a bit beyond our usual date. The Viking age is usually thought to end around 1100, and that will get us to look at the creation of the classic Scandinavian kingdoms. At the start of the Viking age there was no Norway, Denmark, or Sweden as we understand them today. In the course of these lectures I will refer to these areas, but they must really be looked upon very tentatively as geographic regions.

For instance, Denmark in the Middle Ages is twice the size that the modern kingdom is today. It included the entire peninsula of Jutland, all of the Danish islands, and the southern provinces of Sweden, particularly Holland and Skane, which are now part of Sweden. They've been part of Sweden since 1658 but in the Viking age would have been cut off by forests, so they were virtually islands. And they're really attached to the Danish kingdom. Norway was at least four or five distinct areas. No one knew whether this would ever come together as a kingdom or not. In Sweden you're dealing not only with the Swedes, the Svear, that is, the Swedes proper living around Lake Mälaren which is where Stockholm is today, but also people known as the Gotha, or Gotias in Old English, the Goths, in what are now the Swedish provinces of Västergötland and Östergötland, and these were an independent Scandinavian people who had their own rulers through most of the Middle Ages.

You're looking at an extremely diversified and politically divided area. By the end of the Viking age, the kingdoms that we know as Norway, Denmark, and Sweden have come into existence. They are a direct outcome of that Viking experience for two reasons: one, the overseas ventures, especially in the 9th and 10th centuries, netted an enormous amount of booty and wealth, and it also led to the creation of ever more professional armies, warriors who must be counted as some of the best soldiers of the Middle Ages, and increasingly better ships. The classic long ships or the great dragon ships are really from the late 10th and 11th centuries, and with these types of fleets, with this wealth, with these professional warriors sea kings, that is, Scandinavian monarchs who had made their reputations by raiding and battling overseas, could use this military power to impose their control over areas and set up territorial kingdoms. We see this first in Norway, with King Harald Finehair, operating somewhere around 880 to 930, who gives the first definition to Norway and its sea power that enables him to do this. In fact, it's the only way he could ever run Norway, is by the sea.

Less than a generation later the same is achieved in Denmark with a figure by the name of Gorm the Old, who creates a kingdom in Jutland, and eventually that comes to encompass the Danish king of the Middle Ages I just described. It's later in Sweden—the Swedish kingdom is really almost a composite between those two groups, the Swedes and the Goths, or the Gotar, but even by 1100 there clearly is going to be a Swedish kingdom. It's a question of what family is going to rule and which of the two groups is going to have the major say in this. There is a capital, the Swedes have converted to Christianity, and there will be a Swedish kingdom. That's an important point to stress because today in Europe among the various political structures that exist today, with the exception of England, the three Scandinavian kingdoms can quite legitimately trace their descent back to the kings and the institutions that were set up in the Viking age. Now only England has that same claim that it has a continuous monarchy—there's a slight interruption with Cromwell— that goes back into the Middle Ages as well. That is an extraordinary achievement coming out of the Viking age that these kingdoms were forged.

The emergence of those territorial kingdoms go hand in hand with another important development, a development that helps end the Viking age, and that is the reception of Christianity. We will spend a fair amount of time on that issue. Not only the question of conversion, that is, Scandinavians embracing, usually, Christ as a legitimate God but also the Christianizing of the society whereby slowly—this takes 300 years. It's in some ways not completed until the 12th century, until after the Viking age. But it sees the substitution of the ancient martial ethos that I'll be talking about in the first third, the old heroes, with the Christian vision, with the acceptance of the Christian doctrines of the transcendent God, with the notions of Heaven and Hell, and the setting up of institutions of Christianity.

I often make the distinction between conversion and institutional Christianity. Institutional Christianity would be bishops, the churches, the whole structure of the medieval Western church, which those territorial kings, those sea kings, will impose. Very often, the imposition of Christianity is closely linked with successful Viking sea kings who often convert to Christianity while serving overseas. They come into contact with the great cathedrals, the monarchies of England and France, and any monarch, and especially an aspiring monarch, loves to have bishops because bishops do neat things for you. They give you coronations, create great ceremonies; you build neat churches, and it makes you look a big league power. Many of these early Christian kings, King Cnut of Denmark, Norway, and England at one point, St. Olaf of Norway, later kings of Sweden such as Olaf and his son Anund Jakob, all of them want the ceremony, the legitimacy, the high services associated with bishops in Episcopal structure. And therefore their monarchies are often very closely promoted at the same time that institutional Christianity is imposed, setting up bishops, benefices, and the like.

In the last third of the course, we're really looking at two things: one is the political transformation of Scandinavia into these kingdoms, which is a direct result of Viking age; and the second is the reception of Christianity and its adaption, its assimilation into a Scandinavian civilization, and that, too, is part of the Viking heritage. Those first missionaries got to Scandinavia because of the trade routes and the attacks of the Viking age. Starting very early in the 9th century, one of the ways of halting Viking raids came to Louis the Pious, probably one of the most original, probably the only original thought Louis ever had, which is try to convert the Northmen, make them follow Christians so they'll stop attacking us. This is carried out over the course of the 9th and 10th century with little success. We'll go into that, why it's difficult for the first missionaries to have any impact on the Scandinavians, but once we get into the late 10th and early 11th centuries where we have these powerful sea kings after 250 years of Viking activity, they're able to give the backing to the bishops and the missionaries to make Christianity not only a religion of victory but the religion of a monarchy and acceptable to the Scandinavian populations. That conversion to Christianity and that Christianizing of Scandinavian society is one of the reasons why the Viking age eventually passes. The Scandinavians are essentially brought into the wider European community.

I'll close with a few thoughts on what that meant for Scandinavia, above all for the early Christian kings coming after 1100. What they did with that martial ethos is essentially reinvent it as a crusading activity. The final two lectures will look at Scandinavia in the immediate aftermath of the Viking age and how these Christian kingdoms redefine themselves and how particularly Denmark and Sweden attempted to direct their energies in crusading activities in the Baltic regions, particularly the eastern and the southern shores of the Baltic, hoping to carve out larger Christian kingdoms. In the case of both Scandinavian kingdoms, Sweden and Denmark, in the long run it didn't succeed, but it is an important way of measuring how civilization had changed and really why the Viking age eventually comes to pass. With that, we will close with this course.

Lecture Two

Land and People of Medieval Scandinavia

Scope:

Scandinavia as a political and cultural term is more than the peninsula shared by Norway and Sweden, because it includes Denmark, the Faeroe Islands, and Iceland, settled by the Norse in the 9th century. In the Viking era, Scandinavia was cut off from Central Europe by dense forests, and only a single road, Haerveg (the "army route"), linked Jutland with Germany. Scandinavia, which is defined by the Baltic Sea and the North Sea and Atlantic Ocean, was best traversed by water. In the enclosed, nearly freshwater Baltic Sea, Swedes and Danes learned navigation early, then applied these lessons to the dangerous, rough waters of the North Sea and Atlantic Ocean. For all the diversity of landscape in their homeland, the medieval Scandinavians were bound by a common way of life based on the sea and a common culture, ancestry, and worship of ancestral gods.

Outline

I. This lecture introduces the land and peoples of Scandinavia and stresses some of the major features of the Scandinavian landscape, notably the northern climate, the forests, and the seas, that dictated the course of Scandinavian history. The lecture also introduces the ancestors of the Scandinavians, those who gave rise to the Danes, Swedes, and Norwegians.

II. The term *Scandinavia* is used geographically to define the peninsula that is shared by Norway and Sweden. Norway is cut off from Sweden by the Kjolen ("Keel") mountain range and faces toward the North Sea and the Atlantic. Sweden is oriented east toward the Baltic. Thus, when we use the term *Scandinavia* in this course, it has much more of a cultural sense than just a geographic term.

    A. In this understanding of *Scandinavia*, we also include Denmark, which encompassed Jutland; the four large Danish islands, Sjaelland (Sjaelland), Funen, Lolland, and Falster; islands in the Baltic; and the islands of Öland and Gotland.

B. The Aland Islands and Finland were linked culturally to Sweden and, therefore, to Scandinavia.

C. Finally, colonies established in Iceland during the Viking Age are also considered to be part of the cultural unit of Scandinavia.

III. We begin with some of the key features of Scandinavia that will influence the culture and history of its people.

    A. First and foremost, the winters in Scandinavia are brutal, especially in Norway and Sweden. Sailing is possible for only five or six months of the year, and the icebergs in the North Atlantic posed serious threats to any early vessel.

        1. We shall learn more about these conditions as we explore the Icelandic sagas. Our first record of the harsh Scandinavian winters comes from a Greek explorer, Pytheas, who traveled up the rivers of Gaul, took passage to Britain, sailed across the North Sea, and landed on the northern coast of Norway, near the Arctic Circle.

        2. Pytheas tells us that the natives grew barley and vegetables, which they were able to do because of the long hours of sunlight. He also speaks of the aurora borealis, assumed by later Scandinavians of the Viking Age to be the Valkyries of Odin riding across the skies.

    B. Scandinavians learned to adjust to this landscape and exploit its possibilities early in their history. They engaged in trapping and hunting in the winter, as well as local and regional trade. Thanks to the creation of skis, sleds, and skates, the early Scandinavians were quite capable of travel in winter.

    C. The long winters preconditioned a number of social habits and attitudes in Scandinavia. For example, it was wrong to deny hospitality to travelers, particularly in winter; in later Scandinavian legends and myths, such travelers were frequently gods. Further, in the early spring, before planting and sailing were possible, the great halls of Scandinavian leaders were the centers of festivals and religious activities.

    D. Another important feature of the landscape influencing Scandinavian history was the great forests.

1. In the Viking Age and before, Scandinavia was covered by dense forests and largely cut off from the rest of Europe by those forests. The only overland access into Scandinavia was a narrow track, the Haerveg ("army route"), which ran from Germany to the northern shore of Jutland.

2. Denmark was largely cut off from outside influences in the 9th and 10th centuries; there was no real threat of external invasion. This was also true of Norway and Sweden.

3. Of course, the forests were also an important resource to most Scandinavians. Denmark, parts of southern Norway, and the regions around Lake Mälaren in central Sweden contained deciduous forests, especially oak, which was important for shipbuilding and fuel.

4. Almost 75 percent of Sweden was covered with forests in the Viking Age. The conditions were even more extreme in Norway, where only 3 to 5 percent of the land was arable. Seventy percent of Norway above the tree line is mountain, and perhaps 25 percent is pine forest.

E. The sea is a third feature of influence throughout Scandinavian history. Knowledge of the sea was, perhaps, the common experience that bound all the Scandinavians together before and during the Viking Age.

1. The sea was the fastest means of travel. According to Adam of Bremen, writing in c. 1070, the journey by land from Roskilde in Denmark through central Sweden to Uppsala would require about four to six weeks. This same journey by ship took only three to five days.

2. Adam also gives us sailing distances along the shores of the Baltic. To reach Hedeby on the eastern shore of Jutland in southern Denmark from any of the Baltic ports took a week by sea but four to eight weeks by land.

3. Norse legends always account travel by land as long and arduous, whereas travel by sea is quick and relatively easy.

F. Their closeness to the sea gave the Scandinavians several advantages in seaborne commerce.

1. Scandinavia is washed by the Baltic and by the North Sea and the Atlantic. The Baltic is an enclosed sea, almost a freshwater lake. Despite its squalls and mists, it can be navigated easily and is teeming with fish. Further, the Baltic's patterns of currents and winds favored travel from west to east; therefore, Hedeby in Jutland, ports in Sjaelland, the Swedish island of Gotland, and the Swedish market towns on Lake Mälaren became prime ports for sailing.

2. The Scandinavians, starting with their first efforts at shipbuilding in the Neolithic Age, gained critical navigation skills and experience that would serve to their advantage in the Viking Age. They were accustomed to memorizing landmarks and experimenting with shipbuilding in the enclosed waters of the Baltic, expertise that could then be transferred to tackling the North Sea and the Atlantic.

IV. We shall close this lecture with a brief look at the peoples living in Scandinavia in earliest times and through the Viking Age.

A. Unfortunately, our archaeological evidence is not particularly good; we must depend on literary descriptions of Scandinavians written at later times. These include descriptions by Roman authors, starting with Julius Caesar in the 1st century B.C.; Christian writers of the medieval period; and Arab geographers.

B. Such writers uniformly give us the impression that the Scandinavians were tall and had fair complexions, light eyes, and blonde or reddish hair. By the standards of the Mediterranean and Western European worlds, the Scandinavians were large, probably the result of their diet. All the southern sources agree that the Scandinavians were, above all, hardy.

C. The Scandinavians did not seem to be conscious of any racial distinctions among themselves. A peculiar poem, the *Rigsthula* (c. 9th–10th century), refers to the creation of the classes in Scandinavia, the aristocrats, the farmers, and the thralls, all fathered by the god Heimdall. All three classes seem to take on the qualities of various figures in Norse mythology.

D. What really seemed to matter to the Scandinavians was speaking the Norse language, worshiping the ancestral gods, and being part of the Norse community, which was shaped by the landscape. In the next lecture, we shall look at these cultural and linguistic factors.

Further Reading:

John Haywood. *The Penguin Historical Atlas of the Vikings*. New York: Penguin Books, 1995.

Gwyn Jones. *A History of the Vikings*. Oxford: Oxford University Press, 1968.

Questions to Consider:

1. How have the climate and natural resources of Scandinavia influenced the course of civilization since the Neolithic Age (4000–2300 B.C.)? What resources were crucial for sustaining population growth and long-distance trade?

2. How have the seas united and challenged Scandinavians? Why did Scandinavians excel in seafaring and shipbuilding? How important a role has seaborne commerce played in Scandinavian history?

Lecture Two—Transcript

Land and People of Medieval Scandinavia

In this lecture, I plan to introduce the lands and peoples of Scandinavia, and this is an opportunity to stress some of the major features in the Scandinavian landscape. And that will notably be the Northern climate, the forests and the seas, that will dictate Scandinavian history really from the start of agriculture in what we call the Neolithic period, starting somewhere in 4000 B.C., through the entire of our course, to the end of the Viking age in 1100 A.D. and even beyond.

I also want to introduce the ancestors of the Scandinavians—the people who eventually gave rise to the Danes, Swedes, Norwegians, the people of the Viking age. And again, there will be some important points to stress that this population of Scandinavians or their ancestors, going back at least into the Bronze Age, were a relatively homogeneous group of people, and the Scandinavians in the Viking age were therefore the heirs of a very, very long cultural continuity, a continuity of settlement, which is going to be an important feature about Viking age civilization.

Well, first I should start with the term "Scandinavia." The term is used geographically to define the peninsula that is shared by Norway and Sweden. And in that restricted sense, it's correct to speak of the Scandinavian Peninsula. And that peninsula is really rather deceptive because it doesn't imply the unity that most maps would tend to give the viewer. A map is a two-dimensional reproduction of a three-dimensional reality. Norway is cut off from Sweden by a really impressive mountain range, the "Kjolen" or the "keel," which essentially breaks off the two kingdoms, the two future kingdoms. So Norway faces to the North Sea and the Atlantic, whereas Sweden orients east on the Baltic.

And so when Scandinavia is used in this course, it is more than just that geographic term. It refers to the Scandinavian peoples. It has much more a cultural sense. And there we have to include Denmark. And Denmark, as I noted in the first lecture, politically is much larger than the modern kingdom. It's over twice the size. But Scandinavia includes the peninsula of Jutland, which is partially German territory today. Most of Schleswig is now in German territory. It would have been part of Denmark in the Middle Ages. It includes the Danish islands, notably the great island of Sjaelland, or Sjaelland, as we say in English, Fyn, or Funen, as it's sometimes rendered, Lolland, and Falster, which are the four big islands. It includes the islands in the Baltic, Bornholm, now part of the Danish kingdom, and the islands of Öland and Gotland, which are attached to the Swedish kingdom. And Gotland will play an extremely important role in commercial activities, well, really from the very start of the Bronze Age and running through the Viking age and beyond.

Finland—notably the islands between Sweden and Finland today, the Aland Islands, which are really inhabited by Swedish speakers but are now part of Finland, were awarded to Finland by the old League of Nations, and Finland, notably its southwestern and southern shores, are culturally very closely linked to Sweden and therefore to Scandinavia. And even today, Finland is often included in Scandinavia in that cultural sense. Because the Fins came under very, very profound influence from Scandinavian civilization, we will find that actually Fins team up with Swedes to form part of the Rus, the Vikings who operated in Russia from the 8th through the 11th centuries. And so Finland, while inhabited by peoples who speak a completely different language—Finnish is a glutenin language with its own structure, very, very different from the dramatic languages of Scandinavia—nonetheless, culturally Finland is part of this world. And, finally, Iceland, the Faeroe Islands in the north Atlantic, these are colonies that are established in the Viking age. They too are part of that Scandinavian cultural unit today.

Well, with that definition, let's look at some of the key features that will influence Scandinavian history and the landscape that will shape very much human activity and the culture that emerges in Scandinavia by the Viking age. Well, first and foremost, the northern climates, this is something that most viewers are familiar with. Scandinavia immediately denotes a cold place, and understandably so. The winters can be brutal, especially in Norway and Sweden. Denmark is more favored because it's much farther south and it receives many of the benefits of the warmer climate being generated by the North Atlantic drift, or the Gulf Stream, as we call it.

But even Norway benefits from that Gulf Stream so that habitation and certain types of farming and stock raising is possible in Norway, all the way up along the northern shores of Norway, Halogoland, that is, areas that are just below the Arctic circle, just beyond the Arctic circle. It's extraordinary how far north the Norwegians will be able to plant their settled life. Nonetheless, the winters are harsh. Sailing conditions are often obstructed. Sailing, perhaps five months a year, six months a year, is the best you can get. The icebergs in the North Atlantic would pose a very, very serious threat to any early vessel. And so it always must be remembered, as we lecture in the Viking age, that the harsh winters, these conditions are just a given fact in Scandinavian history. And they're easy to forget, although the Scandinavians themselves make reference to them all the time in the literature of the Viking age, especially in the Icelandic sagas that we'll draw upon to discuss much of what we know of Viking age history.

The earliest explanation of some of these conditions comes from a Greek writer, a fellow named Pytheas of Massilia. Massilia is the ancient city, which is now represented by Marseille in Southern France, and Pytheas traveled north following the rivers of Gaul, today France, took passage over to Britain and sailed across the North Sea somehow and landed in a place called Thule, or Tulle, as it's sometimes called, *Thule Ultima*, which to him was the edge of the world, and by best guess this is the northern coast of Norway. It could have been somewhere around Trondelag, or more likely Halogoland, up by the Arctic circle. He is the first southerner, actually the first writer of anywhere, who observes the fact that the natives in this area, and he seems to be describing the ancestors of the Norwegians, can grow barley and vegetables. And they're able to do this, even though the growing season is short. In those high latitudes, you have long hours of sunlight or twilight—this is the land of midnight sun, and Pytheas is the first person to describe it—and this allows you to cultivate crops that otherwise would have been impossible.

He also makes a number of important observations of astronomy on the latitudes and longitudes of the earth, and it was all eventually published in a book on the oceans. And later, classical authors cited Pytheas's work about the northern peoples, and it was premised on the earth as a globe until the 6th century, where Pytheas comes into criticism by Christian authors who were convinced that the earth is flat, and Pytheas suffers a decline in reputation in the Middle Ages. He's usually called a fool. And it turns out that Pytheas was right—

the earth is a globe—but so much for publishing and perishing, if you make the wrong conclusion.

Furthermore, you're in those northern climates. Again, we get this from Pytheas that the spectacular emissions of light, the so-called Aurora Borealis, which the later Scandinavians of the Viking age assume were the Valkyries of Odin, the great war god, that is, his warrior princesses riding across the skies. It is really quite a spectacular landscape. And, furthermore, Scandinavians very early learned to adjust to this landscape and exploit its possibilities even in the winters.

For one, a great deal of trapping and hunting could occur in the winter, as well as a fair amount of local and regional trade. From an early day, the Scandinavians, and before them, the Lapps, the people now known as the Sami, who were in the extreme sections of Scandinavia and Finland and Northern Russia, learned to travel at winter by the creation of skis and of sleighs and skates. There's a considerable amount of travel that can go overland on frozen rivers, and there are occasions when the Sund or the *erra Sund* of that narrow strait between the Danish island of Sjaelland and of Southern Sweden, Skane, will freeze. And you can actually move people and goods across the ice. And so the winters in some ways turn out to be a way of transportation.

Furthermore, the long winters preconditioned a lot of social habits and attitudes we'll see in Scandinavia. It was wrong to deny hospitality to travelers, particularly in the wintertime. And in later Scandinavian legends and myth, those could be gods. And if you turned aside, it could be the god Thor and Loki traveling in disguise. You certainly don't want to turn away strangers for that. Poets, bards, men who were expert in the recitation of the great poems and legends, would always find a welcome in the great halls of kings and jarls—jarls is the Scandinavian equivalent of an earl—whenever they came knocking in the long wintertime.

In the early spring before you could do the planting and the sailing, the great halls were generally the centers of all sorts of festivities, boasts, religious activities, and so from the start, the northern climate will precondition or influence a lot of the social, and even religious, attitudes of Scandinavians. And I mentioned two in passing, and one is the fact that in the Scandinavian conception of the afterlife, the worst conditions one can come up with is cold and the blue color of death, and hence Niflheim, the underworld of the Scandinavians, is a cold place. And I often wonder what early pagan Vikings must have made of Christian missionaries talking about Hell as a place of fiery torment. That made no sense to Norwegians and Swedes. This is the image of the fire in the garden being imported from the Near East.

And even the depiction of the Devil in later European art, starting from the 14th and 15th centuries, where he's depicted as blue, that comes out of an old dramatic tradition of the blue color of death, hell. The daughter of Loki who presides over the underworld is actually described as bluish in color or half-bluish in color. And so the physical reality of Scandinavia will influence not only their social and economic conditions but even their religious outlook.

Another important feature in Scandinavian history will be the Great Forests. And here we really have to remove our preconceptions of what Northern Europe in general looks like in antiquity and the Middle Ages, the farms and the villages and towns with their beautiful churches and steeples. The very carefully manicured landscape of Western and Northern Europe today is something that has evolved over the centuries. In the Viking age and before, Scandinavia was covered with dense forests. And Scandinavia was largely cut off from the rest of Europe by those forests. The only overland access into Scandinavia was a track, later turned into what is known as a corduroy or wooden road. It's essentially laying logs down. This is known as the *Haerveg*. In Scandinavian accounts, it means the "Army Way." And that was a route that traveled from Germany across Jutland to the northern end of Jutland—it dead-ended at the northern shore of Jutland—and it was a pretty narrow track. And it was essentially the only route for transportation into the Danish Peninsula, and then from there you would have to take passage by sea.

And so Denmark was largely cut off from outside influence in the 9th and 10th century. There was no real threat of an invasion. And this is also true of Norway and Sweden much more. There was never an external threat. And throughout the entire of the Viking age, the Vikings could raid their opponents at will, not only because they had the ships; there's no need to maintain armies, the fortifications, the necessary defenses and institutions that would be essential if you shared a common border with an opponent.

Furthermore, those forests turned out to be an important resource to most of the Scandinavians. Denmark, which included parts of Southern Sweden today, the areas of Skane, Halland, and Blekinge, those regions, which only passed to Sweden in 1658, are parts of Southern Norway, the area around the city of Oslo today, the Viken—that's the great fjord that cuts deep into Southern Norway— and the regions especially around Lake Mälaren in Central Sweden. There you had deciduous forests, especially oak, extremely important for building material, especially for shipbuilding and for fuel. Pine trees covered most of Northern Scandinavia. By one estimate, anywhere from perhaps two-thirds to 75 percent of Sweden was covered with forests in the Viking age. Lumber was one of the biggest commodities the Swedes had, and it only was over time, especially after 1100, after the Viking age, when they really begin to clear the forests and put the area under cultivation. So the forests are a major feature throughout Scandinavia.

In Norway, the conditions are even more extreme. The best estimate today is about three to five percent of Norway is really arable, and that's located in the sheltered fjords along the west and in the area around Oslo and its hinterland, the uplands. Seventy percent of Norway is mountain above the tree line. Perhaps close to 25 percent of it is pine forests.

So the forest proved to be a barrier in some ways, and, on the other hand, it is also a major resource. And it's no accident that Scandinavians excelled in shipbuilding, in woodcarving, all types of timbered construction and really never developed masonry architecture. I mean the material is not there. You're not in the Mediterranean world where you have just lots of limestone and marble hanging around, the way the Greeks and Romans can work it.

The third feature that I mentioned at the start of this lecture was the sea. And the sea has to be stressed constantly throughout Scandinavian history. It is perhaps the common experience that binds all the Scandinavians together, certainly in the Viking age, but even in these earlier periods. It is the fastest way to move around. And there are some very, very good figures on this from the later Middle Ages, provided by the account of Adam of Bremen, who wrote the history of the archbishops of Hamburg and Bremen, that is, the German archbishop who claimed authority over Scandinavia. And he gives us some very telling distances.

For instance, in Roskilde, which is on the island of Sjaelland, the capital of Denmark, if you try to travel to Sweden, which would be Central Sweden today, to Uppsala, the great sanctuary of the gods, it would take four to six weeks under the best conditions during the summer to travel by land. You had to go through some major forest zones. On the other hand, if you took passage by ship, you could be in Uppsala perhaps within three days, certainly within five days.

Sailing distances are likewise given for along the shores of the Baltic. To reach Hedeby, on the eastern shore of Jutland in Southern Denmark, to any of the ports of the various Baltic peoples, which today would be Latvia or Lithuania, you're talking travel time anywhere from four to six weeks by land, maybe two months in some instances, whereas, at most, it's a week by sea, depending on what type of vessel you take and the sailing conditions. To be sure, you can only sail in certain times of the year. But the sea is the key link. And in the case of Norway, it's all-essential. Travel in Norway is always by sea. The unification of Norway will be by sea power, starting with Harald Finehair at the end of the 9th century. And here again, we have very good information on the traveling conditions in the Viking age.

We are told in this important document, written at the Court of King Alfred the Great in the 9th century, a Norwegian merchant prince, whose name is Ottar, who hunts walrus and trades with the Lapps up near the Arctic circle, explains that it is a month's travel from the distant reaches of Norway to the south to Kaupang, the main market town, which is in the general vicinity of Oslo. And he's traveling on a slow cargo-moving vessel, which is trading along the way. And he says it's about a month's travel. It's well known. And you have to remember, that is a remarkable achievement. Norway is over a thousand miles of coastline, and Norway is essentially half the length of Europe.

So these daunting distances can be traversed by the sea. And that is very, very well captured in Norse mythology, where arduous travel is always through dense forests and mountains, whereas in the legends and the myths, traveling by sea is quick; it's speedy actually. You get changes of scenery and of action in Norse myths and saga by simply saying, "Well, they took passage and now they're at the next court." This occurs very illogically in the Volsung saga where Gunnar and some of his friends traveled to the Court of Attila the Hun by sea.

This happens to be located in Central Europe, but we won't get into the details of geography and legend.

Therefore, Scandinavia will always depend on seaborne commerce, and here the Scandinavians have several other advantages. For one, Scandinavia is essentially washed by two different seas, or big bodies of water. One is the Baltic, and the other is the North Sea and the Atlantic. It's anyone's guess where the North Sea ends and the Atlantic begins. The Baltic is an enclosed sea. And sometimes it's compared to the Mediterranean, that is, the northern version of the Mediterranean. It is almost a freshwater lake; that is, it was created with the retreat of the glaciers after 8000 B.C. It receives an enormous amount of fresh water from the great river systems of Central and Eastern Europe, the Oder, the Vistula, the Dvina, the Niemen, all these great rivers that drain what are now parts of Russia and Poland, then dump water into the Baltic, as well as the different rivers—the lesser rivers—of Sweden and Finland.

And so the Baltic is a sea that can be navigated fairly easily. It's teeming with certain types of fish, especially at the Sund, or *erra Sund* as it's often called, that narrow strait between Sjaelland and Southern Sweden. That's a prime herring area. It becomes an important fishing zone for commercial fishing in the later Middle Ages. Furthermore, the Baltic's patterns of currents and winds favor travel from west to east and therefore the Danish ports, especially Hedeby and Jutland, or ports in Sjaelland, the Swedish island of Gotland and, above all, the Swedish market towns on Lake Mälaren, and Lake Mälaren is virtually this arm of the Baltic that cuts deep into Sweden. Those are prime ports for sailing. That is where most of the sailing goes; it goes from west to east. So the Scandinavians from the start have an advantage over the other peoples of the Baltic because it's much easier for them to navigate; the winds and currents go clockwise.

Furthermore, Lake Mälaren offers sheltered ports. And you can move your ships into places like Helgö or Birka, important ports in the age of migrations in the Viking age, respectively, load up with lots of goodies and then take off for points east. The Baltic is not an easy sea to navigate in many ways. It's subject to sudden squalls, storms, and, above all, mists. And mists are perhaps the most dangerous conditions for sailing in the Baltic and are always seen as ill omen. And immediately, if your ship is encased in mists, someone, some sorcerer is throwing a spell over you. And you better invoke Thor pretty quickly to dispel it, who was the god of the skies and the god of rain. And the advantage that the Scandinavians gained, starting with the first efforts at shipbuilding in the Neolithic Age—the first effort at sailing—gives the Scandinavians of the Viking age certain critical advantages and navigational skill and experience. They become very accustomed to sailing in the Baltic, memorizing landmarks, experimenting with shipbuilding, and the argument is that the Scandinavians were able to experiment with shipbuilding and navigation in the enclosed waters of the Baltic and then take those skills and expertise and apply them to tackling the North Atlantic and the North Sea, which were far more daunting oceans, bodies of water, to tackle. And there's a great deal of truth to this observation. We can't prove it archeologically, but it makes sense.

Even in Western Europe, that is, the linking of Norway and Denmark to Western Europe, again currents and winds favored the sailing from Scandinavia to England and Northern France. And the Scandinavians, with all of their expertise gained in the Baltic, could apply those skills in sailing to England, sailing to the North Atlantic islands, eventually to Iceland. And so Scandinavia had this position where it faced west, towards Western Europe, and it faced east into Russia. And the key connection was of course travel by sea, the fastest and most economical way of moving people and goods around.

The final point I would like to make and close with is what we know of the peoples living in Scandinavia in earliest times and through the Viking age. And in this case, our evidence isn't particularly good. We actually lack skeletal remains. There's relatively a limited number of skeletons that can be studied from any period of prehistory and really even in Viking age history. So we're depending on literary descriptions of Scandinavians penned at later times.

These include descriptions by Roman authors, starting with Julius Caesar in the 1st century B.C., and running through Ammianus Macellinus in the 4th century A.D., Christian writers of the medieval period, Arab geographers, particularly a fellow named Ibn Fablan, who will keep reappearing in this course, who met many Swedes in Russia on the lower Volga in 921-922. And they uniformly give us an impression that these people are tall, that they are fair in complexion; hair color is generally blonde or reddish, a lot of red-haired types, light eyes, and by the standards of the Mediterranean world and the Western European world, these people are big. Part of that is diet. Given the conditions in Scandinavia, stock raising is often preferred over farming. Farming is extremely difficult, particularly in grains. Barley and wheat are the earliest grains used. Cattle are prized in early Germanic society. So the diet comprises a lot of meat, beef, pork, and, above all, dairy products. That influences the size of a population. That can be demonstrated, and the Roman author, Ammianus Macellinus, made that observation back in the 4th century: The reason they're so tall is their diet.

There also may be genetic reasons behind it. Certainly one thing is true: this population is hardy. All of those southern sources, that is, from the Arabic world, the medieval west, and from the Classical world, agree that you're dealing with a population that was inured to cold. Often the generalization is they can handle cold and lack of food far better than the lack of water and heat, an observation that's repeated century after century.

The Scandinavians themselves, when we get their records about them, are not really conscious of any kind of major racial distinctions, as the modern world would think. And this must have been very disappointing to not see ideologues when they went back into the records. There is a very, very peculiar poem, which is the closest thing we have to any kind of racial consciousness of these people. It's known as the *Rigsthula*. It's probably composed in the 9th or 10th century, and it refers to the creation of the races, the classes of Scandinavia: the aristocrats, the farmers, or as they're known, bondi, and the thralls, the slaves.

And the god, Heimdall, who is the benevolent god to mankind, he guards the bridge of Bifrost, the rainbow bridge that links Asgard to the middle earth where mortals dwell, and later will slay Loki in the final battle of Ragnarök. Heimdall, in the disguise of Ríg, which means "king," travels the world, and he fathers the different mortals, the aristocrats, who are depicted as the Nordic hero, the farmers who, in their description, are very much like Thor—they're reddish-haired, barrel-chested, strong and healthy, with a big hearty appetite—and then he fathers the lowest class, the so-called thralls. They're described as dark-haired and swarthy. Some have tried to look into this as some kind of racial connotation. And, really, if you look at the description of those three classes—and it's an etiological myth; it's a creation myth—the thralls are really described like dwarfs or elves, the people who inhabit Elfheim in Scandinavian mythology, guys living under the earth, really clever making lots of things, working away; their most famous product is the cord that's used to bind the wolf Fenrir, the child of Loki, in the famous myth of the binding of Fenrir.

And the bondi, the karls, as they're sometimes translated, as the farmers, the yeomen, they're described as Thor, with the red beard. Now I always think Thor's red beard is taken from the color of the sky. The old Boy Scout, "Red sky at night, sailor's delight. Red sky at morning, sailor take warning," that is probably an adaptation of the physical reality to the description of the god of the skies and the rains. And most farmers and sailors worshiped Thor, and so they're effectively described as Thor in the myth. And then, likewise, the aristocratic heroes are probably taking on the qualities of Odin.

Other than this very, very peculiar poem, which some scholars now put down to a 13th- or 14th-century creation, and I don't think that's right, but that argument has been made, there's no indication that the Scandinavians had anything like a kind of racial prejudice that hair color, size, actually denoted people's status or ethnicity. There are lots of reports of people being fair-haired, dark-haired. And, furthermore, we know that overseas the Vikings were more than willing to intermarry with local populations.

In Ireland, we will see this, where they intermarry with the Celtic population. It gives rise to a very unique Hiberno-Norse culture. They intermix with Slavic peoples in the East. In Western Europe, English-Franks, Frisians, these people physically look very much like the Vikings.

And as far as we can tell, what really matters—what will count—will be whether you speak the Norse language, you worship the ancestral gods, whether you're part of that Norse community that is very, very much shaped by the landscape; that is, the real test is culture and language. And in the next lecture, we're going to deal with the origins of that culture and language.

Lecture Three

Scandinavian Society in the Bronze Age

Scope:

Since 8000 B.C., bands of hunters living in the lands around the Baltic Sea exploited the dense northern forests as the glaciers of the last Ice Age retreated. Into the Viking Age, many Scandinavians depended on hunting and fishing as a major source of food. From 4000 B.C. on, peoples learned cultivation of wheat and barley, and hence, Neolithic villages appeared in the core lands of southern Scandinavia: Jutland, the Danish islands, Skane, the lake districts of central Sweden, the lands of the Vik, and the western coastal districts of Norway between Rogaland the Sogne. These peoples, whose language and identity are unknown, cleared forest using slash-and-burn techniques, which quickly exhausted the soil. In 2500–2300 B.C., a new people speaking an Indo-European language migrated into Scandinavia. At the same time, the ancestors of the Lapps (Sami) and Finns (Suomi) appeared in their homelands. Trade with the lands of the eastern Mediterranean and Near East proved the catalyst of change. By 1750, Scandinavians had mastered the metallurgy of the Bronze Age. In the Northern Bronze Age (1750–1100 B.C.) were laid the foundations of later Scandinavian civilization. Grave goods and votive offerings, notably the gilt sun chariot found at Trundholm, attest to extraordinary prosperity. Scandinavians traded amber and furs to obtain finished goods from the Near East. But this prosperity waned after 1100 B.C. with the collapse of the great civilizations in the Near East.

Outline

I. This lecture discusses the earliest civilizations in Scandinavia, starting with the Late Paleolithic and Neolithic periods (c. 8000–2300 B.C.) and moving through the Bronze Age (2300–450 B.C.).

   A. The Neolithic Age represents a fairly sophisticated level of human development, including expertise in creating flint and obsidian weapons and tools. This period also sees the advent of agriculture and the domestication of animals.

B. Developments in the Neolithic and Bronze Ages clearly established the fundamentals of Scandinavian civilization. As we will see, the Viking Age drew upon these cultural traditions in the Scandinavians' conception of the gods, the practice of shipbuilding, and other customs.

II. Human habitation in Scandinavia came relatively late, only from about 8000 B.C. on.

A. The earliest inhabitants of Scandinavia were the hunter-gatherers of the Paleolithic Age. These inhabitants were well concentrated in the core lands of early Scandinavia: the Jutland peninsula; the Danish highlands; southern Sweden, especially the region of Skane; the Baltic islands of Gotland and Öland; the region around Lake Mälaren; and the southern shores of Norway. These regions offered easy access to the sea, along with deciduous forests teeming with game.

B. By 4000 B.C., a significant change came to Scandinavia with the advent of agriculture and domesticated animals. Knowledge of these practices was brought into Scandinavia from other areas.

1. Goats, sheep, and pigs for domestication came from the Near East.

2. The cultivation of barley and wheat allowed for stock-raising.

C. With these practices came the appearance of villages; these were far smaller than those that have been found in Central and Western Europe and the Near East.

1. One important aspect of these communities was an emphasis on stock-raising, particularly cattle.

2. Both Julius Caesar and Tacitus tell us that Germanic peoples preferred cattle-raising to farming.

D. Contact with Central Europe and the Near East also brought important innovations in weapons and tools to the Scandinavians. In contrast to the Megalithic peoples of Western Europe, however, the Scandinavians did not have the population and resources to raise great stone monuments, such as Stonehenge.

E. Older hunting patterns held on in Finland and the northern reaches of Scandinavia with the ancestors of the Finns (Suomi), the Lapps (Sami), and the Karelians.

F. We have indications that trade took place between the Scandinavians and Western Europeans in the Neolithic Age, via the great river systems, notably the Elbe, Oder, and Vistula.

III. Around 2300 B.C., we see another significant change in Scandinavia, usually associated with the arrival of newcomers.

A. From limited physical evidence, scholars have surmised that starting around 2300 B.C., the beginning of the Bronze Age, new people arrived in Scandinavia, speaking a language that was destined to evolve into the Germanic languages.

B. The new population did not eliminate the older one; instead, intermarriage and assimilation probably took place.
   1. This speculation is borne out by the fact that Germanic languages, in contrast to other Indo-European languages, have an unusual number of basic words of unknown origin.
   2. The most common example cited by linguists is *dog*, a word unrelated to the variations of *hound* from Indo-European languages.

IV. The advent of the Bronze Age was, obviously, important for a number of reasons.

A. First, the use of bronze enabled the manufacture of weapons and tools that were far more efficient than those made of stone. Along with metallurgy came the production of ceramics, which allowed for the use of storage vessels to protect grain from rats. Skills in metallurgy enabled the creation of swords, axes, and jewelry.

B. The need for metals to create bronze weapons, especially tin and copper, meant that the Scandinavians had to engage in long-distance trade. Access was required to Central Europe and, ultimately, to the trade centers of the eastern Mediterranean—the Greek world and the Near East.

C. What did the Scandinavians have to trade? First and foremost were the products of the Arctic climate, including sealskins, furs, whalebone, and walrus ivory. Honey, wood, flax, and amber were also popular products for commerce. Finally, slaves, captured from the Scandinavians' neighbors, were also in high demand. By 1550, long-distance trade had spawned villages of fairly substantial size and enabled local chieftains to accumulate great wealth and power.

D. Scandinavia was tied economically and, in some ways, culturally to the Mediterranean world and Western Europe through trade and, eventually, through political institutions and religion. During the Northern Bronze Age (1550–1100 B.C.), the Scandinavians adapted imports from these regions to their own context, creating a uniquely Scandinavian civilization that can be compared to the more successful and better known Bronze Age of Greece and the Near East.

E. Populations increased and villages expanded, but agriculture did not change significantly from the Stone Age to the Bronze Age. Most agriculture was pursued through a slash-and-burn technique, which was used almost until 1100.

    1. Despite the expansion of villages, Scandinavia remained a land of scattered settlements and farmsteads up until the end of the Viking Age.

    2. The population shifted with relative frequency as a result of soil exhaustion.

V. Physical evidence suggests that the conception of the gods known to us from the Viking Age was already taking shape in the Bronze Age.

A. The most spectacular piece of evidence we have is a gilt-bronze chariot found in Denmark at Trundholm, dating to circa 1200 B.C. The chariot originally had a pair of horses, but only one survives. The iconography of it suggests that the chariot is the one described in the *Prose Edda* (which we shall discuss in a later lecture), in which the sun is pulled across the sky each day by two horses, Arvak and Alvsinn. The sun is being pursued by an enormous wolf that wants to swallow it and bring on Ragnarök, the end of days.

B. Other representations in rock carvings and grave goods are also suggestive. Clearly, there are representations of a god associated with a hammer, giving rise to the primary god of the Viking Age, Thor, lord of the skies. Thor's goat-drawn cart is regarded as a symbol of sacred royalty among all the Germanic peoples.

C. We also find representations of fertility gods, known later as the Vanir. These are the gods of prosperity and are associated with the boar.

D. We have very little indication of the classic war god of the Viking Age, Odin. Odin did not acquire his importance until the Roman Age (2nd–3rd century A.D.), but he became the quintessential god of the Viking Age.

E. Another aspect of religious life that can be detected in the Bronze Age is the importance of burials.
   1. Elite families deposited luxury goods into the burial sites of their members and, eventually, began to construct large barrows for burials of multiple generations.
   2. Families probably conducted certain rituals in veneration of their ancestors, a feature of Scandinavian worship that would hold through the Viking Age.
   3. This feature of Scandinavian life climaxed in the rich burials of the Vendel Age (4th–6th centuries) in Sweden and the great ship burials of the 9th and 10th centuries found in the Oslo area.

VI. Sometime after 1100, long-distance trade seemed to break down.

A. Starting from about 1200, the great political orders of the Late Bronze Age, such as imperial Egypt and the Hittite Empire, collapsed, resulting in a general decline of organized, literate civilization in the Near East and a decline in markets and demand for the products of the Arctic. Repercussions of these collapses were felt across Central Europe and in Scandinavia.

B. Nonetheless, in the 5th century B.C., trade began to revive as a result of the emergence of La Tène civilization in Central Europe, the Iron Age civilization of the Celts, which opened up a new chapter in Scandinavian history.

Further Reading:

Colin Renfrew. *Archaeology and Language: The Puzzle of Indo-European Origins.* 2nd ed. Cambridge: Cambridge University Press, 1989.

Herbert Schutz. *The Prehistory of Germanic Europe*. New Haven: Yale University Press, 1983.

Questions to Consider:

1. What are the value and limits of archaeology in revealing societies before the advent of writing? In what ways can archaeology document material and social changes in early Scandinavia? What questions can archaeology not answer?

2. How important were innovations in technology and long-distance trade in the development of civilization in Scandinavia? What were the principal trade routes, and what were the prime goods exchanged? How could disruption of trade routes affect civilization in Scandinavia?

Lecture Three—Transcript

Scandinavian Society in the Bronze Age

In this lecture, I plan to discuss the earliest of civilizations and cultures in Scandinavia, starting in what is known as the Neolithic Age, which technically means the new Stone Age. And this is a fairly sophisticated level of human development, where there's great expertise in making flint and obsidian stone weapons and tools. And also, it is a period that sees the advent of agriculture and domestication of animals. And we're going to carry the story through what is known as the Bronze Age, and in Scandinavia the Bronze Age lasts a particularly long time, starting around 2300 B.C. and ending around 450 B.C.

This is a great deal of history to cover, but, again, we have no really written sources on this. We depend very heavily on archeology and anthropology to uncover what these people were like, and we're looking at their material remains. Even so, taking the material remains in tandem with what we know of the historical geography of Scandinavia as well as what we know of later Scandinavian civilization, it is clear that developments in these periods set many of the basic fundamentals in Scandinavian civilization in place and that the Viking age drew upon these traditions, these cultural traditions, perhaps the conception of the gods, as well as burial practices, the importance of shipbuilding already detected in the rock carvings of this period. And so when we turn to the Viking age, it's very useful to remember that the Scandinavians are the heirs of a very, very long tradition in their homeland.

Well, with that said, let's turn to these earliest cultures that we can recover from archeology. I noted in a previous lecture that human habitation in Scandinavia is relatively late that the area was covered with glaciers from the last Ice Age, and it is only about from 8000 B.C. on that humans could actually move into the area. Until then, it was just impossible. It was a vast glacier and snowfield. And the earliest inhabitants of Scandinavia were the usual hunter-gatherers that we call peoples of the Paleolithic, the so-called "old Stone Age."

And, again, by the time these people arrive in Northern Europe, they are descendants of people who have perfected hunting skills, going back deep into the Stone Age; they are probably represented by the later Lapps, or the Sami, as they prefer to call themselves, who ultimately evolve into the Arctic nomads, people who domesticate the reindeer and become absolutely expert in traveling the Arctic wastes, exploiting the hunting opportunities among the various sea birds and sea creatures, especially sea mammals, seals, and even being able to get whales and cut them up. And, therefore, your earliest residents would have been in what is often called the hunter food-gathering stage of human history.

They are particularly well concentrated also in the regions I keep referring to as the core lands of early Scandinavia, and that would be what is today, Denmark, or, more accurately, the medieval kingdom of Denmark—that is, the Jutland Peninsula, the Danish Islands, often known as the "belts" since they act as a belt that connects Jutland to the Scandinavian Peninsula; Southern Sweden, notably the region of Skane that is associated with Denmark; the Baltic Islands, Bornholm, Öland, and Gotland; the region around Lake Mälaren, that is, the core of Sweden today where Stockholm is located; and the southern shores of Norway, especially the regions which are around the Oslo fjord and the Vest fjord area.

There, the conditions were ideal. You had deciduous forests. They were teeming with game and fish. You had easy access to the sea, and a great deal of our knowledge of the earliest people in this area is based on studying their campsites, their tools, and also their refuse, particularly what are known as the "kitchen middens," the discarded, mostly sea creatures and shells that were just stacked up as the garbage heaps for these early community.

By 4000 B.C., there is a significant change in Scandinavia, and that comes with the advent of agriculture and domesticated animals. Now, this knowledge was brought into Scandinavia from the outside. The domestication of animals, notably goats, sheep, and pigs—these are creatures of the Near East, especially the Levantine regions—and barley and wheat, those two grasses which have been domesticated into the cultivated grains, those arrive somewhere around 4000 B.C. and that allows for the cultivation of cereals and stock raising. That is an extremely important change.

Contrary to what most people would think today about Scandinavia, rye and also oats, by the way, are not introduced until after 1100 A.D., that is, after the Viking age. Those are part of the benefits of becoming Christianized and getting linked up with Western

Europeans and learning their superior agriculture. So, in any case, villages begin to appear. These villages are rather small, certainly far smaller in comparison to those that have been detected in Central and Western Europe and certainly far smaller than what we know of in the Near East, where the origins of agriculture are to be found.

One important aspect already of these communities seems to be more of a stress on stock raising than on agriculture, and particularly the raising of cattle. And, again, this is a surmise that is based on physical evidence. We really are speculating here. But it is a feature of Scandinavian and early Germanic society in general that cattle were regarded as the prime wealth. We're told this much later in classical sources, starting with Julius Caesar, also with the Roman historian Tacitus, who penned this work known as the *Germania*, written around 98 A.D., where he describes the customs of the Germans. And from the start, the Germanic peoples, by which Roman authors meant Central Europe and Scandinavia, preferred cattle over farming, that cattle was the mark of rank and was to be preferred over farming, which was often treated as a more despised occupation; or at least not as noble an occupation. It's something you had to do.

The contact with Central Europe and ultimately the Near East—it wasn't Near Easterners who suddenly arrived and brought all this change; it obviously passed through different hands before it reached Scandinavia—also brought important innovations in weapons and tools, their superior tools for agriculture. Carts begin to appear; these are usually documented on rock carvings. And in contrast, however, to Western Europe—these people who are part of a wider, what is known as megalithic, big stone, that late Neolithic culture—the Scandinavians just don't have the populations and resources to raise the great kind of stone monuments one associates in this period with, say, Stonehenge in England, where you have much a more successful—economically, anyway—society where you have the population to raise these great monuments. There isn't any effort at megalithic monuments beyond you raise some dolmans, your circle of stones. Fundamentally, your population in Scandinavia is considerably smaller than Central and Western Europe. And that will be a fact through the whole of Scandinavian history.

Older hunting patterns of course were important, held on especially in the areas of Finland and the northern reaches of Scandinavia, where speakers of the Finno-Ugarian languages—these are a glutenin of languages that are related to Turkish and Mongolian languages. They are not related to the Indo-European languages, the Germanic family or the Romans, the Greek, the Celtic languages, or the Iranian, the Indian language. It's a whole different language structure. Those people eventually give rise to the Finns, or Suomi, the Lapps, the Sami, and the Karelians, who are the cousins of the Finns dwelling in what is now Russia. They're immediately to the east of Finland. And these people were expert hunters, and among them come the Arctic nomads, who attained the northern climates, or exploited the northern climates for the Arctic goods.

In the Neolithic Age, there's already indications that there is trade with Western Europe going across the river systems, notably the Elbe, the great river that bisects Germany; the Oder, which is now essentially part of the border between Germany and Poland; and those two river systems lead from the Baltic to the upper basin of the Danube and ultimately to ports on the Mediterranean. And a good deal of influence comes from the Mediterranean over these river systems into the Baltic.

Well, there's a significant change that occurs somewhere around 2300 B.C., and it's usually associated with the arrival of newcomers. There is a surmise that there must have been a migration. And again, we largely depend on physical remains. Now starting in the Bronze Age, the period from 2300 B.C. on, we do get graves. And since the burial is inhumation, that is, in the ground rather than cremation, there are some skeletal remains to study, and they're still in the preliminary stage of understanding what this means. But before then, we have very, very little in the way of skeletal evidence. We have no written records. But the argument that at least is made now is that in 2300 B.C. people arrived speaking a language destined eventually to evolve into the Germanic languages, from which the Scandinavian languages are descended, and other Germanic languages, such as modern German, Dutch, and English. And there's a long way to go before that evolution takes place.

So we believe there was a major infusion of a new population. That doesn't mean the older population was simply eliminated. The best guess is, is that there was intermarriage and assimilation, and it ran a bit both ways. This is borne out by the fact that Germanic languages, in contrast to other Indo-European languages, have an unusual amount of words of unknown origin for basic items. The most common example cited by linguists is "dog," a word that is not represented among other Indo-European languages. That word is hound, *hund* in German, *canis* in Latin, *cuon* in Greek. "Dog" is of some unknown origin, and it's suspected that a number of basic words were taken over by the ancestors of the Scandinavians, the Germanic-speaking people, from the existing population there. Some of these people may have been related to the Finns, the Lapps. We just don't know who they are. What is important is that populations coalesced into more or less a single group, which we can study from their physical remains.

The Bronze Age is of importance for a couple of reasons: one, the new technology—the bringing in of bronze—enabled the manufacture of weapons and tools that were far more efficient than those of stone. The bronze for a long time is, of course, kept more for weapons than tools, but the advent of metallurgy and, with it, ceramics, is a major improvement in material culture. Ceramics allow you, for instance—especially ceramics made on a potter's wheel—to turn out storage vessels for grain that protect you against rats; essentially, pottery is created as a rat-proof device. Skills in metallurgy lead you to fashion all sorts of objects that you couldn't do in stone. For instance, swords, you can make out of metal in a way you can't with stones. A sword is essentially an elongated knife. Different types of axes and hand axes can be made and, above all, jewelry and personal ornamentation, which becomes an extremely important feature throughout Scandinavian history.

One of the ways that Scandinavians expressed their artistic genius is in the decorative arts, particularly in metalwork, not in monumental architecture or sculpture, but rather in metalwork. And that is already seen in many of the objects coming out of the finds in the Bronze Age graves. And these are very rich grave goods that we find. And I always like to speculate that one of the most remarkable is these enormous horns that have to be held with essentially two hands. What their purposes are, we don't know. In textbooks you read that they're for cultic purpose, which means, essentially, we don't know what they are. We assume they're used in ceremonies. And I always like to think that that horn is the origin of the great Gjallarhorn of Heimdall, the watchman of the gods who will sound the final days of Ragnarök. But there's no way to prove it, but I would like to think it's true.

Also, the need for metals, especially tin and copper, to create the bronze weapons meant that you had to have long-distance trade on a scale that you did not have in the Neolithic Age. There are no tin sources in Scandinavia. You have to bring the tin in. And copper is in pretty short supply as well. And that meant the core lands of Scandinavia, Southern Scandinavia, which are going to eventually turn out to be the heartland of early Germanic civilization, had to get those metals from somewhere. That meant trade routes into Central Europe and ultimately to the centers of the Eastern Mediterranean, the area of the Aegean, that is, the Greek world, and, above all, the Near East where you had great urban civilizations in Egypt and Mesopotamia.

What did the Scandinavians or these ancestors of the Scandinavians have to trade? Well, there are a number of important products. First and foremost were the products of the Arctic climate. This would include skins, furs, all sorts of neat items, always in high demand – prime furs. Often these had to be obtained by trading with the Arctic nomads, that is, the Lapps. This is a feature running throughout Scandinavian economic history, that the Germanic speakers, the speakers of Norse, trade with the Lapps of the north. They would get all sorts of products—walrus, ivory, whalebone, skin, sealskins, furs. In return, they would swap finished goods, such as metal goods or well-worked wooden goods, which the Lapps themselves could not produce. And this symbiosis goes back certainly to the Bronze Age, if not earlier, and will continue through the entire of the Viking age. And we have some really excellent information on how the later Norse continued this trade on a wider scale with the descendents of these earlier Lapps.

There were also timber products, honey, wood, flacks, various items, and, above all, amber. Amber is essentially a prehistoric sap, or gook even, that has hardened into the quality of a stone. And it was in high demand in the Mediterranean world from the Bronze Age right through the Roman period. It was regarded as a precious stone. Much of the best of the amber was washed up on the shores of Denmark, the Danish Islands. And this was a high commodity product. You could trade this item and get an awful lot of tin and copper for it, as well as gold and silver, which you then could bring back to Scandinavia and work into all those marvelous objects that we find in the graves.

And, finally, there was undoubtedly slave trade, distressing to us, but through most of history the slave trade labor, in one form or another, was one of the biggest commodities. And the easiest way to obtain slaves was to essentially raid and enslave your neighbors, who may be people very closely related to you, but since you're dealing with a society that is probably very localized, and ties are very much based on family and kinship, there's no problem in enslaving your neighbors, particularly if you have a limited supply of goods. And from the merchant's viewpoint, it was really rather cost-effective. You simply have the slaves carry all your skins and amber down to the Mediterranean world, and then you just sell everything and then go back north, rather distressing to us. But I'm sure many of the goods transported out of Scandinavia to the Mediterranean world were being carried by slaves who would then be sold at the other end. It was a common feature of slave trade through much of history.

So what happens is that the long-distance trade allows, by 1550, villages of fairly substantial size to be sustained. And it also allows enough concentration of power into the hands of local bigwigs, usually called chiefdoms in anthropological models, that you have families of great wealth and rank who could afford to deposit all those grave goods in the inhumation graves of the Bronze Age. And that is an index of the amount of wealth, as well as the importance of long-distance trade. And so this is another feature I must stress that we see in the Bronze Age, and that is the ties of Scandinavia to those civilizations of the Mediterranean in Western Europe. They're always there. Ultimately, Scandinavia is economically and, in some ways, culturally tied to those other worlds through trade, material goods, and eventually political institutions and religions as well will pass over those trade routes, starting certainly in the Celtic age and running through the Middle Ages.

The question in Scandinavian history is not that there are these links or these contacts but what did the Scandinavians receive and what did they do with what they took from these other cultures. And, again, in the Bronze Age, from what we can see, it was a matter of adapting the imports to a Scandinavian context. And while, yes, these ancestors of the Scandinavians depended on long-distance trade, they did create a uniquely Scandinavian civilization, so much so that the years about 1550 to 1100 B.C. is usually called the Northern Bronze Age, a very, very distinct period, a distinct material culture that implies a certain amount of opulence and success and invites comparison to the more successful and better known Bronze Age of Greece in the Near East with what we call the so-called late Bronze Age. That is the era of imperial Egypt, the great palaces of Mycenae, the Hittite Empire in Asia Minor. And these great political orders were linked to Scandinavia through these trade routes across Central Europe.

As a result, population must have risen. The villages are expanded and agriculture does not change very significantly really in terms of animals and crops from the Stone Age to the Bronze Age. Most agriculture is pursued by what is known as a slash-and-burn technique. And this technique is going to be used really up until almost 1100. Certainly it's used in the Iron Age, that is, the period after about 450 B.C. And Scandinavia must be remembered as really a land of scattered settlements, farmsteads, and villages. There aren't any real towns or cities. These do not emerge until the very end of the Viking age.

And in this early period, especially in the Stone Age and the Bronze Age, there is a fair shifting of population. And this is a result of soil exhaustion; that is, you clear an area, you burn it down by burning the trunks of the trees. You try to destroy the roots. You cut them down. You plant your barley or wheat. For the first generation, you get a lot of success, and eventually the soil exhausts. You move to a new area. You carve out a new village. The old village falls out of use. The area fills up as forest land. And there's a lot of very good study going on, on how the population moves essentially from village to village. And so there is a certain amount of migration or movement stretched over generations still going on, and in that way agriculture remains in this state really until major improvements in the later Middle Ages.

Well, the success of this northern Bronze Age civilization depended a great deal on long- distance trade, and it brought in the metals and the raw materials to work those goods. And, again, we don't have written sources, and we're depending very, very much on the physical evidence. But that physical evidence is very suggestive. In one area, we can make some speculations. We don't know what these people are speaking. We assume it's an early form of Germanic or Indo-European at least. But we have a number of objects coming out of the graves, as well as rock paintings, that suggest that already the conception of the gods, as they're known to us in the Viking age, is taking place.

The most spectacular of these is a gilt bronze chariot that was found in Denmark at Trundholm in Sjaelland—that is, the great island of Denmark—dated generally around 1200 B.C. Only one of the horses survived. The original had a pair. And it's remarkable that you got a chariot anyway; that's a pretty sophisticated item that's invented fairly late in the Near East. This was one of their earliest examples of a chariot in Northern Europe. And the iconography of it, the great bronze symbol that looks like the sun, suggests that what you're dealing with is essentially the chariot described in Snorri Sturluson's *Prose Edda*, pulled by the two horses, Aravak and Alvsinn. And in Norse mythology—and this is a very, very famous mythological handbook written around 1220 by this absolutely witty Icelandic author known as Snorri, Snorri Sturluson, the son of the Sturl. And names in Scandinavian are essentially patronymics. You're simply named as the "son of" or the "daughter of" your father. They are not last names in the modern sense.

So Snorri, which is what his real name is, writes about this myth in which these two horses pull the chariot carrying the sun each day, and the sun is being pursued by this enormous wolf that wants to swallow it and bring on Ragnarök, which in Norse mythology is the end of days. And there's also a similar chariot carrying the moon with another nasty wolf after it. And this object apparently is a representation of this notion that is already evident in the Bronze Age.

There are other representations in the rock carvings and in the objects found in graves that are suggestive. Clearly, there's a god associated with an axe or a hammer, and that gives rise to the primary god of the Viking age, at least for most Scandinavians, who was Thor, the great red-bearded, barrel-chested, heroic god, a little dimwitted, but a good guy generally and easy to appease. And he is the lord of the skies. I have mentioned earlier that he may get his red hair from the color of the skies at night and the morning, whether there's going to be rain or not. He also drives a goat chariot, which is a very, very primitive cart, and a cart that goes back to the Bronze Age. And it's suggestive already that Thor in some fashion is being worshiped. And the goat-drawn cart is regarded as a symbol of royalty—sacred royalty—among all the Germanic peoples in Gaul in the 5th and 6th century. The Franks, the Germanic peoples who moved into the former Roman province and took it over and whose kings are known as the Merovingians—this is the family of Clovis—they were paraded around in a cart drawn by goats, which is a very, very old notion going back deep into Scandinavian and Germanic mythology.

There are also representations of what are clearly fertility gods. These would be known later as the Vanir, that is, the gods of prosperity. They're associated also with the ancient animal, the boar, that is, the undomesticated pig, and that is a common feature that will come through Scandinavian art; that is, the boar as a heroic creature associated especially with the god Njord and his two children, Frey and Freya, who are the gods of prosperity and worshiped throughout Scandinavia.

There is very little indication of the classic war god of the Viking age—that is, Odin, as he's known in English—"Woden." And as we'll see later on, that god in many ways is a creation, not a creation, but Odin doesn't acquire his importance as the primary god in Asgard, that is, the Norse Olympus, perhaps until the Roman age, 2nd or 3rd century A.D., and really becomes the quintessential god of the Viking age. It is the Scandinavians who will endow Odin with all of his powers and his really inimical powers and his changeable nature, starting from the 8th and 9th centuries.

On the other hand, another aspect of religious life that can be detected in the Bronze Age is the importance of burials. I mentioned that you must have elite families that can afford to put all of these displays of goods into the inhumation graves, and eventually they start building very large barrows for multiple generational burials; that is, various members of the family over time are buried in the same spot. And there has to be—I mean, again it's a surmise—there has to be repeated family rites around these graves, around these barrows, where the family comes and venerates the ancestors. And this is a feature of Scandinavian worship through the Viking age.

One of the most powerful indications of the fact that you're dealing with Vikings or Norse overseas is, if you have Scandinavian type burials, and these are burials—they could be cremation or inhumation. But they include all sorts of grave goods and some kind of monument erected where rites continue to the ancestors, that they continue to be venerated. And in many ways—and we know this from Icelandic saga—if you don't, the dead will rise up and walk the earth and do all sorts of nasty things to you. And the Scandinavians don't have—unlike the Mediterranean people, the afterlife isn't some sort of intangible spiritual world the way Homer describes it in the *Odyssey*. The dead physically get up and do nasty things. And especially if they're sorcerers from Hebrides, it can be a real problem.

From the start, in the Bronze Age we see this feature that becomes a major feature of Scandinavian life and will climax in the very, very rich burials of the Vendel age in Sweden in the 4th through 6th centuries and the great Scandinavian ship burials that will be found in the Oslo area in the 9th and 10th centuries.

Well, ultimately the Bronze Age did depend on long-distance trade for its great success. And sometime after 1100, this trade seems to break down. There are fewer grave goods. There is a shift after 1000 from inhumation to cremation. And that starts to restrict our record because we just don't know as much when you're burning everything up and you're dealing with the remains of a cremation burial. And so part of our impression of the succeeding generations down to about 450 B.C., that it's a period of relative poverty, is simply the fact that we don't have the rich burials that gave us the physical evidence to surmise aspects about the society.

Yet we do know, from good historical records, that in the Near East, starting from about 1200 or 1220s on, the great political orders of the late Bronze Age do collapse—Imperial Egypt, the Hittite Empire—and that there is a general decline of organized, literate civilization in the Near East, and with that a fall of markets, a fall of demand for the northern goods, the amber, all of those products of the Arctic, and, as a result, repercussions are felt across Central Europe and ultimately to Scandinavia of the Bronze Age. And there just isn't the same demand.

And so some families must have gotten poorer. The grave goods get poorer and, therefore, our physical evidence does reflect a certain important economic change. And for several centuries, our information on Scandinavia is rather limited. Nonetheless, starting probably in the 5th century B.C., that begins to change. Trade revives, and it revives not so much because of the revival of civilizations in the Near East but the emergence of a new civilization in Central Europe. This is the La Tène, the Iron Age civilization of the Celts. And that civilization will open up a new chapter in Scandinavian history.

Lecture Four

Scandinavia in the Celtic and Roman Ages

Scope:

Trade and prosperity returned to Scandinavia in the later Iron Age (450–50 B.C.) as Celtic merchants, craftsmen, and immigrants arrived in the lands of the Baltic Sea. The burgeoning towns (*oppida*) of Celtic La Tène civilization offered markets for Scandinavian forest products and the skins and ivory of the Arctic land. From the Celts came iron and shipbuilding technology, as well as better tools to extend the arable. Yet Scandinavia remained culturally distinct, with the Germanic language emerging in this era. Far more profound was the impact of imperial Rome. Julius Caesar's conquest of Gaul (58–50 B.C.) disrupted the Celtic world, allowing Germanic-speaking peoples to migrate into Central Europe between the Rhine and Vistula rivers. The Roman historian Tacitus penned the earliest account of these Germans, whose gods and customs resembled those of Scandinavians in the Viking Age. Trade linked Scandinavia with the Roman cities of the Rhineland and Britain. The scale and range of Roman imports enriched all classes, foremost, petty monarchs who emerged with retinues of armed warriors (*comitatus*) by the early 2nd century. Roman civil war and barbarian invasion disrupted these links in the 3rd century, and the ultimate fall of Rome in the 5th century would open a new chapter in Scandinavian history.

Outline

I. This lecture deals with Scandinavia in the Celtic Age and the succeeding Roman Age, but we should keep in mind that these are only chronological references; although the ties were close, Scandinavia was never assimilated into either of these two civilizations.

II. The Celtic civilization that had an important influence on Scandinavia was the La Tène civilization, which emerged about 450 B.C. with the Rhine as its heartland. This culture represented the climax of a series of Central European civilizations characterized by skill in metallurgy.

    A. Celtic Europe, consisting of Gaul, southern Germany, and the Lowlands, also saw the emergence of towns, called by the Romans *oppida* (singular, *oppidum*). These were enclosures of several acres, with specialized areas for manufacturing and agricultural purposes. They were the urban basis for the success of Roman provincial civilization in Britain, Gaul, and the lands of the Danube starting in the 1st century A.D. and running to the 5th century A.D.

B. These towns had enormous appetites for labor, luxury goods, and foodstuffs; thus, Scandinavia regained prominence as an area that could be tapped for raw materials and prestige objects.

C. Scandinavia prospered with the emergence of the Celtic La Tène civilization in Central Europe, as we see in its acquisition of expert metallurgy and iron work, and in the construction of carts and ships.

D. Celtic civilization also enriched and transformed the aesthetics and the arts of early Scandinavia in this period through prestige trade objects, such as the Gundestrup cauldron (c. 100 B.C.), a Celtic object found in Denmark depicting heads, marching warriors, a sacrificial scene, and gods that could easily be associated with Scandinavian divinities.

    1. The Scandinavian gods, or ancient Germanic gods, were, thus, enriched with the iconography and rituals of the Celtic world, a phenomenon that is common in many ancient religions.

    2. Tacitus, a Roman historian writing c. A.D. 100, mentions in his *Germania* that Danish tribes paraded the cult statue of the goddess Nerthus in a sacred cart, probably a ritual that came from the Celtic world.

III. This influence did not mean that Scandinavia was part of the Celtic world. From around 450–500 B.C. on, distinctively Scandinavian developments also emerged.

A. For example, by 500 B.C., the early Germanic language was spoken. This language was quite distinct from Celtic, Latin, and Greek.

B. In their burial practices, Scandinavians adhered to ship imagery, never adopting carts in their burials.

C. Despite all the trade and activity with central Europe, Scandinavians never built towns, largely preferring scattered villages. This feature of early Germanic civilization lasted well into the Roman Age.

D. The Romans saw a difference in religious practices between Celts and Germans; namely, the Scandinavians had no equivalent to the Druids, a priestly caste. Sacrificial rites in Scandinavia remained particularly Scandinavian. The Tollund man, excavated from a Danish bog, was probably strangled or hanged as a sacrifice to an early form of Odin.

IV. This distinctive Scandinavian civilization was unexpectedly given a chance to expand by the Romans.

A. From 58–49 B.C., Julius Caesar conquered Gaul and began the Roman conquest of Central Europe up the Danube; this conquest was completed by Caesar's successor, Augustus. Within less than a generation, the Celtic world was shattered, the Celts had been incorporated into the Roman Empire, and most of Central Europe was left open for migration by Germanic peoples.

B. With the Roman conquest of Gaul and the upper Danube, Germanic tribes spread from the Scandinavian heartland to the lands between the Rhine and the Vistula and north of the Danube. The Romans called this region *Germania*, meaning Central Europe and Scandinavia.

V. Trade between the Celtic Age and the Roman Age increased dramatically.

A. The Roman demand for goods was enormous. For example, 150,000 Roman soldiers were stationed along the Rhine. Scholars have now demonstrated that most of the cattle industry of western Germany and Denmark was devoted to feeding the Roman army on the Rhine.

B. The Romans also had a tremendous need for labor, including slaves, day laborers, and auxiliaries, that is, warriors recruited into the auxiliary army. Large numbers of German tribes also moved to the region under Roman arrangements to settle as agriculturalists.

C. The volume of imported goods from the Roman world into southern Scandinavia was extraordinary. The range of goods found in the Danish Isles and southern Sweden, including fine tableware, glass, and Roman ceramics, indicates that the material life of the upper classes had significantly changed with Roman contact. According to Tacitus, the Germans had also become accustomed to drinking wine and would "gamble their freedom" for fine imported vintages.

D. Other items that traveled to Scandinavia, including superior weapons, were more alarming to the Romans. Our earliest chain mail, probably offerings to an early form of Tyr or Odin, was found in Danish bog deposits dating from A.D. 200–400. Other discoveries include finely wrought swords, weapons of choice for Roman Age Scandinavians.

E. The trade goods coming into Scandinavia allowed consolidation of power around petty kings or dynasts.

    1. In the 1st century A.D., Roman historians were confident that the Germans were disorganized, but from A.D. 100 on into the 4th century A.D., this was no longer the case.

    2. Trade enabled some warlords in Scandinavia and Central Europe to amass wealth and make themselves kings. Some of them kept retainers (*comitatus* in Latin), professional warriors. Tacitus's description of these retainers is quite consistent with the description in Norse literature later on of the *berserkers*, that is, frenzied warriors inspired by Odin to fight for their lords.

    3. In turn, these warriors strengthened their fighting skills over time. Tacitus and later Roman authors describe the German soldiers forming a wedge (*cuneus*, "shield wall"), a dense infantry formation that could serve offensive or defensive purposes. In Norse legend, the wedge was a gift from Odin.

    4. By A.D. 260, in Central Europe, major confederations of Germans had emerged, including Franks, Saxons, Alemanni, and Goths.

F. A warship from a burial at Nydam in Denmark (c. 350) and the impression of a ship from Sutton Hoo (c. 625), suggest another important benefit of Scandinavian contact with the Roman world: familiarity with the use of sails. The Roman historian Ammianus Marcellinus attests to the Germans' use of sails in 4th-century raids.

1. Such vessels were important for launching Viking-style raids on the Roman Empire in the 3rd and 4th centuries and for propelling the migration of the Anglo-Saxons from Denmark to Britain when the Roman Empire began to break up in the 5th century.

2. Scholars have argued that enough Germanic-speaking peoples traveled from Denmark and northwestern Germany to Britain to linguistically and culturally change Britain into England.

3. Further, the Goths, if they came from Sweden, probably crossed the Baltic, followed the amber routes, and moved into the Roman Empire, a voyage, again, enabled by improved shipbuilding.

G. Contact with the Roman world benefited Scandinavia enormously—through trade goods, the demographic safety valve offered by the Roman Empire, and the importation of weapons and ship technology.

1. These developments led to the emergence of petty kings served by retinues of warriors—confederations that were, in essence, the embryos of Viking civilization described in legends and sagas.

2. The drawback to this contact was, of course, that the empire collapsed in the 5th century, and with it came the loss of the trade benefits. The succeeding centuries, from A.D. 400–600, would see a new chapter in the development of Scandinavian civilization.

Further Reading:

H. R. Ellis Davidson. *Myths and Symbols in Pagan Europe: Early Scandinavian and Celtic Religions.* Syracuse, NY: Syracuse University Press, 1988.

Herbert Schutz. *The Prehistory of Germanic Europe.* New Haven: Yale University Press, 1983.

Questions to Consider:

1. In what ways did trade with the Celtic world transform life in Scandinavia in the Iron Age? Why did this trade stimulate the emergence of a distinctly Germanic culture?

2. What was the impact of imperial Rome in shaping society in Scandinavia? How decisive was contact with Rome in changing political and military institutions? How important was trade for the prosperity of Scandinavia?

Lecture Four—Transcript

Scandinavia in the Celtic and Roman Ages

In this lecture I wish to deal with Scandinavia in what is often called the Celtic age and then the succeeding Roman age. These are a bit deceptive terms because they give the impression that Scandinavia is part of a wider Celtic or Roman civilization, and that's not really the case. The terms are really used to indicate the chronological distinction, that is, a Scandinavia contemporary with Celtic and Roman civilization. Again, there's a great deal of trade and exchange that goes on, but in neither instance—either in the Celtic or in the Roman age—should we think of Scandinavia as somehow being assimilated into those other civilizations or as an adjunct or as a peripheral part of it. The ties are close but, again, as I've stressed in a previous lecture, Scandinavians pick and choose what they want and in many ways retain many of their cultural distinctions and heritage going back to the Bronze Age. So with that provision in mind, let us use these terms, Celtic and Roman age, that way.

The Celtic civilization that exercised such an important influence over Scandinavia was actually what we called the La Tène civilization. This was a later stage centering especially on Eastern France or what the Romans would call Gaul. It emerged about 450 B.C.; its heartland was the Rhine and the rivers of Eastern France which drew the Celts up to the North Sea to the British Isles and by trade routes into Scandinavia. This is the last of a series of civilizations in Central Europe. It's really the climax of a tremendous skill in metallurgy. Furthermore, Celtic Europe, which would be Gaul, Southern Germany, the Lowlands, sees an emergence of towns. The Romans call them *oppida*. These are large enclosures, including many acres with specialized areas for manufacturing, areas enclosed for agricultural purposes, and they really are the urban basis for the success of Roman provincial civilization in Britain, Gaul, and the lands of the Danube, starting the 1st century A.D. and running through the 5th century A.D. When you're dealing with the La Tène civilization in Celtic Europe, you're dealing with an extremely sophisticated, almost certainly town-, if not urban-style civilization. Being towns with large populations specializing in metallurgy, mining, all sorts of activities, there was an enormous appetite for labor, for luxury goods, and for foodstuffs.

Scandinavia, all of a sudden, springs into prominence again as one of those areas where Celtic merchants can tap in for raw materials and luxury goods, and these would be the same goods we saw in the Bronze Age, that is, the products of the Arctic, the slaves who would be sold off to supply labor in the Celtic world. Amber is a commodity in high demand; the Celts will work it into their own jewelry techniques. Above all, apparently a fair amount of timber and products of the forest begin to also arrive. Scandinavia prospers a great deal with the emergence of Celtic towns in Central Europe. It can be illustrated by a couple of examples on how life was so enriched. The most obvious is the acquiring of expert metallurgy and ironwork. Starting from 450 or 400 B.C., Scandinavians—either imported Celtic smiths or they learned or were trained by Celtic smiths—are beginning to turn out some quality ironworks. Still in limited supply, they depend a great deal on imports, but this is a significant difference from the experimentation in ironwork that went on in Sweden around 800 or 700 B.C.

Another important area where they gain in technology is in carts and even in ships. These are two areas where the Celts excelled—one is in carts and harnessing. This is seen, for instance, in the Latin language. Romans were the first to admit that the Celts were first-rate in wheeled vehicles, and many of the words for various types of carts in Latin are actually Celtic-loaned words, that is, the Romans had borrowed them from the Gauls. We suspect the same was going on in Scandinavia where we begin to get first-rate carts and harnessing systems, compliments of the Celts. It's an interesting aspect of Celtic civilization. The burials in the La Tène, you know when you're dealing with a Celtic burial because there's a cart there usually, and the Celts always think going to the other world is by cart, whereas the Scandinavians and the people of the Mediterranean always think it's by water. Scandinavian burials always have ship imagery just as you very often get in the Mediterranean world, and the Celts in between of course have the carts.

In any case, shipbuilding was also affected by Celtic trade. Our first paddle boat, if you want to call it that, is the Hjortspring ship which was excavated from a Danish island around 200 or 300 B.C., and it is the first effort to create a coastal vessel propelled by, I think, 20 men using paddles rather than oars. It's of wooden construction, and it shows some of the features of Celtic construction, which is using ribs and skin boats, only you're applying it to wooden construction, and this boat seems to be based on Celtic experimentations, and it will be the first in a line of archaeological finds that lead us from this first effort at a coastal vessel and will climax in the great ships of the Viking age. That is a very, very important gift coming from the Celtic world, that is, superior skills in shipbuilding as well as carts.

Also, Celtic civilization enriched and transformed the aesthetics and the arts of early Scandinavia in this age. Again, this doesn't mean that Scandinavia became part of the Celtic world per se but many fine prestige objects arrived in trade, by which I mean jewelry, a plate. Later with the Romans you get glassware and other types of objects which the noble classes could afford. The most remarkable of these is known as the Gundestrup cauldron which is a beautiful silver repoussé work. It's again coming from Denmark, and it's in a find of a grave good, and what it is is a Celtic object that depicts heads. The Celts were big on head. Taking, so there's always worship of heads, and also what are clearly marching warriors and human sacrificial scenes. Again, we have reports of this with Druids and Celtic traditions and a god wearing antlers and other gods that could easily be associated with Scandinavian divinities, the Vanir of the Viking age. What we have here is a Celtic religious object which could be very easily applied to a Scandinavian religious context.

There must have been many instances of this, where the Scandinavian gods or the ancient Germanic gods, if you will, because the Germanic peoples who emigrate from Scandinavia worship these same gods, that in many ways they're enriched with the iconography and the rituals of the Celtic world. They're still Germanic gods, but they have been elevated and ennobled by being associated with the rites and the objects of the superior civilization to the south. This is a feature that is common in many ancient religions where you have this type of exchange. It doesn't necessarily mean that the ancestral gods have been abandoned. They've simply been articulated and enriched in their conception by contact with other peoples.

This explains, for instance, why Tacitus, a Roman historian writing around 100 A.D. in *Germania* mentions that the Danish tribes move the cult statue of a goddess—he calls her Nerthus, which seems to be a feminine form of the later Scandinavian god, Njord—around in a sacred cart, probably a ritual that came from the Celtic world which by Tacitus's day is quintessentially Scandinavian, that is, some 300 or 400 years later. One could even argue that perhaps the Germanic gods were rather abstract figures until they came into contact with the Celts, and they became more humanized and more myths created about. We're not sure, but clearly the gods were conceived differently as a result of this exchange and contact with the Celtic world.

On the other hand, it's important to keep in mind that all of this influence does not necessarily mean Scandinavia was part of the Celtic world—far from it. I said the irony is we're using this term chronologically and it is in this period from, say, 450 or 500 B.C. on that several important features are clearly noticeable about Scandinavia. One is, at this point philologists' best guess is we have the early Germanic language being spoken. This language in its structure and vocabulary is very, very distinct from Celtic, from Latin and it's related Taoic languages, from Greek, which were all Indo-European languages being spoken in Europe at the time. There were others as well. The Germanic language has a distinct verb system, a whole different set of nouns as a result of continental shifts; there are significant changes in Germanic pronunciations from other Indo-European languages. By 500 B.C. or 400 B.C., those Germanic languages have emerged in the core areas of Scandinavia, and all the Germanic languages ultimately descend from that earlier Germanic language. They are not part of the Celtic world linguistically.

Burial practices, Scandinavians never adopt using carts in burials. They very much adhere to the ship imagery which goes back very early in Scandinavian traditions. There are also switchovers to burying of deceased males with weapons, notably spears and shields, a tradition that will continue long into the Viking age. The Scandinavians never adopt towns, despite all the trade and activity with Central Europe and the fact that maybe some of these Scandinavians may have seen a Celtic oppidum. There is no movement to the sort of town life that we see in Central Europe. Scandinavia still remains largely a land of villages sustained by this long-distance trade which allows expansion of villages more arable perhaps or brought under control, improved tools, carts, harnessing, but still the pattern of life essentially the same as it was in the Bronze Age. You are living in relatively scattered communities and this is a feature of early Germanic civilization that lasts well into the Roman age also.

Roman authors can distinguish very carefully and accurately between Celtic populations who live in towns as opposed to Germanic peoples who live in villages. From the Romans, it's always from the military viewpoint. The Celts are so convenient to fight because they run into towns and the Romans can bring up their artillery and batter them senseless and capture the towns; there's the military objective. The Germans are nasty because they run out of their villages into the swamps and bogs and you never can find them. So the Romans are extremely annoyed with the Germans; they don't play fair. That distinction is clearly made in Julius Caesar. It's also made later on in Tacitus, that there is a difference in the social pattern and economic life, especially the German's putting stock-raising special cattle above agriculture.

The Romans also noticed a difference in religious practices between Celts and Germans, and these are not just stereotypes. One aspect about this contact between the Celtic and Scandinavian world is the Scandinavians never seem to adopt a priestly past. There is nothing equivalent to the Druids, subject to a lot of myth and rumor and modern re-creations of the 19th century, but there is not the kind of religious caste of Druids that you have in Celtic Gaul ever appearing in the Germanic world, whether in the Roman age or even later in the Viking age; that is, the worship of the divinities is not organized into some sort of overall hierarchy. Furthermore, sacrificial rights in Scandinavia are particularly Scandinavian. The Tollund man, who is a poor fellow who was excavated from a Danish bog, was probably strangled or hanged as a sacrifice to an early form of Odin, and the sacrificial rites of human sacrifice in Scandinavia that we can detect in the Celtic and Roman age are completely consistent with what's later on described in the Viking age. For all of its contact, in many ways the contacts of that Celtic world precipitated the formation of a very, very distinct Scandinavian Germanic civilization.

That civilization had. a chance to expand unexpectedly, compliments of the Romans. A German scholar and a friend of mine, colleague, is always a bit annoyed whenever I make the point that the reason Germany exists is because the Romans created it. Julius Caesar, between 58 and 50 B.C., conquered Gaul and began the Roman conquest of Central Europe up to the Danube. His successor, adopted son, Augustus, completed it, and what the Roman conquest did within less than a generation was to shatter the Celtic world, to incorporate most of it into the Roman Empire, and leave Central Europe open for migration by Germanic peoples. Somewhere between maybe 100 B.C. there was already Germanic movement into Central Europe, but with the Roman conquest of Gaul and the upper Danube regions and their incorporation into the Roman empire, the Germanic tribes spread out of the Scandinavian heartland and essentially filled up the lands between the Rhine and the Vistula and north of the Danube. This is the region the Romans called Germania, by which they meant Central Europe and Scandinavia, which was predominately but not exclusively Germanic-speaking peoples. All of these Germanic-speaking peoples, the West Germanic people who later became the Franks, the Saxons, the Anglos and Jutes who eventually moved to England, the East Germanic peoples, the Goths who invaded the Roman Empire in the 3rd, 4th, and even 5th century A.D., all of these peoples ultimately traced at least part of their back to that Scandinavian heartland; so that the Roman conquest of the Celtic world had a major impact on Scandinavia.

The second important impact was that the scale of trade and contact between the Celtic age and Roman age, the difference was geometric, not arithmetic at all. The Romans had enormous demands for goods. The Romans, for instance, stationed 150,000 soldiers on the Rhine. These men had to be fed. Most of the cattle industry of Western Germany and Denmark was feeding the Roman army on the Rhine—that has now been demonstrated archeologically—that is, there was an enormous market for Germanic and Scandinavian beef. There was also an enormous market in labor, slave trade, obviously, but also the Romans needed just day laborers; they needed auxiliaries, that is, warriors. They recruited into the auxiliary army. There were large numbers of German tribes that moved in under Roman arrangements to settle as agriculturists. What happens is the Roman world becomes part of a safety valve, at least demographically where the Scandinavians and their kinsmen in Germania, Central Europe, can export their excess population into the Roman Empire. And, as a result, there are still no cities in Germania or Scandinavia.

The volume of imported goods from the Roman world into southern Scandinavia is truly extraordinary. The Danish Isles and southern

Sweden, Skane, which would have been part of the later Danish kingdom, show a range of goods that indicates that at least for the upper classes their material life had significantly changed with that Roman contact—fine tableware, including glass, silver, all sorts of fine Roman ceramics. We believe at this point the Germans are accustomed to drinking wine. Tacitus, writing his *Germania,* which is a highly romanticized version of the Germans—it's hard to describe Tacitus; I always think of him as a cynic who does history as a sideline—he writes his *Germania* largely as a way of saying, see how noble the Germans are and how depraved and decadent the Romans are, and yet Tacitus is clearly not running off to live in Scandinavia. He wants to live in Rome. In any case, one of the points, Tacitus says, "Well, we're unnerving those Germans because we give them wine and they gamble their freedom away in order to get vintages." Archeological evidence does bear out that Scandinavians and Germans become accustomed to drinking wine as a prestige item. This notion survives through the Middle Ages. There are references to consumption of wine by the great heroes in the Walsung saga, later the early Danish heroes of the 6th and 7th century A.D. These are not anachronisms. There's enough testing of residue to indicate that the import of wine was a very important commodity to the upper classes in Scandinavia in the Roman age.

Besides wine, ceramics, and jewelry, there are other items that get to Scandinavia, which is a little bit more alarming to the Roman government. This includes really good weapons and armor. Our earliest chain mail armor comes from Danish deposits. These are dedications probably to an early form of Tyr or Odin. One is from Vimrose in Denmark. It's a chain mail or *brynja* as you'd say in Norse. It's a big hunk of chain mail that's been thrown in as a dedication, which meant you had the money to throw armor away, which indicates there's a fair level of trade going on despite imperial regulations not to export weapons and arms. We also find a number of finely wrought swords, and in the Roman age swords become the weapon of choice and are remembered as the weapon in heroic legend, the weapon of Odin that he gives out to his favorite heroes. That is one of the benefits of Roman trade, the superior weapons, armor, helmets, all sorts of equipment very often recovered from deposits from 200-400 B.C. This is understandable. The Romans appreciate the skills of the Germanic peoples. Many Germanic tribes have served in Roman armies. Some of it is coming through the simple fact that the veterans being discharged are returning home carrying their weapons, and in other cases it's through trade goods. Roman impact on Scandinavia is dramatic and substantial.

Another feature of this Roman trade, and again this is one of the reasons why one makes the argument I do in the Bronze Age, is the trade goods coming into Scandinavia again allowed consolidation of power around petty kings or dynasts. The Roman historians assure us in the 1st century A.D. that the Germans are extremely disorganized, and they're very happy about this. They're always inciting tribes to fight each other. But from 100 A.D. on, and this starts with the description of Tacitus, into the 4th century A.D., as Germans begin to move into the Roman Empire, steadily the Germanic peoples of Central Europe and Scandinavia become more organized. There are several reasons for this. One is that the trade enables people to amass wealth in Scandinavia or Central Europe and make themselves kings, *reges* as the Romans would call them. We are told that some of these kings keep around them retainers, a *comitatus*, is how Tacitus tells them. These are professional warriors who are devoted to their lord. They have taken service with their lord. They're expected to fight and serve him, and the description that Tacitus gives of these warriors is quite consistent with the description you get in Norse literature later on of the berserkers, that is, the great warriors who worked themselves up into a frenzy and charged into battle—bare shirts as it means. They're impervious to weapons. They have been inspired by Odin, the god of ecstasy and warfare, to fight for their lord. Tacitus is already describing these groups, around warlords, around the year 100 A.D., and this is probably a change emerging as a result of the arrival of more arms and prosperity which allows some of these petty dynasts to set up great halls served by these warriors. And you already have an embryo, those military societies so important in the Viking age.

Another feature about those warriors is they become increasingly better at fighting. Tacitus and later Roman authors mention the Germans forming up what is called a wedge, in Latin, *cuneus*; that is, a shield wall is the term that's often used in the Norse sources, fighting as dense infantry formations with a great yell and charge. The *baritus* in Latin is what they call it, and in Scandinavian legend and myth, the wedge, the secret of the wedge, that is, the dense infantry formation that can be defensive or offensive, is the gift of

Odin to his favorite heroes like Hrolf Kraki or Harold Wartooth or Ivar the Far Reacher or all these great figures of the 6th, 7th, and 8th centuries. Again, this is because the Germanic peoples are taking their political and military hierarchy from the Roman army by close association, and by the year 200 to 300 in that 3rd century, as Germans raid the Roman Empire more frequently, as this is a result of Roman civil wars and other obligations, they get increasingly better at organizing themselves politically and militarily. This is a feature of Germanic life that's common across most of Germania and Scandinavia. The emergence of what you would call incipient kingships is how some scholars would call that.

By 260 A.D. in Central Europe, for instance, already major confederations around kings have emerged, Franks, Saxons, Alemanni, the Goths, who are apparently immigrants from Sweden, who arrive on the eastern frontiers of the European province of the Roman Empire in the 250s and 260s. So that organization is one of the gifts that come to Scandinavia, more political organization, as a result of that contact with the Roman world.

Another important benefit which is still being debated quite a bit because people don't really associate ships with the Roman world, and that's largely because of the Roman conceit, and that is, there are two important ship burials. One is at Nydam in Denmark about 350 A.D. and the other is the impression of a ship burial in England in East Anglia called—it's really a cenotaph—it's an empty tomb—and we don't have the ship, but we have the impression in the sand. And it's at a site called Sutton Hoo about 625 A.D. These two ships are very, very controversial. They're both funerary burials, and there are various grave goods that are put in the center of the ships. But enough of the construction has been recovered to indicate that the commercial contact with the Roman world, the Scandinavians and the German peoples dwelling on the shores of the North Sea, particularly the Fresians and the Saxons who will play such an important role in the early Middle Ages, that all of these people are probably becoming familiar with using sails with ships, which is a feature of Roman ships. If we are to believe the extent of Germanic raids on the Roman Empire in the 3rd and 4th century, these raids must be conducted by ships that are propelled by sails.

One of our best authors, Ammianus Marcellinus, the last great imperial historian of Rome, tells us that these Germans sail their ship, not row—*navigare* is the Latin word. He means they are sailing. Now the two ships that have survived in the archeological record do not preserve sails and often it's argued, well, Ammianus got it wrong anyway. He's from Beirut and what does he know. Actually, Ammianus served in the Rhineland in Northern Europe quite well, and both of those vessels are funerary vessels, and the best guess is that the mast that was there was removed because that's where your funeral goods were put. So you're not really looking at a complete vessel—you're looking at a burial vessel—and it's perfectly likely that by 350 A.D. the Germanic peoples figured out how to put sails on their ships, which is a very important innovation that leads us to our Viking ships.

Finally, if that's the case, those vessels that were constructed by the 4th century were extremely important for launching not only Viking style raids on the Roman Empire in the 3rd and 4th century but in propelling the migration of the Anglo-Saxons, that is, the ancestors of the English, from Denmark to Britain when the Roman Empire begins to break up in the 5th century A.D. And the argument is that enough Germanic- speaking peoples got over to England from what is Denmark and Northwestern Germany that they linguistically and culturally changed Britain into England. If you have sailing vessels, your ability to move large numbers of people increases dramatically, rather than open rowboats. The second important point is that the Goths, if they did indeed come from Sweden, they probably crossed the Baltic, followed the amber routes, and ended up in the Roman Empire, and that migration of a large number of Gothic people out of Sweden would have again been facilitated in the late 2nd and 3rd century by the improved shipbuilding. There's every reason to believe that the contact with the Roman world probably resulted in superior ships for the Scandinavians and was an important step on the way leading to the Viking ships that emerged at the end of the 8th century.

As a result of the contact with the Roman world, Scandinavia benefited enormously with its trade goods. The trade acted as a demographic safety valve, the importation of all sorts of weapons, ship technology, that allowed for the consolidation of petty kings around halls served by retinues of warriors who in many ways had no sense of nationality. The loyalty was personal; it was to their lord. It was to the war god, which you have already seen in many ways is the embryo of that Viking civilization which is described in the legends and sagas that will be coming up very soon.

However, the drawback to this is that in the 5th century the Roman Empire, at least in the West, collapsed. The barriers were breeched. Germanic people settled in Britain, in Gaul, and with the collapse of that Roman political order also went all the trade benefits. The succeeding centuries, from 400–600 A.D., known as the age of Migrations, was a very mixed benefit to Scandinavia. In some ways it benefited, because all these excess tribes had left. But in other ways it had broken down old trade routes, had realigned the peoples of Western Europe, and would open a new chapter in the development of Scandinavian civilization.

Lecture Five
The Age of Migrations

Scope:

The migration of Germanic tribes into the western Roman Empire in the 5th century created a common Germanic culture centered on the lands around the North Sea. Angles and Jutes from Jutland joined Saxons to settle and transform Roman Britain into England. King Clovis made his Merovingian family and the Franks the dominant Germanic state in the former western Roman Empire. Protected by the Merovingian king, the Frisians dwelling on the lower Rhine developed trade between Scandinavia and Western Europe. Scandinavians emulated the ethos and material culture of Merovingian Gaul, as attested by rich grave goods found in Denmark and Sweden. Scandinavians also celebrated as their own the legendary heroes of the *Volsung* cycle, who were based on historical Gothic, Burgundian, and Frankish figures. From the mid-7th century, these bonds were loosed as Anglo-Saxons and Franks embraced Christianity. In the 8th century, the Scandinavian language underwent changes in morphology and syntax so that a distinct Norse tongue rapidly emerged. By 790, the Scandinavians of the Viking Age had arrived.

Outline

I. This lecture deals with three important developments during the period A.D. 400–600, an era often known as the Age of Migration, reflecting the fact that many Germanic tribes from Scandinavia and what is now West Germany migrated into the former Roman Empire.

    A. The spread of Germanic civilization into the former Roman Empire had major consequences for the Scandinavian heartland and will be the first development discussed in this lecture.

    B. We shall then examine the bonds that linked the Scandinavian homeland with the Germanic societies that were now transplanted to the Roman world. These ties formed part of a general Germanic culture (or *koine*) and led to the transmission of legendary material from the Germanic kinsmen of the Scandinavians back to Scandinavia. As we will see, both groups of Germanic people shared a martial ethos and a set of common values that would become quintessentially Scandinavian in the Viking Age.

C. In the third part of this lecture, we shall look at how this common Germanic culture began to split in different directions after A.D. 600, and how changes in Scandinavia removed the Scandinavians from their German kinsmen. By 790–800, the Germanic peoples of Western Europe had evolved into Christian Europeans, while the Scandinavians had evolved into a distinct Germanic pagan culture.

II. We begin with some of the important ethnic changes in the political and linguistic landscape of northwestern Europe.

A. In the Age of Migrations, three major groups removed themselves from the Scandinavian heartland into the former Roman world.

1. The first of these groups included the Angles and Jutes from Jutland and the Saxons, who migrated to England. Large numbers of Saxons also settled along the northern shores of France, the future area of Normandy.

2. These Germanic-speaking people in England were very conscious of their Scandinavian origins, as we see expressed in the epic *Beowulf*. The epic was composed in England around 675–700 by a cleric, a man of noble class, in Germanic alliterative verse, yet it tells of the Goths of southern Scandinavia. The story was brought to England by settlers from Scandinavia and gives us a great deal of detail about rulers in the 6th century from parts of Norway and the Danish kingdom.

3. These connections are also borne out by archaeology, particularly the Sutton Hoo treasure, which is quite similar to contemporary burials in Sweden.

B. Likewise, the ties were very close between Scandinavia and the Germanic people who moved into Gaul, primarily the Franks.

1. The Frankish kings under Clovis (r. 486–511) were nominally Christian, but they remained similar in their habits to their contemporaries in Scandinavia. The

political assassinations perpetrated by these Frankish kings, as described by Gregory of Tours, seem remarkably similar to actions depicted in *Beowulf* or the *Volsung* sagas.

2. The Franks were the most successful people in Western Europe; they gave political unity to the former western empire and renewed trade connections with the Scandinavians. Archaeological finds suggest that Swedish and Danish monarchs, for example, coveted the material culture of their Frankish contemporaries.

C. The Frisians, from the islands along the shores of Holland and Germany, moved into sections of the Low Countries and along the lower Rhine.

1. The Frisians were the premier merchants, developing the trade networks between Western Europe and Scandinavia.

2. Their primary market town was Dorestad, which emerged around 675 and served as the nexus of the trade routes going into Jutland and southern Sweden. Later, the Vikings would follow these trade routes in reverse.

D. Geographically distant but linguistically close to the Scandinavians were the Goths, who migrated from Sweden and ended up in the Mediterranean world in Spain and Italy.

1. Until the Goths' departure to the Mediterranean West in the 5th century, most of Eastern Europe was under nominal Gothic control or, later, under the Huns, particularly Attila (r. 433–452). Scandinavia was thus tied to Eastern Europe through various trade routes.

2. Some Goths returned to the Scandinavian world later in the 5th century, as attested by large numbers of Roman gold coins found in Sweden.

III. Literary traditions document Scandinavia's role in a much wider Germanic world. Most of our literary sources are prose sagas, based on earlier alliterative verse, preserved for us in manuscripts from Iceland.

A. Early Germanic poetry is based on a qualitative verse form. In contrast, classical Greek poetry was, essentially, a mathematical equation, in which the number of short syllables and the number of long syllables must be equivalent. In Germanic poetry, the key is not the number of syllables in a verse but the number of stressed syllables.

B. This type of composition is for oral recitation, not written communication. Runic inscriptions, which will be discussed in a later lecture, were used for communication with the gods, rather than for composing poetry.

C. We find common features of these cultures in Germanic verse: Rulers maintained great halls, which also functioned as the ceremonial and religious centers of the communities. During the long winters, at social gatherings in the great halls, poets recited stories, running 300–500 lines long, for entertainment.

D. Significantly during this period of migration, the Scandinavians shared in the same oral poetry as their kinsmen in other regions. Remarkably, the first heroes in Scandinavian poetry, who were based on historical figures, were not Scandinavians; rather, they were Germanic heroes of those various peoples who had moved into the Roman world.

   1. These heroes came from a Gothic tradition of the early 4th century, as well as from traditions of the Franks and Burgundians. This poetry also celebrated Attila the Hun, known as Atli in Norse.

   2. The legends tell us nothing of the Roman world; rather, they focus on great heroes and deeds linked to the ancient gods and mythological traditions.

   3. One outgrowth of this poetic tradition was the cycle of three poems from which any poet could recite episodes. The most well-known of these cycles concerned the Burgundian king Gunnar, his half-brother Högni, and their sister Gudrun, historical figures destroyed by the Huns in 437.

   4. In Norse and Germanic legend, these figures lived on as heroes of the Rhineland and became associated with the cursed treasure of the Niflungs. Gunnar and Högni were lured to the great hall of Attila the Hun, where they were killed in a heroic battle. Their deaths were avenged by Gudrun, who had been reluctantly married off to Atli but kills him and sets fire to the hall.

5. This independent cycle was also linked to a cycle of Frankish heroes, which included the famous couple Sigurd and Brynhild, again based on historical figures of the late 6th or early 7th century.

6. In the Norse tradition, Sigurd won Brynhild after he had slain the dragon Fafnir. In the Scandinavian version, the stories of Gunnar and Sigurd are merged; Sigurd marries Gudrun, Gunnar's sister, changing the action of the story. The primary figures become the two queens, Brynhild and Gudrun, with Brynhild arranging for the death of Sigurd and the story ending with the destruction of the hall of Atli.

7. This tradition became the basis of the *Volsung* cycle and served as grist for the mill of new legends told about Scandinavian heroes later in the 6th and 7th centuries. In the process, the West Germanic heroes became quintessentially Scandinavian.

E. Indeed, by 625, the West Germanic kinsmen of the Scandinavians had converted to Christianity and had begun to forget their own stories. Between 650–700, new Christian cultures emerged in England, in the Frankish world, and in Frisia, which led to a parting of the ways between the Scandinavian heartland and the new states in the former Roman Empire.

IV. Starting around 700, the Scandinavian language underwent a major morphological change, becoming unintelligible to the West Germanic peoples by about 800.

A. The general term for this morphological change is *syncope*, which describes a shortening of words in Scandinavian. We see this readily in the names of heroes in *Beowulf* and their Scandinavian equivalents. For example, Hrothgar, the host of Beowulf, is rendered Hróarr in Old Norse.

B. We look at another illustration of this change, a runic inscription on one of the gold horns from Gallehus in Denmark (c. 400). The inscription is in a West Germanic dialect, probably close to English, that contains 13 syllables. When rendered in Norse of about A.D. 800, the same inscription has been reduced to 8 syllables.

C. The Scandinavian languages tended to drop final consonants, so that the German word *fahren* ("to carry," "to bear") became simply *fara*.

D. Vowel sounds also experienced significant change. We see this in the example of the cognates for Old English *scyld* and Norse *skjöldr*, "shield."

E. This change in the Norse language is indicative of many other cultural changes that would redefine the Scandinavian identity by A.D. 800 as it evolved into the identity of the Viking Age.

Further Reading:

R. Hodges and W. Bowden. *The Sixth Century: Production, Distribution, and Demand.* Leiden: Brill, 1998.

Gwyn Jones. *A History of the Vikings.* Oxford: Oxford University Press, 1968.

Questions to Consider:

1. How did trade and the celebration of common Germanic heroes foster bonds between Scandinavians and their Germanic kin in Gaul and Britain in 400–650? Why did Scandinavians admire the civilization of Frankish Gaul?

2. How did Christianity transform the Franks, Frisians, and Anglo-Saxons into Europeans between the 6th and 8th centuries? How did these developments separate Scandinavians from their Germanic kinsmen?

Lecture Five—Transcript
The Age of Migrations

In this lecture, I plan to deal with three important developments during the period from about 400–600 A.D., and this is often known as the period of the age of Migrations. It refers to the fact that many Germanic tribes from Scandinavia and what is now West Germany migrated into the former Roman Empire. These would be notably Franks in what the Romans called Gaul, and it's destined to become France, various people who move into the Low Countries, notably, the Frisians, Germanic tribes that come from Denmark and Northwest Germany that move into Britain and turn Britain into England. That re-peopling of the northwestern provinces of the Roman Empire had important demographic changes in Scandinavia as well.

This period is really in reference to a group of folk or ethnic migrations that essentially spread Germanic civilization deep into the former Roman Empire and has major consequences for the Scandinavian heartland, those core areas where Germanic civilization had emerged. Those migrations formed the first part of this particular lecture. Then what I would like to look at is the bonds that linked the Scandinavian homeland with those Germanic societies now transplanted to the Roman world, and those ties were very important because it not only formed part of a general Germanic culture, or *koine*, if you want to use the Greek term, a common culture, but it also led to the transmission of very important legendary material from the Germanic kinsmen of the Scandinavians to Scandinavia. These include the heroes of the Volsung saga which is one way of documenting this contact, and that led to the development of important Germanic poetry, epic poetry, and a whole martial ethos, a set of common values that were shared by all the Germanic peoples and became quintessentially Scandinavian in the Viking age.

And then the third part of this lecture, I want to talk about how that common Germanic culture that existed, say, around 600–625 A.D., began to part in different directions—that is, the Germanic peoples of what are Gaul and Britain, the former Roman provinces, evolve into English and Franks; the people in the Low Countries, predominantly the Frisians of Holland, likewise evolve into a separate distinct Germanic people—and how changes in Scandinavia will remove the Scandinavians from those German kinsmen, so that by 790 or 800 at the opening of the Viking age those Germanic peoples of Western Europe have evolved into Christian Europeans whereas the Scandinavians have evolved into a very distinct Germanic pagan culture. And it explains a great deal of the animosity and differences between these two groups at the opening of the Viking age. The Scandinavians came to regard these people as potential foes, victims for their raids. There were no longer those close ties that you had seen back in the 5th or 6th century A.D. There are three major issues, three very important issues, and it also opens up a discussion of epic poetry and pagan beliefs and the heroic ethos which is so important to the Scandinavian people in the Viking age because it's being clearly, if not necessarily formed, certainly defined and shaped by the legends that emerged at this particular time.

Let's look first at some of the important ethnic changes in the political and linguistic landscape of Northwestern Europe. The age of Migrations led to three major groups that removed themselves from that Germanic heartland into the former Roman world. The most important group that Americans would be familiar with is the Anglo-Saxons, which is really a term that no one ever used in the Middle Ages. The English themselves call themselves the English, or they might call themselves Saxons if they came from Wessex; that is, they are related to the people of Northwestern Germany. There are also people known as Jutes, but the Germanic migrations between approximately 450 and maybe about 650 A.D. or 600 A.D. came from various parts of Scandinavia. We know in the southwestern areas of Norway, there were people who migrated from the famous fjords of Rogaland and Hordaland. These were later dens of Vikings; they settled in northern England, particularly in the region known as Bernicia, which is the northern half of the later kingdom of Northumbria. Numerous tribes moved out of Jutland.

There is archeological evidence to document that there was a significant drop of population in Denmark. Many Germanic peoples removed themselves to England. These include Angles, Jutes, but other lesser tribes whose names are unknown to us, so that Scandinavia had a constant outpouring of people from Jutland, Southwestern Norway, into England but also along the northern shores of France, Gaul, the future areas of Normandy where large numbers of Saxons settled. And classical authors, notably Procopius, who wrote the rather strange history of the Emperor Justinian, a classic history of writing about great achievements and not crediting the man who performed them, talk of these migrations. He's very, very familiar with Northern Europe and the relationships among these Germanic peoples.

That led to the creation of a Germanic-speaking civilization in England, the various Anglo-Saxon kingdoms, and in this period of the age of migration those people were very conscious of their Scandinavian origins, foremost expressed in the epic of *Beowulf*, well known to students of English literature. This epic is composed somewhere between maybe 675 and 700 A.D., perhaps in the midlands of England, Mercia, the central kingdom, or perhaps in Northumbria by a cleric, a man of noble class, in Anglo-Saxon, that is, Germanic alliterative verse. And yet this epic talks not about English heroes but about Beowulf, who is a Geat—Geatas is the plural—or Gotar or Gautar, that is, Goths of southern Scandinavia probably dwelling along the western shores of Sweden today, pretty close to Lakes Vattern or Vanern, that is, in the southwest of Sweden, areas that were actually historically linked to Norway in the Viking age.

That epic was brought by English settlers from Scandinavia who remembered these figures who give us a great deal of detail about rulers of largely the 6th century A.D. in what became parts of Norway and the Danish kingdom. There are also references to the kings of Sweden at Uppsala. These connections were also borne out by archaeology, particularly the so called Sutton Hoo treasure, that is, the objects found in the great ship burial dated about 625 A.D. It's an empty tomb. It's thought to be a tomb of a king of East Anglia, which is today Suffolk and Norfolk of southeastern England. It's a pagan burial tradition to a king who may have been nominally Christian, so it's technically a cenotaph, and the helmet that comes out there of the excavation—there are marvelous objects from all over the Mediterranean world, including some coins from Merovingian and Gaul, objects from the Byzantine world, but other objects show very, very close connections to contemporary burials in Sweden, particularly burials at Vendel where similar types of helmets, particularly figures sporting boar helmets—the boar was a sacred animal of the Vanir, that is, the brother and sister of Frey and

Freya who were important divinities in the Germanic tradition. So the ties are very close between these English people and the Scandinavians.

Likewise, the ties are very close to those Germanic peoples who moved into Gaul, primarily the Franks, and the Frankish kings under Clovis who converted to Christianity sometime around 490 A.D., and his conversion is very indicative of conversions of many Germanic peoples and we will re-encounter this with the Scandinavian kings. Essentially he prayed to the Christian God who gave him victory in battle. He remembered that one of his wives was Christian, and he tried Christ and it worked. Christ as the lord of hosts was understandable. Clovis immediately became baptized. That didn't mean that conversion led to a Christian life. The Frankish kings were very, very similar in their habits to their contemporaries in Scandinavia. One could read the pages of Gregory of Tours who is a Christian author who's of Gallo-Roman descent, and he writes in Latin about these Frankish kings. If you read the lives of these Frankish kings, the lurid politics, the murders, the assassinations, they sound remarkably similar to what's going on in the great Scandinavian halls as described in *Beowulf* or the Volsung Saga, which is the saga that talks about the early great heroes, or the saga of Hrolf Kraki; so that the great halls of the Frankish kings in Gaul were not too different from the great halls in Denmark and in Sweden described by the legends written down in Iceland centuries later.

Furthermore, the Franks were the most successful people in Europe. The Frankish kings went on to forge a very, very effective kingdom and gave some kind of political unity to forming the Western Empire, and whatever the trade connections had been between Scandinavia and Rome, they had been disrupted in the 5th century and economic conditions had changed with this large migration of people out of the Scandinavian area, but certainly by 500 A.D. trade connections renewed, and in many ways the Danes, particularly, were Frankish wannabes. Most Danish monarchs, from what we can tell from the burial goods, or Swedish monarchs, especially from Vendel, would very much have liked to have had the material culture of their Frankish contemporaries. There's a lot of archeological evidence to suggest that swords were imported from the Frankish world. They had the best manufacturer in the Rhineland. This goes on through the Viking age. Many of the jewelry objects are similar;

what you would find in a Frankish burial is also common in what you would find in Scandinavian burials. The ties between the Franks and the Scandinavian world were very close, and Frankish kings, while they were nominally Christian, were not very good Christians. Frankish kings kept multiple wives. Christian authors usually called them concubines, but they were just multiple wives, as most Germanic kings married a number of wives for political purposes. It wasn't really until after about 625 when the Frankish kings began to become really Christian kings, and that was owed to the fact that Irish monks showed up and started to explain to them what their Christianity meant.

The third important people who moved into Western Europe and are extremely important throughout this period of the age of Migrations in the early Viking age are the Frisians. The Frisians spoke a Germanic language which to this day is the closest related language to English. They had dwelled along the islands on the shores of Holland and Germany. They moved into sections of the Low Country. They dwelled among the rivers of the lower Rhine, and they were the people who developed the trade networks between Western Europe and Scandinavia. They are the premiere merchants, usually operating under the protection of the Frankish kings. They remained pagan for a very long time. They are not really converted until the 7th and 8th centuries. Their primary market town would be Dorestad which emerges around 675, and that would be the nexus of the trade routes going into Jutland, into southern Sweden, and those trade routes are actually the trade routes that the Vikings followed in reverse. There is a reference in *Beowulf* to the Gautor, or the Gotar, that is, the Gothic king, the Geatas in *Beowulf*, Hygelac, as raiding Frisia, Holland, about 523 A.D. It's a reference in the poem which was also picked up in the chronicles, and he's killed in a Viking-style raid. It almost looks like a preview of the Viking age. Those three groups were all-important in establishing new kingdoms and eventually new societies in Western Europe.

There were also distant relatives of the Scandinavians, geographically distant, but linguistically very close, Goths, people who had migrated from Sweden I mentioned last time, and they ended up in the Mediterranean world, in Spain and Italy. Up until that departure into the Mediterranean world in the 5th century, most of Eastern Europe was under some sort of nominal Gothic control or later under the kings of the Huns, particularly Attila the Hun, and the Huns very much depended on their Gothic subjects. Scandinavia was tied to Eastern Europe through various trade routes across the great rivers of Central and Eastern Europe, the old amber trade routes. The Gothic language is very, very close to the Scandinavian languages in some ways, and at the same time there are contacts in terms of common jewelry and memories. The Goths remember they had come from Sweden. Again, our classical sources tell us that some moved into the Mediterranean world. Some of those Goths went back to the Scandinavian homeland, and that's borne out again by the archeology, where large numbers of Roman gold coins, largely of the 5th century, some from the early 6th century, show up in Sweden, particularly at Gotland and in the areas around Stockholm today, that is, the Lake Mälaren area. And the best guess is they're being carried back to the old Gothic homeland by those Goths who remembered those origins and trekked back to Scandinavia some 200 years after their ancestors had departed.

You could see that Scandinavia was really part of a very, very wide Germanic world where these migrations had led to the settling of Germanic peoples across large portions of the Roman world. That is most dramatically documented in the literary traditions. These literary traditions, to which I will return, survive in Scandinavia largely from manuscripts composed in Iceland. These are prose sagas which are based on earlier poetry. The poetry is a German alliterative verse, a type of verse in which the crucial elements in each line of poetry were the stressed syllables—Germanic poetry is based on what is known as a qualitative rather than a quantitative verse form. A classical verse which goes back to Greek models is essentially a mathematical equation. So many longs and so many shorts have to equal out; whereas, in Germanic verse, which is close to the cadence of the spoken language, the key is not so much the number of syllables in a verse but the number of stressed syllables, and particularly those syllables that are stressed should alliterate so that you combine these two half lines in different patterns by the alliteration on the crucial words. That's the type of verse that's used in the epic of *Beowulf* and the type of verse that is innovated in the Viking age in Norse and is represented in the Icelandic manuscripts. This type of composition is for oral recitation; that is, poets did not use writing. The runic inscriptions which we'll talk about in an upcoming lecture were really used for communication with the gods, not for composing poetry, so it's recitation of the great heroes and the gods that counted, not composing literary epics that people actually read. That is very, very indicative of that common Germanic heroic culture that existed in all these areas, and that is, the rulers maintained great halls which also functioned in some ways as the ceremonial and religious centers of the community. And you can imagine you spend a great deal of time indoors anyway during the winter.

So the halls of a great prince would obviously be the center of social activities, and this was captured in the poems and in *Beowulf* as well. The poets would recite stories for entertainment, and most of these poems probably ran somewhere between the order of, say, 300 and 500 lines of verse. And they were based on traditional heroes who were well known to the audience and the poet really did exploit anticipation over surprises as a dramatic technique. What's really significant in this period of migration is that the Scandinavians, being part of this wider Germanic culture, shared in the same oral poetry, and what is a remarkable point about heroic poetry in Scandinavia is the first heroes who are based on historical figures celebrated by Scandinavians were not Scandinavians. Rather, they were Germanic heroes of those various peoples to whom they were related who had moved into the Roman world. These included heroes from a Gothic tradition, from the early 4th century. It also included Franks and Burgundians, that is, people who removed themselves to Gaul, and, above all, it included Attila the Hun, known as Atli in Norse, who is regarded as, well, just another Germanic ruler. They really didn't make much of a distinction between the Huns and the Germans. He was just a great figure.

The legends know nothing of the Roman world. They don't tell us anything about the economic or the social breakup of the Roman Empire. Rather, they focused on great deeds and figures and heroes who got linked to the ancient gods, legendary mythological traditions. What developed was a cycle of three poems. They're not really a single poem, but they're a cycle of episodes and tales in which a poet could recite episodes in a particular hall in a particular night, and the whole story was pretty much well known by the audience. The most famous, the central story, concerned these Burgundian heroes, particularly the King Gunnar and his half brother Högni and their sister Gudrun. They were historical figures of the

Burgundian kingdom who were destroyed by the Huns in 437 A.D. A Hun army showed up and wiped them out on Roman orders. In Norse and Germanic legend these people lived on as a heroic group of kings on the Rhineland. They became associated with the treasure of the Niflungs, or the Nibelungs, in the German tradition, this cursed treasure. And they were lured to the great hall of Attila the Hun, Atli in the Norse tradition, where they were killed in a great heroic battle at the hall and avenged by their sister Gudrun, who had reluctantly been married off to Atli. She kills Atli and burns the hall down in retribution for the death of her brothers. That cycle, which was an independent cycle, was also linked to another cycle of Frankish heroes. These included the famous Brynhild, or Brünnhilde, as she's known in the Wagnerian opera, and Sigurd, or Siegfried, as he's known in Wagner as well. That's the West Germanic version. These, this pair, were apparently a group of Frankish rulers from the late 6th, early 7th century with some really wild and wooly stories told about them in Gregory of Tours.

They captured the imagination because of all their deeds and misdeeds. And in the Norse tradition Sigurd won Brynhild after he had slain the dragon Fafnir. And this is depicted on a famous rune stone in Sweden. He was one of the favorites of Odin, the war god. He slew the dragon by artifice, seized the golden hoard the dragon had brooded over. This was a hoard that had been cursed because of Loki, who had killed the brother of the dragon, known as Otr or Otter, and Sigurd took the hoard, got a famous horse, Grani, and a sword from Odin, rode off with Brynhild as his bride. She was a Valkyrie who was asleep because she had offended Odin. She awakens and teaches Sigurd all the secrets of the runes, and then in the original tradition they got married and lived as berserker and Valkyrie, as heroes of Odin.

The Scandinavians took those two traditions apparently and put them together. In the Scandinavian tradition, what happened is Sigurd doesn't marry Brynhild but goes off and ends up marrying Gudrun, the sister of Gunnar in the Burgundian tradition. That changes the entire action of the story, and it's very, very Norse because the primary figures become the two queens. Brynhild had been promised to Sigurd, but she ends up marrying the brother-in-law, the lesser Gunnar. And this results in a tension between the two queens, and Brynhild eventually arranges for the death of Sigurd, claiming, "I will not suffer two men in one hall." She had been first taken by

Sigurd who then went off and was magically induced to marry Gudrun, and when Brynhild understands that she had married a lesser man, then she eggs on her relative, that is, the younger son of a brother of Gunnar, to slay Sigurd treacherously. Then the whole story ends up with the destruction at the Hall of Atli. Brynhild dies; she joins Sigurd on his funeral pyre, and in death they are reunited in a way they were not in life.

They then go off to Valhalla. Gudrun ends up avenging her brothers at the Hall of Atli, but that's a whole story that has to be reworked. A spell is cast over her and she forgets the fact that her husband had been done in by other brothers. That tradition, which becomes the basis of the Volsung saga, is transmitted from the West Germanic peoples to the Scandinavians. The Scandinavians take these heroes, particularly Sigurd, who slew the dragon, who won the famous Valkyrie and was done in by treachery because he married the wrong woman, the powerful Brynhild who's a Valkyrie of Odin. Gunnar, who, while he treacherously has his brother-in-law Sigurd slain, dies heroically fighting against Atli, is thrown into a snake pit where he plucks the strings with his toes until he gets all the snakes asleep, but one of them comes and gets him, but he dies heroically. All of this material becomes the grist for the mill of turning out new legends about Scandinavian heroes in the generations later, in the 6th and 7th century.

These West Germanic heroes become quintessentially Scandinavian heroes. The names Sigurd, Gudrun, Gunnar keep reappearing in the Scandinavian nomenclature. They embrace these West Germanic heroes as their own. However, by 625, their kinsmen, the people who gave rise to these legends, are forgetting these heroes. They have converted to Christianity. They are coming under the influence of the Latin literary culture, and between 650 and 700 A.D., new Christian cultures emerge in England, in the Frankish world, and eventually in Frisia. That leads to a parting of the ways between the Scandinavian heartland of Germanic civilization and these new states that have emerged on the former Roman Empire. You can trace the fact that starting around 625, 650 A.D., there aren't any more heroes coming out of the West Germanic peoples. The heroes being celebrated are now Scandinavian heroes based on the figures in the Volsung saga.

There's also another important linguistic change that occurs at the same time, and that is, starting around 700 or a little earlier, the

Scandinavian language goes through a major morphological change. You have to keep in mind that these are not written languages in a modern sense; that is, there's not a standard literary form. These are various dialects of Norse, various dialects of English, Frankish, Frisian. Now the West Germanic peoples are beginning to write their languages down in literary form. *Beowulf,* for instance, is the first major literary monument we have in English. It leads to the development of a literary language in English. The Scandinavians, on the other hand, because of the use of language, you speak it, it changes. It gets mutilated in common speech. We're all familiar with the spoken vernacular as opposed to the written. That gives rise to a series of changes in which the Scandinavian languages are transformed into quite a different set of dialects, so that they're mutually unintelligible to the West Germanic peoples by 800 A.D.; that is, in 450 A.D., someone from Denmark could probably talk to someone in England; by 800 A.D., that's no longer possible. There are several fancy linguistic reasons for it; the general term is known as syncopy. There's a general shortening of words in Scandinavia. You can find this very easily illustrated when you look at the names of heroes in *Beowulf* and you look at their Scandinavian equivalents. Very often the Scandinavian name is two or three syllables; the Old English name is three or four syllables. Hrothgar, the host of *Beowulf,* becomes Hróarr, just two syllables in Old Norse.

There are also changes in verb forms, the dropping of certain consonantal forms. The result is the languages really go in two very different directions. They're at the point where you could recognize that Norse is related to English or Frisian or Germanic Frankish, but understanding a complicated sentence is very difficult when you're dealing with any kind of sophisticated ideas. It can be illustrated by two very short examples. One is a runic inscription. One of the rare ones we have is from this period dating around 400 A.D. on one of the great horns from Gallehus in Denmark. These gold horns are actually only known through reproductions. They were destroyed in 1802. There's a very early runic inscription which is in a West Germanic dialect possibly close to English which, when translated, reads, "I, Hlewagastir of Holt made this horn"—*ek hlewagastiR holtingaR horna tawido*. It runs thirteen syllables, rendered in Norse of about 800 A.D. and later it's *ek Hlégestr hyltingr horn táža*. It's reduced to eight. This can also be seen in the way languages diverge. The Scandinavian languages drop final consonants so the German

©2005 The Teaching Company Limited Partnership

word *fahren* "to carry or bear" becomes simply *fara*. Many words in Norse end in vowels, which makes the language ideally suited for poetry.

The shortening of many of the Norse words also make the Norse language very well suited for poetry. There are enormous changes in vowel sounds, especially when you take the basic root word and you, in effect, turn it into what are known as the oblique cases; that is, you turn it into an accusative, a genitive, or a possessive. Those familiar with Latin know that what you're, in effect, doing is conjugating nouns the way we conjugate verbs. Again, a very simple illustration will show the difference. *Skjöldr* is shield in Old Norse. *Scyld* is shield in Old English, pretty close. You can recognize them, *skjöldr*, *scyld*. But when you start putting it in the oblique cases, when you want to use it as an object or as a possessive, you see that that English stays pretty much the same, *scyld*, *scyld*, *scyldes* (of a shield), *scylde*, *scyldas* (plural), *scyldas* (as an objective plural), *scylda* (as genitive plural), *scyldum* for you use with prepositions, but in Norse there's all sorts of internal vowel changes that occur in that basic conjugation. It goes *skjöldr*, *skjöld*, *skjaldar*, *skildi*, *skjildir*, *skjoldu*, *skjalda*, *skjoldum*; that is, there are so many vowel changes.

If you encounter that basic root word in a sentence. you're not going to know what it is. In a complicated sentence, a Norse and an Englishman, they might recognize the basic word. but any kind of sophisticated communication is not possible. That change in the Norse language is indicative of a whole bunch of other cultural changes that is redefining the language in new ways and is one of the best baselines we have for the emergence of a Scandinavian identity by 800 A.D., and that is the Scandinavian identity of the Viking age.

Lecture Six
The Norse Gods

Scope:

Scandinavians in the Viking Age were defined by their worship of the ancient Germanic gods, who are known from classical sources and archaeology. Devotion to ancestral gods was linked with respect to the graves of ancestors. The Eddaic poems composed in the Viking Age and the *Prose Edda*, penned by the witty Snorri Sturluson (1179–1242), preserve a remarkable vision of the Norse gods. The cosmos was conceived as distant worlds resting in the world tree, Yggdrasil. Asgard, citadel of the gods, and Midgarth, the land of mortals, were defended by good-natured Thor, frightful Odin, and mischievous Loki against giants and monsters. Creation itself was provisional, for the gods were destined to destruction in the final combat of Ragnarök. Yet the gods reflected the values and conditions of the Viking Age, and they rewarded and protected those who performed the ancient rites. Foremost, Odin, lord of poetry and ecstasy in battle, inspired the heroes of legend and the sea kings of the Viking Age. Thor, lord of the skies, was invoked at sea, and even trickster Loki reflected the Norse appreciation for wit and deceit. Worship of the gods united Scandinavians, divided them from their Christian neighbors, and inspired the martial ethos and daring of the Viking Age.

Outline

I. As mentioned in the last lecture, one of the great common bonds among the Scandinavians was their devotion to the ancient Germanic gods.

   A. This lecture will stress the literary images of these gods that have come down to us in Norse poetry and saga.

   B. We shall also examine archaeological and classical sources, both indicating that these divinities were worshiped for quite some time in Scandinavia.

      1. The Germanic gods were closely associated with veneration of the ancestors, which is well represented in burial practices.

2. We have found both symbolic ship burials, containing model ships or stones arranged in the pattern of a ship, and full ship burials, reserved for the deceased of great rank. Descriptions of these ship burials include one from *Beowulf* and one dating from 921–922 by an Arab observer, Ibn Fadlan.

3. The gods were associated with important social customs and perpetuation of family traditions, and the adherence to worship of the ancient gods was one of the hallmarks of Scandinavian civilization in the Viking Age.

II. Literary traditions report much about these ancient Germanic gods.

A. Some of these literary sources have come under considerable question in recent years because they date from the 13th and 14th centuries, much later than the original tales would have been told. Nonetheless, without the literary sources, we would be unable to explain much of our archaeological evidence.

B. Our two main sources for the myths of the Norse gods are the *Poetic Edda*, a collection produced in Iceland that contains some poems dating back to oral traditions of the 9th and 10th centuries, and the *Prose Edda* (c. 1220), a handbook composed by Snorri Sturluson and based on Eddaic poems and other accounts now lost.

C. The gods depicted in these traditions are marvelously witty and creative and often serve as foils to human figures. Mythology reveals a great deal about the values of Scandinavian paganism, its importance in motivating society, and its close links to the heroic ethos, associated especially with the cult of Odin, Norse god of war.

III. The *Prose Edda* is one of the literary masterpieces produced in the aftermath of the Viking Age. It was written in three parts as a means of instructing aspiring Icelandic poets in using ancient Norse mythology and poetic techniques to gain patronage at court.

A. The author, Snorri, cleverly recasts the Norse gods as "heroes of old" who came to be viewed as gods by later generations. In Anglo-Saxon England, in Frankish Gaul, among the Frisians of the Low Countries, and in Saxony in West Germany, the ancient Germanic gods were expunged from the records by later Christians, but they are preserved in Scandinavia because of Snorri's literary conceit.

B. Snorri poses most of the mythological material in the form of a dialogue conducted by a disguised king of Sweden and three mysterious figures. The king is Glyfi, but he is disguised as Gangleri ("wanderer"), and he is being instructed about the lore of old.

C. In this account comes a coherent view of the Scandinavian cosmology in the Viking Age. Snorri's prose account is closely based on the first poem in the *Poetic Edda*, the *Voluspa*. The earlier poem is cast as the prophecy of a *völva* ("prophetess") describing the creation of the world, the progress of the gods, and ultimately, the day of destruction, Ragnarök.

D. In the *Voluspa*, the *völva* sings of creation, which is conceived as an ice-bound chasm. There, a giant dwelled, Ymir, fed by a primeval cow. By licking the ice blocks, the cow uncovered the imprisoned god Buri, whose later offspring include the three creator gods, Odin, Vili, and Ve. These three gods slay Ymir and use his body to create the world.

    1. The world that is created is conceived as a huge, sacred tree, Yggdrasil, containing worlds in its branches. This conception corresponds well with the reality of Scandinavia in the Viking Age, divided, as it was, among various forests. These worlds included Midgarth, the middle world of the mortals; Asgard, where the gods dwelled; and Alfheim, home of the elves. The distances between these worlds are vast.

    2. The gods create humanity by breathing life into Askr and Embla, formless creatures who represent primeval trees.

    3. In this cosmology, the deceased return to great halls, such as Valhalla, the hall of Odin. One's station in the afterlife depends on one's activities in life. For example, women who die in childbearing, a noble death, go to the hall of Frigg, the wife of Odin. Those who die of old age or sickness were seen as despised and are consigned to the lower world of Niflheim, presided over by Hel, daughter of the trickster god Loki.

4.   The sacred tree that embodied all these worlds was the centerpiece of the mythology and of many Germanic rituals. We are told that most great halls were built around a sacred tree. The tree is constantly under attack by dragons and serpents, and it constantly renews itself. The tree has three great roots, where the representations of destiny reside, and a wisdom well, from which Odin drinks. Odin actually hangs himself from the world tree for nine days as a sacrifice to release the power of the runes.

5.   At some point, the forces of chaos are expected to be released and will bring about the day of destruction, known as Ragnarök. Odin's task is to populate Valhalla with great warriors for the final battle.

IV. These ancient Germanic gods probably date from the Bronze Age and were articulated in the Celtic and Roman periods. As they come down to us in the Viking Age, they are a very different set of divine forces than any Christian would recognize.

A.   The supreme god was Odin, known as Wotan in German or Woden in English. He grew in importance from earlier times to become the lord of warriors and poets in the Viking Age. He is associated with ecstasy in all its aspects. He inspires the berserkers, as well as poets, because poetry was an ecstatic state in which great deeds were celebrated.

1.   Odin was also driven to attain wisdom. He sought the power of the runes, an alphabet dating back to about 200 B.C., devised from north Italic scripts, that was used to show possession of weapons or jewelry and had magical powers. Casting of runes was a powerful form of prophecy and magic that gave one victory in battle and enabled communication with the gods.

2.   Odin is remembered in the myths as handing out swords and horses to his warriors, but one did not take service with Odin lightly. Although he had great power, Odin was also jealous of his followers and would collect them at the appropriate time so that they could populate Valhalla for the final battle.

B. Other powerful gods of the Viking Age included Thor, regarded as the son of Odin. Thor is a red-haired, barrel-chested, good-natured god, quick to arouse to wrath but just as quick to appease. He rides across the sky in his goat-drawn chariot, hurling his primitive hammer.

    1. Thor is, in some ways, a parody of Odin. The many myths told about Thor reflect the witty side of Scandinavian storytelling, and his exploits in battling the giants who threaten to bring on chaos are famous.

    2. Thor is matched up with one of the most delightful of all mythological figures, the trickster god Loki. Loki often accompanies Thor on various travels and acts as Thor's clever foil.

    3. Thor is associated with the skies and with sailing conditions and was often invoked by Scandinavians against the Christian God.

    4. Thor is also known for his attempts to defeat the Midgarth serpent who encircled the world. The myths of Thor, as well as others, are depicted in artwork, both in Scandinavia and the British Isles.

C. Finally, the important divinities of the Vanir, Njord and his son and daughter, Frey and Freya ("lord" and "lady"), were associated with fertility, prosperity, and veneration of the ancestors.

V. In comparison to other pagan cults, that of the Scandinavians in the Viking Age did not have the institutional organization that we associate with Greco-Roman paganism or Christianity.

A. Very few temples have been excavated. Most rites seem to have been held in the open air. The great halls of kings and princes functioned as religious centers, particularly in the spring before the sailing and campaigning season.

B. No priestly caste is discernible in the Scandinavian traditions. Prophetesses were dedicated to Odin and Freya and were able to communicate with the other world but were not part of a centralized hierarchy.

C. Individual cults and numerous divinities were in evidence, but again, we don't see the institutionalized religion that we associate with medieval Christianity.

D. Nonetheless, in the face-to-face society of Scandinavia, these gods were well known. The morality and religious rites were understood by everyone; the religion was community and family oriented.

E. Veneration of the ancestors was an important obligation of all Scandinavians. Even the lower classes of society returned to the barrows and celebrated festivals in memory of their ancestors. Not properly propitiated, these ancestors could physically return to walk the earth and perform misdeeds.

F. The Germanic gods had been worshiped for centuries. On the eve of the Viking Age, they served as one of the key cultural values that distinguished the Scandinavians from other peoples of the world.

Further Reading:

H. R. Ellis Davidson. *Myths and Symbols in Pagan Europe: Early Scandinavian and Celtic Religions.* Syracuse, NY: Syracuse University Press, 1988.

Snorri Sturluson. *The Prose Edda.* Translated by A. Faulkes. London: J. M. Dent, 1987.

Questions to Consider:

1. How much does the vision of the gods reported in the *Prose Edda* of Snorri Sturluson correspond with the belief and rites of the Viking Age? Why did Icelanders preserve the memory of the old gods?

2. What features of Scandinavian paganism accounted for vitality of the cults in the face of Christian proselytizing between the 9th and 11th centuries? How did successes of the Viking Age confirm Scandinavians' belief in the power of their gods?

The Norse Gods

In this lecture I want to emphasize and develop the themes of the evolution of an independent Scandinavian civilization starting in the age of Migrations and running into the Viking period. One of the great common bonds among the Scandinavians was their devotion to the ancient Germanic gods. They were not Christianized until really the end of the Viking age and even into the period after the Viking age in the case of Sweden. Many were still worshipping the old gods probably at the opening of the 12th century. The devotion to those ancient Germanic gods is understandable, as we'll see in this talk.

We're going to stress the literary image of these gods that have come down to us from Norse poetry and saga, but also there's an enormous amount of archeological evidence and classical sources that indicate that these divinities were worshipped for a very long time in Scandinavia. They were also very closely associated with the veneration of the ancestors and in burial practices, particularly well represented in ship burials. These are symbolic ship burials. There are many instances where you have a model ship in the grave or the stones are arranged in a ship pattern to give you the impression of a ship, and the goods are put into that grave site. This is common not only in Scandinavia but also in Scandinavian colonies in the Viking age; they've been excavated on the Isle of Man, in the Shetlands and Orkney Islands. Finally, there is the full classic ship burial where the deceased is of great rank and is usually put on that ship with various grave goods. Usually, one of the wives accompanies him, a little reluctantly; she is usually strangled and put on the ship with the warrior or the prince.

We have descriptions of these types of ship burials, one from the poem of *Beowulf,* where the legendary ancestor of the Danish kings, known as Skjöldung in Old Norse, is sent out to sea in a ship burial, or the very spectacular one described on the Volga by an Arab observer in 921–922 when the ship was actually burned at the river bank.

The gods are associated with very, very important social customs, conventions, veneration of ancestors, perpetuation of family traditions, and the burial of the dead. This adherence to those ancient gods is one of the hallmarks of defining Viking-age, Scandinavian civilization and one of the great distinctions between the Scandinavians and their Germanic kinsmen in Western Europe as well as other peoples with whom they come in contact. What we know about this ancient Germanic religion—and, as I've mentioned in previous lectures, we know a great deal in comparison to other pagan cults in Europe prior to the conversion of Christianity—depends a great deal on literary traditions. These have come under considerable question in recent years. How much can we trust literary accounts written largely in Iceland, most of our manuscripts surviving from the 13th and 14th century? Really, the application of writing may be dating to the 11th or 12th century in many instances, so the manuscripts are even later versions of earlier recording of these legends. Nonetheless, if we throw the literature out, we're really pretty much in the dark in understanding our archeological evidence. And the literary sources—granted they are stereotyped; they are sometimes misunderstanding earlier practices—nonetheless do very much illuminate and work in tandem with the other sources.

With that proviso, I do believe that the poems which survive in the so-called *Poetic Edda*—that is, a collection of poems made in Iceland and some of these poems going back to originals of the 9th and 10th century, based on oral, poetic traditions—as well as the prose narratives that have come down to us, foremost, the prose handbook, known as the *Prose Edda,* written by Snorri Sturluson around 1220 A.D., these two literary works in particular are our main sources for the vision of the gods, the myths of the Norse gods who really come out as marvelously witty creative figures, often foils to human figures, and undoubtedly reflect traditions and notions about the gods going back into the Viking age and before. Using this literature, especially in tandem with archeological and historical material and a lot of reports that come to us from Roman authors and later Christian authors, gives us some kind of picture of what Scandinavian paganism was and particularly the values of that paganism, its importance in motivating society, and particularly its close links to the heroic ethos associated especially with the cult of Odin, the supreme god and the god of war in the Norse tradition, which is fundamental to understanding the Viking age. Therefore, I think it's very important to spend some time on these poems and this conception of the gods as it comes down to us, because, otherwise, the Viking age is extremely difficult to understand on its own terms.

The *Prose Edda,* in particular, is a marvelous work. It is clearly one of the great literary masterpieces produced in the aftermath of the Viking age. Snorri wrote that handbook in three parts. It really is a way of instructing aspiring Icelandic poets how to use ancient Norse mythology and poetic techniques in order to get patronage at one of the courts of either the King of Denmark or the King of Norway, where the old poems were recited. And if you couldn't get the royal court, then you head for a jral, that is, an earl, a prominent man who was interested in being celebrated in the old tradition. The other important point about Snorri's work is that Snorri very, very cleverly recasts the Norse gods as heroes of old who came to be viewed as gods by later generations. This is a very important literary conceit that Snorri puts in his preface because many Christian authors saw the gods as demons, as ancient powers, part of the army of Satan. In Anglo-Saxon England, in Frankish Gaul, among the Frisians of the Low Countries, in Saxony in West Germany almost nothing of those Germanic gods survives except very, very brief references because the old gods were rooted out as demons. They were cast down; they were destroyed. Their names survive, for instance, in the days of the week. In English this would be Tuesday, Tyr; Wednesday, Woden, the equivalent of Odin. They would survive in certain place names and a couple of other instances, but, on the whole, the old Germanic religion was simply erased and Christianity was brought in.

This was not the case in Scandinavia, particularly in Iceland, and Snorri's account, therefore, allows us to see the gods in operation as literary figures. Snorri actually poses most of the mythological material in the form of a dialogue between a disguised King of Sweden talking to three mysterious figures. He goes by the assumed name of Gangleri, which means the wanderer, and he's being instructed, this Swedish king, about the lore of old. In that account comes a coherent view of the cosmology, the world order, as apparently the Scandinavians conceived of it in the Viking age.

This prose account of Snorri is based very closely on one of the oldest poems and the first poem in the *Poetic Edda,* the so-called *Voluspa* which is cited by a prophetess, a *völva,* who has gone into some type of trance. In really a very, very archaic form of Icelandic, in a very powerful alliterative verse, she talks of the creation of the world, the progress of the gods, the great halls, and ultimately the day of destruction, Ragnarök, the day when the gods will fight the giants and the forces of chaos will triumph and the sun will sink into the sea and the land will fall away. But there's also a vision of a rebirth, apparently under the god of Balder, which is alluded to at the end of the poem. Snorri is drawing on this poetic tradition, and this poetic tradition is a very, very early oral verse going back deep into the Viking age. So what I wish to do is to give you some sense of what this worldview was and how it corresponded to the Norse's own physical world and then to discuss some of the key divinities who are so important for the Norse society of the Viking age.

In the *Voluspa* she sings of the beginning of creation, which is conceived as a primeval frozen land, which is obvious to Scandinavians living in the homeland that they do. There a great primeval giant, Ymir, dwelled. We have no information of his origin. It's simply a poetic depiction. He lived in this great ice-bound chasm, this gap, He was fed by a great primeval cow, and that cow, by licking the ice blocks, eventually uncovered an imprisoned god, Buri, who, in turn, had offspring. Three offspring of the original god, Odin, along with Vili and Ve, slay the giant Ymir and use the body to create the world. The world that is created is conceived as essentially a huge sacred tree, Yggdrasil, which has various worlds in its branches.

This sort of conception really corresponds very well with the reality of Scandinavia in the Viking age divided up among the various forests. Furthermore, the distance between these worlds—particularly Midgarth, the middle world, where the mortals dwell, and Asgard, the world of the gods, or Alfheim, the world of the elves—these are great distances that have to be traveled in the poems, and in the myths and the accounts that come from Snorri there's always this great travel, this deception. There are dangers; you go through forests and over great mountains. The god Thor is always being deceived. This concept of the world is very much in line with what the Scandinavians' own physical reality was all about. The gods create humanity. They breathe life into these formless creatures, Ask and Embla, who are representing actually primeval trees. Odin gives them life and being.

Another aspect about this cosmology is that there are different halls where the deceased go. The greatest go to the hall of Odin, Valhalla, as we call it in English, or Valhöll, in its proper Norse nominative form. Those are the great heroes who have fallen in combat. Other halls are available to you. Your station in the afterlife was very much dependent on your own activities in life. Women who die in childbearing—that's a noble death—they go to the hall of Frey, who is the wife of Odin. Those who die of old age and sickness are seen as despised; they go down to Niflheim, that is, the lower levels, presided over by Hel, the daughter of the trickster god Loki, where the English word Hell comes from. And while that is a rather grim and gloomy area, it's not necessarily associated with the punishment of a Christian hell. In a very odd way, but very significant way, one's social rank and one's deeds in life actually dictated the type of hall you went to in the afterlife.

The tree was obviously the sacred symbol in which all these worlds were encased. The sacred tree was usually the centerpiece of many Germanic rituals and worship. Most great halls—we're told this in the legends—are built around a sacred tree. Germanic peoples usually associated an oak tree. It's some version of Yggdrasil of Norse mythology. When Charlemagne conquers the Saxons in the 8th century who are worshipping the Germanic gods, the first thing he has to do is run around and chop down sacred trees because that's where the Saxon pagans go to worship. The tree is constantly under attack by dragons and serpents. It's constantly renewing itself. It has three great roots where the njorns—past, future, and present who represent destiny—reside. There's a great wisdom well where the god Odin gives up an eye in order to have a drink in order to get inspiration. This world tree is the central focus of many of the early legends and myths associated with Odin and finding knowledge. Odin actually hangs himself on the world tree nine days, as he says, in the *Havamal,* a sacrifice, a gift unto myself in order to release the power of the runes.

This gets us to the final days of that cosmology; that is, the Norse never quite seem to conceive that it is possible to have an eternal order, given their conditions, and at some point, as Odin often says in poetry and myth, the wolf is watching the hall. At some point, the forces of chaos, the great giants, the wolf Fenris, the offspring of Loki who will devour Odin in the final battle, they will be released, and there will be a great destruction, often known as Ragnarök. That, too, is noted in *Voluspar*, not only the creation but the ultimate destiny, the destruction of the world. Odin's task is to populate Valhalla with great warriors for the final battle. The gods that the Norse conceive, these ancient Germanic gods, as I said, probably date from the Bronze Age. They were articulated increasingly in the Celtic and Roman periods.

As they come down to us in the Viking age, they are a very, very different set of divine forces than any Christian would recognize. To be sure, Christian warriors had a very powerful ethos, and most Christian knights well into the Crusades were very, very good on worshipping Christ and weak on the Ten Commandments, and they loved the Old Testament with the God of hosts. But, nonetheless, this Christian perception of the divine was really quite a contrast from that of their Germanic ancestors. The supreme god was Odin. Known as Wotan in German, or Woden in English, he had become the premiere god by the time of the Viking age.

In Germanic tradition before the Viking age, he probably wasn't all that important. In the Viking age and in the Icelandic saga and poetry, he's the lord of warriors and poets. He's associated with ecstasy in all of its aspects. He is the god who inspires warriors, the great berserkers, into battle, and, yet, he is the god who inspires poetry. That might seem a little odd to us, but to a Scandinavian that was perfectly logical because poetry was essentially celebrating great deeds. It was an ecstatic state just as battle was. The great frenzies that led berserkers into battle was the sort of inspiration that gave a poet the ability to record those great deeds to act as examples to future generations.

These two powers were closely associated with Odin, and one invoked Odin if only one had aspirations of being a great hero. He was a god driven in order to obtain wisdom in all of its aspects, the power of the runes. The runes are an alphabet probably going back to about 200 B.C. devised on north italic scripts that came in as one of the benefits of trade in the Celtic age, and those runes were essentially letters used to show possession of weapons or jewelry. They had powers of magic. One carved runes on weapons so that the weapon would work well to cast spells against the enemy and, again, this was associated with the power of Odin. The casting of runes was a powerful form of prophecy and magic which gave you victory in battle and a way of communicating with the gods rather than an alphabetic script for recording mundane documents as we would imagine.

Odin is remembered in the midst as handing out swords and horses to his warriors. Sigurd in the Volsung saga is one of his greatest heroes. Then the heroes that follow in the 6th and 7th century in the Scandinavian tradition, Hrolf Kraki, for example, the Great King of Denmark who held a hall at Lejre built around a sacred tree probably close to the modern town of Roskilde today, the old Danish capital, he, too, was a great warrior remembered for being devoted to Odin.

One does not invoke Odin and take service with Odin lightly. Odin is a whimsical god, a god who can be summoned up with great power, but also a god in the end who is extremely jealous of his followers and is going to collect them at the appropriate time so they can populate the great hall of Valhalla for the final battle. In the case of Hrolf Kraki—the great Danish king of whom I'll speak later—the legendary king who has this ride to Uppsala and takes on a challenge with his Swedish rival Adils in a great contest of heroes, on his return, he's greeted by this farmer by the name of Hroni who offers him hospitality. Hroni is a man with a hood over his head, and he has one eye. Remember, Odin gave up an eye in order to drink at the wisdom well. He greets Hrolf Kraki, the virtues of his victory over the king of the Swedes, and Hrolf Kraki is quite impressed with all his heroes, and Odin says, "And I give you some weapons to take with you." He says, "Oh, farmer, no, not necessary, we'll go on. We don't need you." He rides on and then realizes those weapons had been offered not by a farmer but Odin in the disguise of a farmer. He had offended the great god and his doom is upon him. You do not turn down gifts of the great god Odin. Those ennoble the giver even more than the person receiving.

Odin is, without a doubt, the god of the Viking age, the god of poets, of warriors, of sea kings, who would launch out on those great raids. This god of Odin is already being celebrated in verse in the age of migration in the generations before the Viking age. In fact, one of the best descriptions of him is by Adam of Bremen who is writing around 1070 A.D., and he says Odin is fury, fury in all of its aspects, writing in Latin.

There were other powerful gods of the Viking age extremely important in reflecting the conditions of that age; foremost and best known to us is Thor. Thor is regarded in mythology as the son of Odin, a powerful red-haired, barrel-chested, good-natured god, quick to rise to wrath, but just as easy to appease, who rides across the skies in his goat chariot hurling his primitive hammer as his prime weapon, Mjollnir, which he throws and it returns to his hand every time.

Thor in some ways is something of a parody of Odin. There are numerous myths told about him, most of them quite good-natured and really reflect the very marvelous, witty, side of Scandinavian storytelling. The stories of Thor, both in the *Poetic Edda* and in Snorri's handbook, are eternal. They're just marvelous accounts to read and have ensured the memory of that god long after a worship has disappeared. His exploits are famous. He is battling the various giants that threaten order and will bring on chaos. These giants are always trying to carry off Asgard or make off with one of the goddesses like Freya or Sif or Ithunn, one of them, and Thor is always there for the rescue. Thor's a good guy. He sometimes doesn't always get it right and half the time he gets frustrated because it gets too complicated, and he takes out his hammer and starts clobbering giants. But he certainly is a god who is invoked by most Scandinavians. He's associated with the skies and especially in sailing conditions.

Helgi the Lean, who was one of the early settlers of Iceland and had acquired some Christianity probably in Ireland or Scotland before he arrived and was sort of a Christian, he said, "On land I worship Christ; and when I'm out to sea I worship Thor. He's the only one that makes sure that the weather is good for me." Thor was also matched up with one of the most delightful mythological figures from all religion, the god Loki, who is the trickster god and really represents the Scandinavian delight in cleverness and deceit. Loki is sometimes, I think, Odin in reverse. He's constantly duplicitous. He's coming up with all sorts of schemes. He usually gets caught in his own schemes and many times he accompanies Thor in mythology on various travels and acts the clever foil to Thor.

The most famous is the travel to the legendary realm of Utgard-Loki, where everything is illusion, and Thor is trying to carry out great tests of strength, but he's being deceived by the giant there. Thor himself was, by most Scandinavians, invoked as the primary god against the Christian god later on. There's a famous story told of an old Icelandic lady who said to a Christian missionary, "Thor has challenged Christ to a duel, and he hasn't shown up." This is typical in mythology. Thor is always fighting giants. And the Christian missionary said, "Christ has just been very polite about this because if he showed up Thor would simply be incinerated." That probably didn't convince the Icelandic lady very well. No show means you lose in Icelandic law. It sort of reflects the attitudes of both sides.

Foremost, Thor is associated with his attempts to destroy the Midgarth serpent, the great serpent that encircles the world. Again these myths—just as the myths of Ragnarök where Odin is being swallowed by the wolf, Thor fishing for the Midgarth serpent, the great dragon that encompasses the earth—these are depicted in artwork in Scandinavia as well as artwork in the British Isles, often in context where you have both Norse and Christian traditions. They are not just stories of myth; they are powerful stories used to educate and explain the gods. They are not the same as necessarily worship. Worship of the gods is far more than just the myths, but, nonetheless, these myths are current with the Viking age and the age of Migrations.

Finally, the important divinities of the Vanir: This is Njord and his son and daughter Frey and Freya, which simply mean lord and lady. These were important fertility gods who were associated also not only with prosperity but veneration of the ancestors. The early kings of Sweden, the Yinglinga kings or Yinglinger kings who took the name Ying or Ing in old English—it's one of the titles of Frey. We see the early Swedish kings of Uppsala were seen as human avatars of the ancient gods.

What is remarkable about the ancient gods of Scandinavia is that in comparison to other pagan cults—perhaps through the whole Viking age this is still under debate—they do not have the kind of institutional organization we would associate with Greco-Roman paganism or with Christianity. There are very few temples that have been excavated. There are reports of such temples, one at Uppsala, by Adam of Bremen, and now excavations in Iceland have revealed what we think were small temples attached to farmsteads. There are at least several examples of that. Most rites seem to have been held in the open air. The great halls of kings and princes functioned as essentially religious centers particularly, in the spring festivals, where before the sailing season, the campaigning season, great boasts were made and toasts and the handing out of gifts. These would be associated with Odin but also rites to the Vanir.

There is no priestly caste that we can discern in the Scandinavian traditions. There are seeresses—that is, a *völva* a woman who is dedicated to Odin and Freya, the goddess of the Vanir—who are able to communicate with the other world. They can cast the runes, but there is not the kind of centralized hierarchy. There are individual cults. There are numerous divinities that all Scandinavians worship. There's a great deal of personal choice what divinities you choose to worship, but, nonetheless, the kind of institutionalized religion that would be associated with medieval Christianity, it just isn't there. And there isn't anything close to the so-called Druid caste apparently in the early Celtic religion.

Nonetheless, in the face-to-face society of Scandinavia, these goods were well known, the stories of the myths and the legends, and you have to remember a large amount of the year was spent indoors during the winter and the autumn, and the retelling of these myths meant that everyone knew who the gods were, that the morality and the religious rites were very well understood by everyone. It was very much a communal and family religion. It was particularly very well associated with the veneration of the ancestors. The funerary rights to which I alluded for the great ones, that is, the noblest members of society, approached the funerary rites that would be expected of the great heroes of the god Odin himself. The great ship burials, or the piling up of great war gifts, this would be associated with people of rank. But even in the lower levels of society, there is a good deal of information that returning to the barrows, the sites where your ancestors were—celebrating with a festival in memory of the ancestors, even if not individually at least collectively—was an important obligation of all Scandinavians. The ancestors, as far as we can tell from Icelandic literature, didn't go so much into a spiritual afterlife.

If you didn't propitiate them, they actually, physically, came up and walked the world and did nasty things. There are all sorts of ways of getting rid of these types of guys in Iceland, especially wizard types from the Hebrides. They're a real problem in Iceland. They never die quietly, and if they come up and walk the earth, you have to get the body and burn it. There are various ways to take precautions if they haven't been properly propitiated. So appeasing those ancestors is a very important obligation. It's associated with the burial and funeral rights and associated with the worship of the ancient gods.

These gods had been worshipped in these sites, in these locales, for centuries. On the eve of the Viking age, they are one of the key cultural and spiritual values that tie all the Scandinavians together and make them distinct for the rest of the world. Perhaps one of the ways to best understand the power of these cults—it's not actually a Scandinavian example—comes from a Frisian chieftain. The Frisians, as I've mentioned, were the people who were dwelling on the shores of Holland who were Germanic people in close association with Scandinavia. They were merchants and remained devoted to the ancient gods well into the 8th century. One of the English saints who showed up and tried to convert the Frisians, explained to them the value of baptism, almost had this Frisian chieftain—it's about 700 A.D. when the incident takes place—on the verge of baptizing. He asked the question, "If I accept this new powerful god Christ, what happens to my ancestors?" This is where the saint blew it. This is Saint Willibrord of Anglo-Saxon England, and he said, "Your ancestors were not Christian; so they're dwelling in Hell. The chieftain looked at him and, "No, I prefer to spend eternity with my ancestors." If that doesn't capture the power and value of those ancient cults of the Germanic tradition, no other incident is better in my mind.

Lecture Seven
Runs, Poetry, and Visual Arts

Scope:

In the 8th century, Scandinavians articulated their Germanic cultural traditions in poetry and visual arts into a distinctly Norse style. The Germanic runes were simplified as the *Short Futhark* of 16 letters and employed for communication with the gods. Scandinavian innovations in metalwork and woodcarving resulted in a succession of imaginative styles that contributed to later Christian art. Above all, Scandinavian poets adapted the alliterative, stressed epic verse common to all Germanic peoples into new meters well suited for the syncopated Norse language. Poets recited the ancient myths and legends orally, using formulaic language and relying on anticipation over surprise. The *Eddaic* poems, composed in the 9th and 10th centuries, gave personality to the Norse gods, and Norse poets recast the legendary heroes of the Age of the Migrations into quintessential Scandinavian heroes. While their kinsmen in England and the Frankish world forgot the old heroes, the Norse celebrated and embraced them as worthy of emulation by warriors of the Viking Age.

Outline

I. This lecture follows up on some of the themes discussed in the evolution of a distinct Scandinavian civilization during the Age of Migrations, particularly concentrating on the runes and decorative arts. We shall conclude by discussing the importance of poetry, how the techniques of oral composition functioned, and how the Scandinavians expanded on the basic Germanic verse. These three topics are all avenues for understanding how the Scandinavian society of the Viking Age emerged.

II. The runes were an alphabetic system in two versions. The first of these was the *Long Futhark*, consisting of 24 letters, and the second was the *Short Futhark*, with 16 letters.

    A. The runes were devised from a north Italic alphabet that had been transmitted north of the Alps to the Celtic peoples, who in turn, had carried it to Scandinavia somewhere between

200–100 B.C. The earliest surviving inscriptions probably date from A.D. 200–300.

B. The runic letters were never applied to the writing of documentary information; they did not lead to a literate society. As mentioned in an earlier lecture, most of the poetry that comes down to us from Icelandic manuscripts is based on oral poetry. Further, continuous prose narratives, such as legal documents or historical records, are not in evidence in Scandinavian civilization.

C. Nonetheless, the runes were extremely important as a method of communicating with the gods. The runes are best seen as a magical version of drawing.

D. The runes that survive are usually found on objects, such as weapons or jewelry, and have two features: First, they denote ownership, and second, they seem to have mathematical qualities, each letter representing a number or a magical power to augment the power of the inscribed object.

E. Runes were also used to cast magical spells, such as to protect one from poison, as evidenced in the *Volsung* saga.

F. The *völva*, a prophetess dedicated to the goddess Freya, cast the runes in a ceremony to foretell the future. This ceremony is reported by Julius Caesar. Often, runes were cast to determine who among a group of prisoners would be sacrificed to Odin by hanging.

G. Again, as a form of drawing, the runes were also used in commemoration of the dead. Large numbers of rune stones were erected in central Sweden in the 10th and 11th centuries to honor warriors and merchant princes.

  1. One example shows episodes from the *Volsung* saga, in which the runic inscription is carved into a depiction of Fafnir the dragon.

  2. The rune stones are often dated based on the decorative motifs, particularly the various types of animal designs, that are also found on woodcarving and jewelry.

III. The Scandinavians were heirs to an ancient tradition of decorative arts that were common among all Germanic peoples.

  A. The animal style and geometric techniques on distinctly English objects come from the Sutton Hoo treasure, including jewelry, a helmet, and shield. These objects show a style close to the Vendel style in Sweden, characterized by elaborate depictions of fantastic animals.

  B. The genius of artistic traditions in the Germanic world is found on personal ornamentation. We can trace the development of these ornamental styles very easily, starting from the Vendel Age (400–600) and running into the early Christian period.

  C. Starting c. A.D. 500–1200, Scandinavian woodworkers, jewelers, and rune masters devised an exquisite succession of stylistic designs.

  1. One of the earliest of these is the Borre style (c. 825–975), characterized by stocky and thick designs, close to the Germanic styles found in Sutton Hoo, or 4th and 5th-century Gothic arts.

  2. From this style, more fantastic and sinuous figures evolved, especially seen in the Mammen style (c. 975–1050).

  3. Scandinavians also borrowed from Western European art; for example, we see floral designs from Carolingian art and geometric patterns from Islamic art.

  D. The climax of the native Scandinavian style can be seen, surprisingly, on door panels of Christian churches of the 11th and 12th centuries. Such panels show episodes from ancient myths, particularly the *Volsung* saga, depicted in the almost Baroque Urnes style (c. 980–1200).

  E. Scandinavian society did not have freestanding masonry architecture, nor did the society have a tradition of sculpture. The Scandinavians' chief building material was wood, also used for woodcarving, but much of the art crafted from wood does not survive. For this reason, decorative arts expressed the Scandinavian identity.

  F. There are also numerous references to tapestries and the weaving of runes in tapestries.

G. These decorative arts repeated the myths and legends of poetry, emphasizing the deeds of heroes, and were important ways of marking rank in Viking society. As the Viking Age progressed, the number of jewelry styles proliferated and the amount of jewelry buried in graves increased significantly. The Vikings identified themselves by their personal ornamentation, which is where their artistic genius lay.

1. The visual arts generally correspond fairly well to what we are told in the myths and legends. For example, we often see Thor fishing for the Midgarth serpent on various pieces of jewelry and rune stones.

2. Perhaps the most famous example of this correspondence is found on some cult statuettes that have come down to us depicting Thor and his hammer, among other subjects.

3. In the *Laxdaela* saga (c. 1240), Olaf the Peacock commissioned the finest craftsmen to decorate his hall with woodcarvings depicting the stories of old. The figures were so skillfully carved that they seemed to come alive and dance when illuminated by the fires in the hearths. Hence, these decorative arts were interwoven with the religious beliefs and the daily lives of the Scandinavians.

IV. Finally, we turn to the poetry and its power in transmitting legendary figures from the West Germanic peoples to the Scandinavians, attesting to the common Germanic culture.

A. This poetic tradition is based on oral poetry devised for recitation. Keep in mind that reciting oral poetry is not a task of memorization. Instead, poets were trained to understand how meters worked.

1. In Germanic meter, the technique was based on a half-line of four or five syllables with two stressed syllables, followed by another half-line with at least one stressed syllable.

2. The line was tied together by the alliteration of the stressed syllables, and the half-lines could be arranged in various patterns.

B. Because the poetry was less concerned with the number of syllables than with the number of stressed syllables, it closely followed the cadence of spoken language. Most poets learned the ability to think in half-lines and composed with a harp, enabling them to keep time.

C. Poets had other techniques to help them in recitations, such as the use of formulas and *kennings*, that is, metaphorical phrases worked out to immediately identify mythological figures and situations.

D. Hence, as poets composed, they were aided by both a structure of verse that followed the cadence of the language and formulaic phrases. The stories they recited were well known, although each composition was independent. The art thus created can be compared to the very structured form of a Bach fugue, which also allows for infinite variation.

E. These poetic recitations were adaptable to the audience and the setting in which they were performed and could encompass any number of digressions and allusions.

F. Again, the knowledge behind the poetic recitations, taken in conjunction with what we know of the decorative arts and the runes, serves as a powerful representation of the bonds of society. Poetry was the main means of communicating and educating within the Viking world. The launching of the Viking raids in the 9th and 10th centuries was a stimulus for a new wave of poetry, for improvisation and innovation on traditional meters, and for incorporating new heroes of the present with the memories of the past.

Further Reading:

Brigit Sawyer. *The Viking-Age Rune-Stones: Custom and Commemoration in Early Medieval Scandinavia*. Oxford: Oxford University Press, 2000.

David M. Wilson and Ole Kindt-Jensen. *Viking Art*. London: George Allen and Unwin, 1966.

Questions to Consider:

1. How did Scandinavians from the 8th century on adapt their poetry and visual arts into distinctly new forms? How did these arts and aesthetics define the Scandinavians in the Viking Age?

2. What were the various purposes of the runes? Why did Scandinavians not employ the runes for the composition of poetry or the recording of documents?

Lecture Seven—Transcript
Runes, Poetry, and Visual Arts

In this lecture I wish to follow up on some of the themes I've talked about in the evolution of a distinct Scandinavian civilization in the age of Migrations. I want to particularly concentrate on the runes, that is, the Scandinavian form of writing that had arrived to the northern lands perhaps as early as 200 B.C., as well as some information on the decorative arts, particularly jewelry, woodcarving, and other objects that are some of our best information from the period of migrations as well as for the Viking age and then conclude with the importance of poetry, particularly oral composition, which I've mentioned briefly in the previous lecture, why that was so important in the lives of Scandinavians and how that technique actually worked, and how the Scandinavians also innovated on the basic Germanic verse so that by the 9th and 10th century the varieties of verse patterns and the means of expression were many times greater in the Scandinavian world than it ever had probably been in that earlier Germanic period when these legends were first recited and transmitted to the north. Norse poetry evolves in a very distinct and beautiful way with all sorts of possibilities in its verse patterns, and that, in part, is a legacy of the Viking age. They become more and more adept about celebrating great heroes who emulated the deeds of the past. These three things, the runes, the visual arts, the poetry, are all avenues into understanding how that Scandinavian society of the Viking age emerged.

The runes have excited a lot of popular imagination and one can go on the Internet and find many examples of popular books of how to cast your runes. Usually, these involve either your love life or, less likely, to do in your rival in business. And in a way that's not a bad use of the runes in the modern age, or abuse, whatever, because the runes were an alphabetic system and come in two versions. There is an earlier alphabet of 24 letters known as the long Futhark. The Futhark is their word for alphabet. It's taken from the first. It's like "alphabet," but it's taken from letters that are put together to indicate the writing system. Then there is a later version used in the Viking age of 16 runes. This is the short Futhark, and that is the type of inscriptions one encounters starting from about 790–800 on.

I think the shortening of that alphabet from the long system used by all the Germanic peoples to the short system in the Viking age is one of the changes associated with the evolution of Scandinavian languages, the reducing of syllables and all of the changes in a pronunciation I discussed in an earlier lecture. The runes are apparently devised on a North Italic alphabet, that is, an alphabet that would have been used by Etruscans or Italic people. That alphabet had been transmitted north of the Alps to the Celtic people who, in turn, had carried it to Scandinavia, probably somewhere between 200 and 100 B.C. We do not have inscriptions from that date. Our earliest inscriptions may be from 200 or 300 A.D. One of the earliest I read in an earlier lecture is inscribed on a very famous golden horn. There's actually a pair of gold horns that were found in Denmark and eventually stolen out of the Danish museum and melted down, we fear, from 1802, but they're known from reproductions and drawings. The runes were very faithfully inscribed in those reproductions and we were able to read them, and that dates from about 350 A.D. That's one of our earliest runic inscriptions.

Based on the letter forms, we can give a pretty good guess of when the inscriptions were first made. The runic letters were never applied to, as far as we can tell, writing of documentary information. It did not lead to a literate society. That's an important point to stress because most of the poetry, as it comes down to us in written form on manuscripts from Iceland, is based on what are known as oral techniques of poetry, that is, poetry that is recited to an audience that is not going to follow with any written text. There is no written text. Most understanding of law and knowledge is going to be by memorization, by reciting, either verse or chanting, and that prose, continuous prose, and narrative documents, legal documents, historical records, et cetera, are not going to be used in Scandinavian civilization. That is something that the Scandinavians learn when they convert to Christianity and acquire the literate civilization based on Roman literature.

On the other hand, the runes were extremely important. They were regarded as the power of Odin. They were a way of communicating with the gods, and in many ways it's best to look upon the runes as a version of drawing, a magical version of drawing. Those runes that have survived are usually found on objects, and they have two aspects to them. One is to denote ownership. They give the name of the owner of an object. This could be jewelry and, particularly, weapons. I mention very often these are swords or sometimes spears; they're given names like Tester or The Cutter, whatever.

Also, we get many indications of the runes simply being the same letter repeated many times. And the best guess is that the runes also had mathematical qualities, that each letter represented a number or a power, so that by multiplying the number of the letter, thorn, the "th" symbol, which actually is used in Anglo-Saxon as well as Old Norse, would be a way of augmenting the power of the sword or the object involved. Runes were seen as ways of casting magical spells. There are runes that are reported to protect you from poisoning. In the Volsung saga, for instance, the reason why Sigmund, the father of Sigurd, the great hero who slays Fafnir the dragon and wins Brynhild, does not die from poison is he has the power of runes. One of Sigmund's sons, who doesn't, drinks poison and promptly dies. He has the power to proof himself against this.

There's a ceremony of casting the runes, usually associated with the völva, who's a prophetess who is dedicated to the goddess Freya, the sister of Frey, the goddess of fertility who has many of the same powers of Odin. She has magical powers. She's conceived as a goddess who can fly as a falcon or a bird; that is, she can go to the other world. Odin also assumes the guises of birds to fly off and understand the other world, the upper regions. This ceremony is an ability to cast the runes to try to understand what the future has to tell. There are reports of this ceremony as early as the time of Julius Caesar.

Very often, runes are cast to determine who among the prisoners is going to be sacrificed to Odin, which is usually done by hanging. Hanging is a ritual to Odin. It's the sacrifice of one of the powerful foes you've captured, and this practice goes on quite frequently in the Viking age. The most famous that comes to mind is in 845 A.D., when the Vikings capture part of a Frankish army, 111 of them, we're told, and hang them on one side of the Seine River. Then Charles the Bald and his army see this and panic and run away, and the Vikings occupy Paris, but we'll get to that. In any event, those hanging ceremonies, those sacrificial rites, were also associated with the casting of runes.

They finally—as I said, as part of a form of drawing—they are finally used also in commemoration of the dead, and that again is in communicating with the ancestors. Large numbers of rune stones were erected in central Sweden, particularly from the 10th and 11th century. These were put up by warriors and merchant princes, as I would prefer to call them, men who made their reputations very often in Russia in the slave trade, serving in Byzantine armies, and in a fair number of them who actually fought for King Cnut in Denmark. They erected these rune stones, or their relatives did, to honor them. Sometimes these rune stones were also associated with drawing. I mentioned the famous rune stone that shows episodes from the Volsung saga in which the dragon Fafnir is this sinuous creature upon which the runic inscription is carved, and then you see figures showing incidents from the legend. That type of artwork is very, very, common on rune stones, and these rune stones are often dated based on the decorative motifs, such as the various types of animal-style designs that are also found in woodcarving and especially in jewelry. We have a great deal of jewelry from the age of Migrations and the Viking age, and very often the runes are lined up with decorative motifs which puts them pretty much in close with jewelry. That's one reason why I always think of the runes as sort of a form of drawing. The runes are therefore extremely important and associated with the cults of Odin, with the commemoration of the dead, communication with the gods, and reinforcing all of those heroic values associated with the cult of Odin.

The Scandinavians were also heirs to ancient decorative arts, a tradition of decorative arts that were common among all Germanic peoples. I've made mentioned of two in particular. One is the Anglo-Saxon objects that have come out of the Sutton Hoo treasure, the distinctly English objects. These include some marvelous jewelry, a great helmet that's almost intact, as well as the decorations on a shield boss. All of these, in what is known as animal style or geometric techniques, are very, very close to contemporary styles that are usually often called Vendel style in Sweden, where again weapons, jewelry, personal ornaments are done in very, very elaborate, geometric patterns or animals. Usually you have an animal swallowing something, serpents, fantastic animals; very often some of these forms of jewelry are depicting what I think of as some version of the Midgarth serpent, the dragon. The genius of artistic traditions in the Germanic world were really put on personal ornamentation.

You can trace the development of these ornamental styles very, very well starting from the Vendel age and running really into the early Christian period, and somewhere from approximately 500 AD to 1200 A.D., Scandinavian craftsmen, jewelers, woodworkers, and rune masters—people carving rune stones—devised an exquisite succession of different stylistic designs. The earliest of them, the so-called Borre style which is in the early Viking age, is a rather stocky and thick style. It is pretty close to the Germanic styles you would have seen in Sutton Hoo or Gothic arts I've mentioned from the 4th and 5th centuries. From it, you evolve into far more sinuous figures; more fantastic creatures come in, especially in the 10th and 11th century with the Mammen style, which is based on a famous inlaid ax. You get very, very imaginative depictions, and the Scandinavians are often borrowing from Western Europe. For instance, floral designs are taken in from Carolingian art. There are certain influences of geometric patterns from later Islamic art. All of this is taken by the Scandinavian craftsmen and really turned into a marvelous, native style of decoration.

It climaxes especially in the 11th and 12th century in, of all things, the door panels of early Christian churches, the so-called stave churches, in which the ancient myths are depicted, particularly the tales of the Volsung saga, Sigurd slaying the dragon, or Gunnar in the snake pit where he's trying to play the harp to lure the serpent to sleep and the one adder is piercing him. Regin the smith, who is the treacherous smith who makes the sword of Sigurd and then is going to do in Sigurd, Sigurd learns of this and slays Regin. All of these incidents out of the Volsung saga appear in one famous set of church doors in Norway done in what is known as the Urnes style. That is the last of these great decorative styles that came out of the Viking age. It's almost baroque in its fussiness and is very, very distinct, really uniquely a Scandinavian form of artwork.

It's important to stress these visual arts just as it is the literary traditions. This is a very, very powerful way in which these people identify themselves. Scandinavian society did not have free-standing masonry architecture. They did not build great monumental buildings as the Romans did and the way early Christians eventually did with their great cathedrals in the Middle Ages, nor did they have a tradition of sculpture. Part of it is simply materials. They don't have all the limestone and marble hanging around the way you do in the

Mediterranean world. Also their major building material was wood, and in wood, the Scandinavians really expressed their genius in woodcarving. Unfortunately, much of this woodcarving does not survive. We have some coming out of ship burials, notably, the ship burial of Oseberg that dates around 834 A.D., probably to the Norwegian Queen Asa who is the paternal grandmother of King Harald Finehair, who's the first King of Norway, or something kind of resembling Norway. That includes some absolutely stunning examples of woodcarving, including two dragonhead posts. One of them is the most famous, in the so-called Academician style. It's very, very close to the Jellinge style, the Borre style, close to some of the styles you see on the rune stones. It also has a cart, which is probably a ceremonial cart, very similar to the carts used to move the cult statues around in festivals to the goddesses, the Vanir goddesses.

Furthermore, there are ordinary objects that are decorated both in metal and wood with human heads. These seem to be totems that either represent the gods or the ancestors. We have numerous reports of this veneration of the ancestors, quite a particularly spectacular report by one of the Arab geographers who explains how Swedes, on the Volga in the 10th century, Swedish merchants, set up posts with heads or totems to their divinities or their protector spirits—they may be the ancestors—whom they invoked for good market. So there's this very, very powerful tradition of woodcarving, decorative arts, textiles, certainly tapestries. There are lots of references to tapestries and the weaving of runes in tapestries. Brynhild in the Volsung saga at one point is visited by her rival Gudrun, and what is she doing? She's weaving a tapestry of heroic deeds and runes at the time. This was undoubtedly a common form of decoration.

These decorative arts repeated the myths and the legends of poetry. They emphasized the deeds of the current heroes, and they were also extremely important ways of marking out rank within Viking society. As the Viking age progresses, it is no accident that the numbers of jewelry styles proliferate, that the amount of jewelry found in graves increases significantly, and that there is also evidence of importation of silk and fabrics.

One way in which the Vikings identified themselves was very, very much in their personal ornamentation. That is where their artistic genius was, and they were a distinct people both in their dress and decoration. This would be everything from ordinary objects, such as belt buckles, to elaborately engraved hilts. That is an extremely important component in the Viking age, personal display, putting your wealth in that way, projecting your rank, projecting your association with your ancestors, with the gods, and with the great heroes. Therefore, the visual arts become a very, very important way of, in effect, testing what we were told in the myths and the legends, and they correspond, generally, fairly well.

As I said, there are certain myths, such as fishing for the Midgarth serpent, that actually appear on jewelry themes and in rune stones. Perhaps the best idea of how this must have impressed all Scandinavians—these constant visual representations of the myths and legends—comes from some statuettes that have come down to us which probably represent cult statues. There's a very, very famous one of Thor standing over his hammer. There's another one of the god Frey. These are often reproduced in most textbooks. These types of statuettes and cult statues, rare in archeological finds, must have been extremely common. It reminds me very much of a passage in the *Laxdaela Saga,* written probably around 1240 or thereabouts in Iceland, and it's really one of the finest romantic sagas, probably the best romantic saga of all of Iceland. In there one of my favorite characters is Olaf the Peacock. He's really incredibly, lavishly dressed, even by Viking standards, and that's how he got the name Peacock. He's illegitimate. His father, Hoskuld, supposedly had an Irish princess that he picked up in Norway on the slave market.

In ant event, Olaf the Peacock makes the journey to Norway, gets prime timber, goes back and builds his own farmstead, which is an Icelandic version of the great hall that you encounter in the legends and myths. We're told in *Laxdaela Saga* that he commissioned the best craftsmen he could find to decorate the hall's interior with marvelous woodcarvings of all the stories of old. We're told these are the stories of the Volsungs, coming up in the next lecture, of Hrolf Kraki and his contest with Otto the King of Uppsala, the myths of Thor, the elements of the cosmology that would be repeated in the Volupsa. The figures were so marvelously done that when Olaf threw his lavish feast—and he really was regarded as one of the top Gothi, or chieftains, who settled legal disputes in Iceland—and you went to his feast, you have to imagine the tapestries there. The figures in the illumination of the great hearth seemed to come alive and dance and almost played out the myths before you. This must have been extremely common in most Scandinavian halls, and so when we look at this material we have to really exercise our imagination to see how it fits in with the daily lives of these people and how it plugs in very much with their religious beliefs and their social values that are so fundamental to the Viking age.

This brings us back, finally, to that third point I want to make in this lecture, and that is, besides the runes and the visual arts, once again, the poetry. I mentioned the power of the poetry, especially in transmitting legendary figures from the West Germanic peoples to the Scandinavians, indicating there was this common Germanic culture that begins to break up in the 7th century as the Scandinavians articulate and elaborate their Germanic civilization into Viking age Scandinavia, and their kinsmen evolve into Western European Christians.

That poetry, that poetic tradition, as I mentioned briefly, was based on a poetry that was devised for recitation. Oral poetry is not an act of memory. It is not a case where the poet sits down and memorizes 2,000 lines. You have people today who will proudly tell you, "I can recite in ancient Greek six books of the *Iliad*. I can recite in Anglo-Saxon *Beowulf* or the Norse prose." That is not how poetic composition occurs in an oral society. The written versions we have of those poems are at the end of a very long tradition. What this poetry involved was training a poet to understand how meters worked, and in Germanic meter that was a half line. That was usually four or five syllables with two stressed syllables followed by another half line with at least one important stressed syllable. The idea was to make sure those stressed syllables alliterated; they had the same initial sound to it. That then tied the line together. Those half lines could be arranged in various types of patterns. You could have two following. You could put together a group of eight as a single couplet where each line is syntactically related. You could break them up into a full line or into two or three short lines. There were an infinite set of patterns of arranging this first, and the poet thought in terms of half lines.

Also, since you're dealing with a poetry that wasn't as concerned about the number of syllables as opposed to the number of stressed syllables, it followed very much the cadence of spoken language. Most poets composed at the harp. We're told this in *Beowulf;* we're told this in Norse poems. That harp allows you to keep time. What the poet had was an ability to think in these half lines, and, remember, he has no writing. It's just that, "Oh, Garm bays loudly before Gnipa cave / breaks his fetters and freely runs./ The fates I fathom get farther I see it / The mighty gods the engulfing doom," which is a very good rendition of one of the refrains in the Voluspa. The power of the poetry almost carries itself along with that alliteration if you have the style.

Furthermore, the poet had a lot of extra techniques to help him out. This included what most linguists and philologists, people who study language and literature, call formula; that is, there were phrases worked out which identified figures for you. These could be metaphorical expressions, Norse poetry, in contrast to the earlier Germanic poetry that's represented in *Beowulf* and some of the other continental poetry which are based on all traditions. They're literary epics. But Norse poetry had a metaphorical expression called kennings, which I'll speak about later on in terms of Skaldic poetry. These were metaphorical phrases that were worked out referring to mythological situations. So Grani's burden, which fills a whole half line, means gold. Grani is the horse of Sigurd in the Volsung saga. He carries off the hoard of the Niflung's, the poisoned hoard, which had been cursed by Loki, in effect, and Gunnar eventually gets a hand to it. It's both a learned illusion and at the same time it fits very nicely a half line. The poet would memorize a number of these kennings and phrases which metrically worked for half lines

As he's composing he not only has a structure, a verse that he knows, follows the cadence of the language. He knows he needs so many alliterating syllables in a line. He knows that he could think in half lines. He could boom two together as a sentence or one as a short sentence or refrain. He also has these phrases he can use. Each composition is independent. He's reciting a story well known, in a poetic form of recitation well known, and, as a result, when he stands in the hall and accompanies himself with his harp, each poetic recitation is an independent creation.

The best analogy I think I can give on that would be to think in terms of the kind of very, very structured form of a Bach fugue. Anyone familiar with organs knows that there is a very, very set standard for a fugue. On the other hand, within that formula there is infinite variation. The same would actually apply to jazz musicians who have their own sort of techniques of composition. Many jazz musicians really don't read music, but they know the form very well, and within that form there's infinite variation. This is the genius of Norse poetry, this infinite variation in oral recitation of stories extremely well known and exploiting the dramatic technique of surprise over expectation.

When the poems are recited, the audience already is anticipating what's going to happen. The poet has all of these marvelous techniques to retell the story, and he can slow it down or speed it up, depending on how his audience is reacting. They could elaborate. For instance, in some of these Norse poems all of a sudden the action goes along; it slows down; we're going to describe the shield of Ragnar and there's everything on it, and there's this delight in explaining all the various images on it. Then he will return to the action and really get to the punch line when Ragnar is captured and thrown into the snake pit of Aelle. Along the way, there are all sorts of marvelous allusions. This is in the famous poem known as *Ragnarsdrapna*, which was probably composed in the early 9th century by Bragi the Old.

There's this marvelous ability to adapt the poetry, the stories, the legends, to whatever setting is necessary. The reciting of these poems and the knowledge of all of these stories and myths and legends, taking into consideration what we know of the visual arts, what we know of the runes, these were powerful bonds of society. The poetry, even though in its fragmentary form, survives in late manuscripts from Iceland. The poetry is the main means of communicating and educating within the Viking world.

The launching of the great Viking raids in the 9th and 10th century actually was a great stimulus for a whole new wave of poetry, for improvisation and innovation on traditional meters, Viking heroes such as Ragnar Lodbrok. I mentioned it briefly with his poem, *The Shield of Ragnar*, *Ragnarsdrapna*. Vikings of the 9th and 10th centuries are known to us not only from the literary accounts of Western Europeans who see them as foes but some of them are known from references to poetry where they are immediately cast into poetry and immediately compared to the heroes of old. The poems become a marvelous way of perpetuating not only the memory of the past but incorporating all these heroes of the present and linking them to those memories in the past, so that for many Vikings and many Scandinavians in the 9th and 10th century, they were just the emulators and continuators of the great heroes that stretched all the way back to Sigurd and Gunnar. There was this almost timeless quality of heroic ethos that was perpetuated in the poetry and in the various legends of the great figures of the past.

That is a very good point to stop this lecture, this creation of a poetic medium for transmitting these traditions. In the upcoming lectures, we're going to look at what some of these traditions were, particularly of the early Scandinavian heroes of the 6th and 7th century who in many ways are going to be presented in this poetic form as the precursors of the Vikings.

Lecture Eight
Legendary Kings and Heroes

Scope:

In the 6th century, noble kings, served by valiant berserkers, ruled from great halls and inspired poems celebrating the earliest Scandinavian heroes. The Skjöldung kings, favored by Odin, ruled from the hall at Hleidr (OE: Hereot) on the Danish island of Sjaelland. At Uppsala in central Sweden, the Yngling kings reigned. The Anglo-Saxon epic *Beowulf* celebrated the deeds of this Gautish warrior performed in the service of the Danish king Hrothgar, or in Norse, Hroar. Icelandic poets and saga writers, too, recalled these great figures, but they recounted the deeds of the generation after Beowulf (who was not remembered in the Norse tradition). King Hrolf Kraki, who gathered to Hleidr the greatest of northern heroes, rode to Uppsala and humiliated his rival, Adils. These traditions of valorous lords and their devoted warriors dedicated to Odin emphasized reckless courage that gave Scandinavian warriors the will to win or to accept a heroic death. Viking sea kings would later set forth in their longships with an ecstatic joy in battle that stunned their Christian foes. Honor, riches, emulation of the ancient heroes, and entrance into Valhalla inspired Viking warriors for the next three centuries to prevail over their far more numerous and better armed opponents.

Outline

I. This lecture concludes our discussion of the cultural and religious background of Scandinavia in the Viking Age, concentrating on the earliest heroes of Scandinavia, celebrated in legend and poetry, those associated with the later kingdoms of Denmark and Sweden. This lecture is an important transition into the Viking Age for several reasons.

   A. The heroes we will discuss date from the 6th and 7th centuries A.D., and in many ways, they were not only characters to emulate but also historical figures, kings who ruled in what later came to be Sweden, Norway, and Denmark. Thus, they had a dual influence on the later Viking Age.

B. These heroes served as models for later kings of Scandinavia, including the Skjöldung kings, who were associated with the great hall at Hleidr (OE: Hereot) on the island of Sjaelland; the Yngling kings in central Sweden at Uppsala; and the Gautar kings (OE: Geats) in what would become the basis of the kingdom of Norway.

C. These legends give us another version of the Scandinavian heroic ethos, as well as window into some of the political geography that was beginning to take shape in Scandinavia on the eve of the Viking Age.

II. How do we know about these legendary figures of the 6th and 7th centuries who came to be regarded as the first kings of Denmark, Sweden, and Norway?

A. One of our sources is the Old English epic *Beowulf* (c. 675–700), which harkens back to the techniques of oral poetry but was created as a work of written literature. It was written as a single epic, combining three or four stories and probably using Vergil's *Aeneid* as its model. *Beowulf* is set in pagan Scandinavia, but it is also imbued with Christian ideas.

    1. The poem reflects events in Scandinavia more faithfully, in some ways, than the later Norse tradition. The Anglo-Saxon settlers who carried these stories to England came from a Scandinavia that had not yet coalesced into anything that looked remotely like the kingdoms of Norway, Sweden, and Denmark; therefore, they more accurately remembered the homeland of Beowulf and his Geats.

    2. These settlers also remembered that the Swedes dwelled around Uppsala and that much of what is now Sweden was divided into independent tribes. There was great distance separating the Swedes from the Danes, who were primarily located on the island of Sjaelland.

B. In contrast, the later Norse sources usually include quotations from earlier poems encapsulated in narrative prose sagas. The most famous of these is the saga of the Danish king Hrolf Kraki (c. 13th century A.D.), which discusses the same figures that are seen in *Beowulf*, but where *Beowulf* deals with figures from the first half of the 6th century, the saga of Hrolf Kraki concentrates on the generation after *Beowulf*.

C. A number of chronicles and legendary histories have also come down to us, written in Latin by Danish authors. The most important of these was penned by Saxo Grammaticus (c. 1150–1216), a Danish cleric writing in the age of the Christian king Valdemar I (r. 1157–1182).

D. Again, the Norse accounts were written without an understanding of the fragmented political geography that must have existed before the Viking Age and in the time of *Beowulf*. These accounts have already cast the heroes of these sagas into the classic three kingdoms.

III. The realm of *Beowulf*, along the western shores of Sweden today, is borne out in the archaeology as a royal center, although Beowulf himself is not remembered in the Norse tradition. (Beowulf may be represented as Bothvar Bjarki, a Norwegian berserker at the court of Hrolf Kraki who fights in the form of a great bear.)

A. Already in the 6th century on the island of Sjaelland, both the Anglo-Saxon and the Norse sources agree, there was a powerful kingdom, ruled from the great hall of Hleidr (OE: Hereot). At the time, the legendary kings ruling there, the Skjöldung ("kings of the shield"), traced their descent to an eponymous hero who was said to be descended from Odin. These Danish rulers had very little control outside of the main island of Sjaelland.

B. Their contemporaries and rivals were the Yngling kings of Sweden, who claimed descent from the god Frey and were remembered in the epics as great opponents. Again, archaeology verifies the fact that there were dense populations around the Uppsala Lake Mälaren area, on the island of Sjaelland, and in the apparent heartland of *Beowulf*. These three regions would become the nucleus for the later Scandinavian kingdoms.

IV. The action of *Beowulf* is concentrated on a hero who travels to Denmark to rid the hall Hereot of the horrid creature Grendel.

A. Beowulf fights Grendel and Grendel's mother in tremendous combats, then returns to rule over his kingdom after his lord is killed. Ultimately, Beowulf dies fighting a dragon that seems to come straight out of Germanic mythology. In the Anglo-Saxon tradition, this story is a fantastic legend embodying creatures and beasts from a primeval past.

B. In the Norse tradition, the legends concentrate on human action and reveal conflicts between personalities. The Norse writers of the 12th and 13th centuries, in other words, saw these earlier kingdoms as the prototypes of the kingdoms of their own day.

V. Hrolf Kraki, without a doubt, must have been a remarkable figure. He probably lived sometime between A.D. 550 and A.D. 575 and was remembered in the tradition as one of the favorites of Odin.

A. Hrolf's birth was the result of an incestuous union between his father, a Viking chief named Helgi, and Helgi's daughter, Yrsa.

B. Hrolf himself is the epitome of a king of the Age of Migrations and of the Viking Age. By his charisma and because of his favor from Odin, he collects around him the greatest heroes of the northland. Hrolf presides over his hall in much the same way that Odin presides over Valhalla.

C. As a result, numerous heroes and figures, many of them probably unrelated to Hrolf or his time period, are incorporated into this Danish legend and become part of Hrolf's group of retainers. In the 6th and 7th centuries and in the Viking Age, these men were probably known as berserkers, although this perspective changed in the later Christian accounts of the 12th and 13th centuries.

D. Hrolf clashed with his contemporary in Sweden, Adils, who eventually married Hrolf's mother/sister. In the legend, Hrolf made a famous ride to challenge the king at Uppsala, a journey through the forests of Sweden that would have taken a month to six weeks.

1. Along the way, Hrolf meets Odin, disguised as the farmer Hrani, who tests Hrolf's warriors. Ultimately, all the warriors fail except for Hrolf's 12 companions, so all the rest are sent back to Denmark. When Hrolf arrives at Uppsala, he is accompanied only by these 12 champions.

2. Hrolf and his men take over the hall at Uppsala, slaying the Swedish warriors who are waiting to trap them. The Swedish king Adils flees, and Hrolf is established as the greater king.

3. Eventually, Adils raises an army and returns, and Hrolf and his companions ride off. In the course of their escape, they throw the gold that they have captured across the fields of Uppsala. Of course, the Swedes dismount and fight over the gold, and the Danes gallop away.

E. The story may seem odd to us, but ultimately, it tells of a test of valor and honor. The clash was not about territory but about who was the greater king. A great king was a man who attracted to himself great warriors and showed an example of generosity to those warriors. In the Age of Migration, this ability was politically important; kingship was acquired through personal reputation and charisma.

F. This same world is captured vividly in *Beowulf* in the boasting that takes place during the feasts at the great halls. Oaths were sworn on rings associated with Odin, and those who made these boasts had to deliver. These traditions were very powerful, and when we look at the legends of Beowulf and Hrolf Kraki, we see the way in which politics was played out.

VI. What was the importance of these legendary figures in the Viking Age?

A. To some extent, they were added to the great hall of heroes going back to the Volsungs. They also reveal an important point that is now being debated among scholars.

B. Revisionist scholars have argued that the impact of the Vikings was greatly exaggerated: They were essentially pirates and were marginal to the development of Western Europe. These same scholars have noted that Western Europeans in Anglo-Saxon England and Carolingian Europe were hardly models of Christian piety. In fact, the Christian warrior caste was also brutal.

C. But the Scandinavians who launched out on raids several generations later than the epics we have been discussing were not burdened with any notion of a "just war." The

Western Europeans were not prepared to face the Scandinavians, who saw themselves as the emulators of their great heroes of the past. The Scandinavians knew that in battle, victory goes to those who have the will and determination to prevail, enabling them, as we shall see, to sweep aside more numerous and better armed opponents.

Further Reading:

Turville-Petre, G. *The Heroic Age of Scandinavia*. London: Hutchinson's University Library, 1951.

The Saga of King Hrolf Kraki. Translated by J. Byock. New York: Penguin Books, 1998.

Questions to Consider:

1. How do the Old English epic *Beowulf* and the Norse sagas about legendary figures associated with the Skjöldung kings of Denmark reflect conditions in Scandinavia during the Age of Migrations (400–600)? How accurate are the depictions of social and religious practices?

2. How important was honor in motivating warriors to serve their lord? Why was Hrolf Kraki remembered as a great lord?

3. Why would the heroes of this legendary past exercise such an influence on the imagination of later Scandinavians in the Viking Age? Why would later Christian Scandinavians also regard these heroes as worthy of emulation?

Lecture Eight—Transcript

Legendary Kings and Heroes

In this lecture I plan to conclude the discussion of the cultural and religious background of Scandinavia in the Viking age. In this particular lecture I want to concentrate on the earliest heroes of Scandinavia who are celebrated in the traditional verse I spoke about in the previous two lectures. These would be heroes associated with eventually the kingdoms of Denmark and Sweden. This lecture is an important transition into the Viking age for several reasons. The heroes date from the 6th and 7th century A.D., and in many ways they were not only examples to emulate, such as the legendary figures of Gunnar and Sigurd from the Volsung saga or the great gods Thor and Odin who were told in the myths, these were figures who were historical characters. They were actually kings who ruled in what later came to be Sweden, Norway, and Denmark. These figures had a dual influence on the later Viking age.

One is, yes, they were great heroes; they were persons you would emulate; and they in turn were probably emulating the heroes before them. But, on the other hand, they also became associated with the great halls at Hleidr or Hereot which are on the island of Sjaelland, or Sjaelland as we say in English, which is the largest Danish island, and therefore acted as a model for the later kings of Denmark who came to unite the kingdom of Denmark in many ways saw themselves as the heirs not only to the courage and the deeds but also to the political legacy of these early kings of Denmark.

The same is true with a group of heroes and kings who are known from the area of central Sweden who are associated at Uppsala, which continued to be a great sanctuary through the Viking age and probably was still operating as a pagan sanctuary into the early 12th century A.D. That was associated with another line of kings, the Ynglingar, or the Yngling kings, who claimed to be associated with the god Frey, the god of prosperity, the god of the other life, associated with boars. There was a great hall there, especially remembered, with the rather avaricious and nasty king Ottos, who is the opponent of Hrolf Kraki, the great king in Denmark who's at the hall at Hleidr. Finally, there is a memory of heroes who would become associated with eventually what became the basis of the kingdom of Norway, even though today that area is part of Sweden.

And these would be the so-called West Gautar, or Gautar, the Geatas of the Old English poem, *Beowulf,* and the hero Beowulf, who's, well, not really remembered in the Scandinavian tradition, is part of yet another political legacy that fed into the creation of the kingdom of Norway.

What the legends give us, and these would be legends covering events from roughly about 490 A.D. to maybe 700 A.D., is not only another version and insight into this heroic ethos but also a window into some of the political geography that is beginning to take place in Scandinavia on the eve of the Viking age as well as the types of sea kings. And I prefer to call them sea kings, rather than chiefs, who would launch the great Viking attacks. What these figures don't have in the 6th and 7th centuries are the ships that will be capable of conducting those Viking raids. And we will discuss the ship technology in an upcoming lecture. That ship technology is going to essentially be revolutionary in its military and political implications and eventually even in its economic implications. These legendary figures of Scandinavia in the 6th and 7th century, the earliest Scandinavian heroes to be celebrated in poem and later in saga, are still dwelling in a world where ships have not yet progressed to the sleek long ships of the Viking age, and a good deal of the trade as far as we can tell from the surviving archeological evidence is really in the hands of Frisian, that is, the west Germanic peoples settled along the islands of Holland who were under the protection of the Frankish kings and carrying out most of the carrying trade between the Frankish world and England and Scandinavia in this period.

How do we know about these legendary figures of the 6th and 7th century who came to be regarded in some ways as the first kings of Denmark, Sweden, and Norway? We have some rather unusual sources on this. One is that Old English epic of *Beowulf,* which I mentioned in another context. *Beowulf* is a very peculiar poem. It is based on all poetic techniques; that is, it goes back to the early Germanic poetry, but it was created as a literary masterpiece. It was written by a man, probably living in a monastery, of noble birth. It's an anonymous composition; it uses the Old English techniques, but it was written as a single epic in which he took really probably three or four stories and combined them, using probably the *Aeneid* of Vergil, the great Roman epic, as his model. It is also imbued with various Christian ideas. *Beowulf* is set in pagan Scandinavia, but this English author, being a Christian probably—his family had been Christians at this point for maybe one or two generations—has updated it religiously so that references to the ancient gods were removed although the action and the ethos in the poem is very, very pagan indeed, in many ways. That epic, which was perhaps composed in its current form somewhere around 675- 725 A.D., survives on a single manuscript that goes back to the Cotton Library, which is a very important library established in the early Modern age. The poem does reflect events in Scandinavia in some ways more faithfully than the later Norse traditions.

The ancestors of the English who carried these traditions over to England came from a Scandinavia that had not yet coalesced into anything remotely looking like the kingdoms of Norway, Sweden, and Denmark. And, therefore, they remember the Geatas, or the Gautar, as an independent group dwelling on what is now the western shore of Sweden, which historically was associated with Norway, would only become part of Sweden under a treaty in 1658, and that is the homeland of *Beowulf* which is often referred to as West Gautland, the western Goths. It's just north of the modern river Gautar that feeds into Lake Vanern and hooks around towards the Oslo fjord. Beowulf's kingdom where he lived in 500 A.D., that of his lord Hygelac, was really in some ways the eventual political basis for the Norwegian kingdom that grew up around the Oslo fjord and the Uplands. They also remember that the Svear—Swede actually is the Anglo-Saxon rendition of the Norse name of these people— dwelled around Uppsala, that they lived around Lake Mälaren, and that much of what is now Sweden was divided up into independent tribes and people. There was great distance separating the Swedes from the Danes who are primarily located on the Island of Zalant. Jutland, the peninsula that most people associate with Denmark, at this point was probably home to a whole bunch of different tribes and had very little to do with the Danes.

The information that comes from the Norse sources is much later. It comes from Icelandic tradition. There were a number of poems associated with the heroes of this period but these poems are usually quoted within prose narrative sagas. The most famous of them is *The Saga of Hrolf Kraki* written in the 13th century A.D. *The Saga of Hrolf Kraki* talks about the same figures that you have in *Beowulf*. Beowulf is talking about figures among the Danes and the Swedes, probably from the first half of the 6th century A.D. *The Saga of Hrolf*

Kraki concentrates on the generation after, on the King Hrolf Kraki who ruled at Hleidr, the great hall of Sjaelland, who was obviously the favorite of Odin, who was in many ways the model king for later Danish kings that would like to think of themselves as descendants of this king in Sjaelland one way or the other, or at least to his political legacy. Nonetheless, he is only a tangential figure in Beowulf's account. He isn't very important in the poem of *Beowulf*. He's only mentioned in passing because Beowulf is really more interested in the Gautish hero, Götar hero, the Gothic hero, from now is what the Scandinavians would have called Norway, as well as the Danes of that generation.

There are a number of chronicles that have come down to us in Latin, written by Danish authors, and legendary histories, and the most important one that I'll mention quite frequently in this course, which is a major source not only for this period but running through the whole Viking age, is a chronicle written by an ecclesiastical historian by the name of Saxo Grammaticus, a Danish cleric writing in the age of Vladimir I who was a Christian king of Denmark from 1157-1182 and in many ways made the Danish medieval kingdom a great kingdom in the 12th century. Vladimir presided over a very important literary revival in Denmark in which there was a great deal of composition in Latin in which these Danish Christian kings are trying to project themselves as the Christian heirs of the kings, going back to Hrolf Kraki and earlier, the so-called Skjöldungar or the Skjöldung kings of Denmark, that is, of the family of Hrolf Kraki. That means that the Norse accounts are written without the same benefit of political geography of *Beowulf*. *Beowulf* is actually much closer to the very, very broken and fragmented political geography that must have existed in Scandinavia before the Viking age, where Denmark, Norway, and Sweden at best were an embryo, whereas the Norse accounts writing of these heroes have cast these heroes already into, well, this is the king of Denmark, Hrolf Kraki. This is going to be the king of Norway. They are thinking already in the classic three kingdoms which are really a result of the Viking age rather than a cause.

The realm of *Beowulf*, which is along the western shores of Sweden today north of the so-called Göta River and bordering on the shore, is also borne out in the archaeology as a royal center. There are a number of important and impressive barrows, some early rune stones from the area. It clearly was the center of royal power. Beowulf himself is never really remembered in the Norse tradition. The best guess is that he is represented as Bödvar Bjarki, who is a hero at the court of Hrolf Kraki, who is said to be a Norwegian. By the time the Norse authors wrote, the region which was Götlan in Beowulf's time, in the 6th century, had long passed under the control of largely Norway, some of it under Sweden. So Beowulf is remembered as a berserker at the court of Hrolf Kraki, or a part of this legendary figure who fights in the form of a great bear. He has actually two brothers who are part animals as well. It's a real wild and rather wooly group that comes out of Norway to serve the Danish king. What we can tell is that already in the 6th century on the island of Sjaelland both the Anglo-Saxon and the Norse sources really agree. There was a powerful kingdom ruled on that island from kings at this great hall which in many ways probably seen as the equal of Valhalla. It's called Heart in the Anglo-Saxon tradition or Hleidr in the Danish tradition.

In many ways it is the predecessor of the latest Christian capital of Roeskilde. At the time, the legendary kings ruling there, the so-called Skjöldungar or Skjöldung kings, the kings of the shield, trace their descent back to an eponymous hero who was supposed to be perhaps descended from Odin. Furthermore these Danish rulers had very little control outside of the main island of Denmark. They may have exercised control in Skane. There's very little evidence that they ruled in Jutland. Their contemporaries and rivals were the Yngling kings of Sweden who claimed descent from the god Frey and were remembered in the epics as great opponents. Again, archeology does verify the fact that there are dense population settlements and graves around the Uppsala-Lake Mälaren area on the Island of Sjaelland as well, as I've mentioned, the apparent heartland of Beowulf. Those three regions end up becoming, interestingly and significantly enough, the nucleus for the later Scandinavian kingdoms.

In *Beowulf,* the legend and action of the poem is really concentrated on this hero who travels to Denmark to rid the Danish hall Heorot of the horrid creature Grendel. To the English poet, Scandinavia is a remote and misty land, populated with Grendel who's a monster who's never really very well described.

There's been several suggestions of what his name means; it might be related to a Norse word of the blowing wind. There's another one where he essentially translates as a bottom feeder. He's some creature from the depth. In the Anglo-Saxon tradition Beowulf fights Grendel, then Grendel's mother, in these fantastic combats. He goes back to rule over his kingdom once his lord Hygelac is killed in a raid in Frisia and dies fighting a dragon, and a dragon that comes right our of Germanic mythology, as in all dragons. Why do dragons get angry? Someone stumbled into the lair and stole some of the gold treasure, so the dragon lashes out, and Beowulf combats and fights this monster. In the Anglo-Saxon tradition, while they do remember the names quite accurately in some ways and the kingdoms, this is all a fantastic legend. It's associated with great creatures and beasts from a primeval past.

In the Norse tradition the legends are quite different. Concentration is on human action, on great kings like Hrolf Kraki, who's the generation after Beowulf, or his rival in Sweden. There are conflicts between personalities. The kings attack each other and are trying to strive for gaining control of the great heroes of the northland. Some of these elements are also in *Beowulf*, but they're not the primary action. The Norse writers of the 12th and 13th century saw these kingdoms as sort of prototypes for the kingdoms of their own days, the foundations of these later states.

Hrolf Kraki, without a doubt, must have been a remarkable figure. He gave rise to a legendary figure, remember, not only in Scandinavian tradition but also in Anglo-Saxon tradition. He probably lived somewhere between 550-575 A.D, and he was remembered in the tradition as one of the favorites of Odin. His great court was built around an oak tree symbolic of Yggdrasil. He was, in turn, the son of a great figure who had been a Viking chief and a rather minor figure in the *Beowulf* poem. He's actually the result of an incestuous union between his father and his sister, Yrsa. The father marries the daughter in a rather complicated etiological myth. His father's name is Helgi, who is remembered also in the Anglo-Saxon tradition.

What's important about Hrolf Kraki is he is the epitome of what not only a king of the age of Migrations is but also a king of the Viking age. It is by his charisma, it is by his gift giving, it is by his favor of Odin that he collects around him the greatest heroes of the northland, and they come from different places, such as Bjarki, from what is now Norway, Hjalti—Svipdag the famous Swedish hero. Much of the traditions about Hrolf Kraki, and there would have been a very, very extensive poetic cycle in which poems would be recited, really concerned his heroes, and in many ways Hrolf Kraki presided over his hall the way Odin presides over Valhalla; that is, Odin's hall is populated with all the great heroes of the past. He is waiting for the final day of doom, *Ragnarök*, and he keeps adding these heroes into his hall, and so Hrolf Kraki, in some ways, is presiding in Denmark in the way Odin presides in Asgard.

The result is numerous heroes and figures, many of them probably unrelated to Hrolf Kraki, and even in that period get incorporated into this Danish legendary king and become part of the great group of retainers. In the era of the 6th and 7th century and in the Viking era, these men were probably known as berserkers, that is, the frenzied warriors who understood the power of runes and could work themselves up into battle rages where they charged into battle without any regard for themselves. The word still survives in English, to go berserk, that is, to go into a rage, and by the time you get to the 13th and 14th century where Scandinavians are Christians, they kind are a little stand-offish on berserkers. This isn't really what you want to recommend. You're thinking more in terms of chivalrous knights, and berserkers don't really work out very well as chivalrous knights, and so in the prose accounts of the traditions of Hrolf Kraki the berserkers become these crazy warriors that the heroes like Hrolf Kraki or Bjarki actually defeat. So they become sort of a class of strange opponents. The berserkers of Hrolf Kraki's court then become heroes who are a little more respectable and Christianized. But they all probably were in this class of berserkers that are discussed in classical and medieval accounts of the professional warriors.

Hrolf Kraki, remembered as a valiant king, clashed with his contemporary in Sweden, and that is a fellow by the name of Adils who in the legend ends up marrying Hrolf Kraki's mother, Usr, who is actually his half sister in the myth. There was a recollection in the legend that Hrolf Kraki had made a famous ride to Uppsala, that he left his court at Hleidr, crossed over into what is known as Sweden, Skane, and with his heroes galloped up to challenge the king of Uppsala. The cause of this attack is a little obscure. It involves treasure; it involves honor; it involves some sort of dynastic issue. This is what always sets the heroes off. Somehow their honor has been in one way or another sullied, and they have to assert it by going off and somehow besting their opponent in contests. In *The Saga of Hrolf Kraki*, Hrolf travels through the forests of Sweden, and, as I mentioned, that is probably a journey of at least a month to six weeks to ride from Denmark up to Uppsala. Along the way he meets Odin disguised as the farmer Roni, and Odin tests Hrolf Kraki's warriors on various occasions. When Hrolf Kraki started out on this ride, he had his 12 companions; he had a bunch of berserkers and 100 other men—in the course of meeting Roni on several occasions—Roni keeps reappearing at new locations—which should have tipped Hrolf Kraki that this guy is not just an ordinary farmer, but you know it's a legend and we won't go into the details too much—and in each case everyone fails but the 12 companions. And so the lesser men are dismissed and sent back to Denmark.

When Hrolf Kraki reemerges at Uppsala, he's only accompanied by his 12 warriors. You're certainly not going to get much political history out of this, but you're certainly going to get a great deal of the social ethos and the warrior ethos in this tale. When they arrive in Uppsala, which would have been a great hall comparable to the one in Denmark, what Hrolf Kraki and his men do is they move into this hall and take over. Hrolf Kraki presides over the hall. There are Swedish warriors waiting to trap them. They slay them hiding behind the tapestries. The Swedish king Adils has to run away. Hrolf's mother comes out and presides over the hall. What is established there is Hrolf Kraki is the greater king. He's moved into the hall of his rival; he's taken it over; he presides over it with his warriors; he starts giving gifts; he takes over the treasure of the Swedish king who's known to be a miserly king, a man who doesn't win much loyalty to him, and as a result he's usurped that position in Uppsala. Eventually the Swedes come back. Adils goes off and raises a huge army, and Hrolf and his companions ride off to escape. In the course of their escape, they throw the gold they've captured across the fields of Uppsala. They throw the gold on Fyrisvellir plain, as it's called. The Swedes jump down and fight over the gold and the Danes gallop away.

It's an odd story to us who think in terms of kingdoms and nation states perhaps, and we would think this raid represented an attempt to assert the hegemony of the Danish. There's all sorts of speculation about it. What it is was a test of valor and a test of who was a greater king. It wasn't a question of taking territory. A great king was a man who attracted to him great warriors, who showed an example of generosity to those warriors, who could assure them of riches, and those riches were given out as gifts that honored not only the giver but also those that received. That is what makes Hrolf Kraki a hero. The fact that he could move into the Swedish court and take over and preside in Sweden just as he did in Denmark is an indication that everyone agreed. He is the greatest king of the northlands, and, yes, he does retreat. He does not stay in Uppsala, but the act of throwing the gold, in which the Swedes jump off their horses to find gold rather than pursue the Danes, is yet another indication to the Scandinavians, who delighted in the story as Hrolf Kraki has just bought the retainers of his rival Adils who are now his retainers as much as they had been of the Swedish king.

That really captures the sense of what politically was important in the age of migration, great kings who could go out on careers, gain riches, gain fame, build a great hall, attract the warriors to them. Kingship was something that you acquired due to your personal reputation and charisma. It was useful that you were descended from other kings, that you understood the profession of arms, that you had the favor of Odin, but kingship was only effective if it was made effective and exercised by that rule. That is an important point to stress because the Viking age will give many men the possibility to become sea kings and gain riches and powers and therefore establish their own kingdoms, whether overseas or later in Scandinavia. That notion is already evident probably in the clashes that you see among those incipient kingdoms in Scandinavia in the 6th century.

That same world is captured very vividly in *Beowulf* in the boasting that goes on at the great halls because halls, as I mentioned, were not only political centers where a king ruled but they were also places where religious ceremonies took place, especially in the spring and early summer before the campaigning season, before sea kings would launch out on raids. Before you would go attack the hall of your rival king to assert your valor, you would have great ceremony; there would be feasting. A lot of mead would pass around and probably wine imported from the Carolingian world. And there boasts were made. Those boasts were extremely important. You raised your toast, you claimed what you were going to do, and when you made those claims you swore it on rings, rings which would be associated with Odin, and then you had to deliver. This fellowship goes on in the epic of *Beowulf*. It goes on in *The Saga of Hrolf Kraki,* and it continues as a theme even into early Christian times among Scandinavian kings.

The most famous of them—we'll mention later—occurs somewhere shortly after 986 when these professional Vikings, the Jomsvikings, show up at the Danish court, and boast, "We're going to punish Jral, or earl, Haaken of Norway because we're being hosted by our great King Sven Forkbeard." They swear all of these oaths and boasts in the great hall in this religious political ceremony, and then the next morning when everyone sobers up and the Jomsvikings are thinking, well, we must have had a great time—I can't remember what I said—Sven Forkbeard immediately reminds them. "Don't you remember you swore on the rings, Odin's rings? And you said you were going to sail to Norway and beat up King Haaken for me," and they say "Oh, yeah, I guess we did," and sure enough, off and running into the great naval disasters of Danish history.

These traditions are extremely powerful to the Scandinavians when you're looking at these early legends of Beowulf and Hrolf Kraki. You're seeing the way politics are played out in the Viking age. They're extremely personal; they're tied to great kings. Great kings make their reputation by going out raiding, by warring, great deeds as warriors. They acquire the wealth, the women, the warriors that allow them to establish a hall, and from that hall they rule as monarch over an area that is really rather vaguely defined. These are not kingdoms in any kind of Roman sense or medieval sense. They are very, very much personal monarchies, and the personal monarchs were very much motivated by issues of personal honor, revenge, pride, all of those motives. The legends in the epic of *Beowulf* capture this aspect of political life far more effectively than any kind of modern analysis of what motivated these rulers. What was the point and the importance of these legendary figures to the Viking age? To some extent, they were added into that great hall of heroes going back to the Volsungs. They were seen as prototypes of what a king could be in Scandinavia, and they also reveal a very important point which is now being debated amongst scholars.

I mentioned there's a revisionist scholarship that has taken the position that the Vikings in some ways have been greatly exaggerated, that they're essentially pirates; they're rather marginal to the development of Western Europe. Most of our information we have about them has been written by monks who were usually the victims of Viking rage, and these guys are generally rather hysterical and they're bound to exaggerate five Viking ships into 50 ships. It is also pointed out that western Europeans in both Anglo-Saxon England and Carolingian Europe were hardly models of Christian piety, that the warrior caste was pretty brutal. There are records of monasteries being sacked or damaged in battles among Christian warriors. There's a great deal of truth to this, and there is a reason to accept some of these caveats.

On the other hand, when you look at the legends and the myths and particularly the legends associated with Hrolf Kraki, the epic of *Beowulf,* the Scandinavians who launched out several generations later from when these epics were placed in time were not burdened with any notion of just war. To be sure, monasteries were sacked in Europe, but that was an outrageous crime and the exception, and not the rule. The western Europeans were in no way prepared for the types of warriors that would descend upon them in those long ships. They are dealing with Scandinavians who see themselves as the emulators of these great heroes who not only exceed all expectations in battle, they revel in battle. They go into battle with ecstatic joy; whether they win or lose doesn't matter because they join the great hall of Odin and honor, riches, entrance into Valhalla. This is what is going to motivate the Vikings more than anything else over the next 300 years. In battle, success goes to those who have the will and determination to prevail, and with figures such as Odin, Sigurd, Hrolf Kraki, the Norse had in these heroes traditions which gave them the will to dominate battlefields, sweep away better and more numerous opponents. And the Western Europeans were really completely unprepared for the type of invasions they were about to experience.

Lecture Nine
A Revolution in Shipbuilding

Scope:

At the end of the 8th century, Scandinavians achieved breakthroughs in ship design and the rigging of the sails that enabled them to perfect warships and ocean-going cargo vessels (*knarr*). For the next three centuries, Viking ships dominated the seas and rivers of Europe. The ship recovered at Nydam (c. A.D. 350–400) indicates that Scandinavians had mastered *clinker* construction and, perhaps, had experimented with sails. Shortly after 750, Norse shipwrights learned to lay down ships based on a keel, with a *keelson* to carry a tall mast. These vessels combined flexibility with strength, allowing Viking ships to ride the waves, rather than battle them. Given their low draught, Viking ships could be beached on sandy shores or sail up the rivers of Europe. Hence, Viking fleets enjoyed strategic mobility, while their cargo ships, capable of conveying 50 tonnes, transported settlers and livestock across the Atlantic Ocean. Under sail, warships recovered at Gokstad in Norway (c. 900–905) and at Skuldelev near Roskilde (c. 975–1050) could attain maximum speeds of 12 knots. The performance of these ships can be demonstrated by the fleet of 120 longships under Ragnar Lodbrok that sailed from Denmark to capture Paris on March 28, 845, covering more than 1,000 miles within a month and defeating a Frankish army en route. No medieval army could counter the speed or daring of Vikings in their longships.

Outline

I. This lecture describes developments in Scandinavian shipbuilding from prehistoric times up to end of the Viking Age, concentrating on three essential issues. Without certain breakthroughs in shipbuilding that were achieved at the end of the 8th century and certain innovations that occurred in the 10th century, the Viking Age, that is, the Scandinavian domination of the waters of Northern Europe from 790–1100, would have been impossible.

   A. The first topic is the evolution of shipbuilding, including why the Scandinavians were able to achieve these breakthroughs.

   B. We shall then turn to the construction of ships in the Viking Age, which had major economic and social consequences for Scandinavian communities. The culture of the sea was one of the quintessential elements of Scandinavian civilization.

   C. Finally, we shall close with an example of what the Scandinavians' skill in shipbuilding meant in terms of military advantages.

II. Viking Age ships represented the climax of a long history of shipbuilding in Scandinavia going back to the prehistoric age.

   A. A number of remarkable rock carvings of 4000–2300 B.C. reveal that the ancestors of the Scandinavians were familiar with constructing ships. These ships seem to have been propelled by paddles, rather than by oars, and they had no sails, but they must have been able to negotiate coastal waters.

   B. The first major ship we have is the Hjortspring ship from Als, an island of Denmark, dating from about 300–200 B.C. Most ships from archaeological excavations are funerary, not working vessels, and these were probably modified for burial operations. Sails and masts were removed, and the ships were filled with large amounts of goods.

   C. The Hjortspring ship is about 40 feet long and would have had 20 men on each side propelling it with paddles; there is no evidence of a sail. It was probably a vessel used for moving people along coastal waters, somewhat similar to a flatboat or ferry.

1. The Hjortspring ship shows the adaptation of Celtic building styles that we know from Roman descriptions, in particular, the construction of skin boats. The Celts first made a skeleton construction of ribs, then covered it with skins and caulked it. Such boats were known as *curraghs*.

2. The Hjortspring ship was also tied together with planks, so that it shows a mixture of Northern European *clinker*, or skeleton, construction and shell construction.

D. The Scandinavians probably started building their first successful warships and cargo vessels as a result of the influence of Roman ship design. Between the 1st and 3rd centuries A.D., large numbers of Roman commercial vessels arrived in the Scandinavian world, sailed by provincials of Celtic and Germanic origins.

1. The most important innovations of the Romans was the sail. Some scholars date the addition of the sail in Scandinavia to 750–790, at most a generation before the first raids of the Viking Age. Others argue that the sail was being used in the 3rd and 4th centuries, based on comments by Roman authors and archaeological evidence from the two surviving ships we have, which are clearly the ancestors of Viking Age ships.

2. The first of these, the Nydam ship (c. 350–400), is again, a burial ship from Denmark. This vessel is 80 feet long and may have had its mast and sail removed for burial. The Nydam ship, too, shows a combination of building styles, but it is propelled by oars, not paddles. Based on several reconstructions, this ship certainly could negotiate the coastal waters of the North Sea quite easily.

3. The Sutton Hoo ship of about A.D. 625 does not give us as much information, because the ship is known only from its impression left in the clay of the burial site. Similarly, there is not much remaining of the timber construction of the Kvalsund ship (Norway, c. 700).

E. Sometime in the early 8th century, the Scandinavians learned how to put down a keel, which became a major feature of Scandinavian shipbuilding. The keel allowed Scandinavians to construct ships that could negotiate the sea and open waters. The keel also allowed for a *keelson*, a base to accommodate a large mast with an enormous sail.

III. Several excavations are important in telling us how these ships were constructed.

A. The Oseberg ship (834), found in Vestfold, Norway, is the equivalent of a royal yacht, rather than a working warship. It has all the classic features of a Viking Age ship: It has a keel and a sail and shows a sophisticated method of construction that involved building up by levels of *strakes* on the keel.

B. The Gokstad burial ship (c. 900–905) is a warship; it is 75 feet long and had a keel and keelson capable of carrying a mast close to 45 feet in height. The sail might have been 750–825 square feet. This ship is a brilliant piece of work in combining strength and flexibility. All such Viking Age ships were built to ride the water, rather than to fight the waves.

C. A third set of five ships, excavated starting in 1962, was found in the Roskilde fjord near Skuldelev, Sjaelland. These ships were probably sunk in the 11th century to block the bay and prevent warships from attacking the Danish capital of Roskilde.

  1. The Skuldelev ships include two classic longships; a *knarr*, which is an ocean-going cargo ship of the type used to settle Iceland; a coastal trader; and a fishing ship. Together, they show us the culmination of Scandinavian shipbuilding.

  2. One of the warships is about 92 feet long with a breadth of 14–15 feet. It is the type of ship that would have been used by the armies of King Cnut (r. 1014–1035) to invade England.

  3. The *knarr* could have carried 30–40 tons of cargo and is of the type that was regularly used in trade between Norway and Iceland.

IV. Thus, by 790, the Scandinavians had constructed a remarkable set of war and cargo vessels that no other civilization possessed. Such ships could be constructed readily from the materials at hand and did not require the same kind of specialized labor and facilities as Mediterranean shipbuilding.

A. Both *knarrs* and longships could be constructed quickly and easily in Norse communities. They could be built close to shore, protected by simple temporary structures.

B. Since Viking ships rode so low in the water, they could be beached anywhere, which was an important tactical advantage for both cargo vessels and warships. They could travel up rivers quite far and were very easy to pick up and carry from one river system to another.

C. These ships were built from the existing hardwoods in Scandinavia, particularly oak. An ideal oak tree was located, maybe 60–90 feet long, and cut down to form the keel. Large branches would often be used as ribs. Green, unseasoned timber was used to maintain flexibility and allow the ship to ride the waves. Altogether, 12 or 13 oak trees would be needed for construction.

D. After the keel was laid down, the *strakes*, levels of planking, would be built up, followed by installation of the ribs and crossbeams for reinforcement. Remarkably, the ships are not heavy; for instance, the bottom planking of a Viking ship is only about an inch thick.

E. The decks were probably movable to enable bailing if necessary. After the strakes were built up, the keelson and mast would be installed, with the mast itself another oak tree. Finally, slots were cut for the oars, which were constructed of prime oak.

F. The level of technical skill of shipwrights overseeing this construction was quite sophisticated, but the actual work could be performed quickly by almost any woodworker.

V. These vessels were built for speed and efficiency in moving people and goods, definitely not for comfort.

   A. Vikings voyaging in these ships on the North Atlantic lived on salted and boiled foods and drank curdled milk. They were exposed to the elements and could not build fires.

   B. The performance of these ships can be deduced by building reconstructions. A standard longship of the 9th century probably carried a crew of at least 50; in the 10th and 11th centuries, the crew probably numbered 100 or 200.

1. Based on these reconstructions, a Viking warship of the Gokstad design, sailing an 8-hour day, could easily average 3–4 knots; running under sail and with the wind, it might make 8–12 knots.

2. As an example, we know that on March 28, Easter Sunday, 845, a large Danish army occupied Paris. The fleet was reputedly 120 vessels and may have been commanded by the legendary hero Ragnar Lodbrok.

3. Working out the times and distances, this force could have covered the 900 statute miles from Scandinavia to the mouth of the Seine in about three weeks. The Vikings would then have sailed up the Seine 150 miles to Paris, which would have taken a week or less.

4. In the course of traveling to Paris, the Vikings met two Frankish armies led by Charles the Bald. They defeated and hanged 111 prisoners from one of these forces on one side of the Seine, and so terrorized the other force into fleeing.

5. In comparison to the speed of these ships, most medieval armies on land could, on average, travel only 12–15 miles a day, assuming that they had ideal conditions and well-maintained roads. Viking fleets, which could negotiate along any coast of Europe and could travel deeply into most river systems, could move three to five times faster than any opponent on land.

C. Given the fact that the Scandinavians held a monopoly on sea power, it is no surprise that the Vikings could raid and attack at will before most of their opponents could even get their armies in the field. This strategic advantage would be held by the Vikings for the next 300 years.

Further Reading:

A. W. Brogger and Haakon Shetelig. *The Viking Ships: Their Ancestry and Evolution*. New York: Twayne, 1971.

John Haywood. *Dark Age Naval Power*. London/New York: Routledge, 1991.

Unger, Richard W. *The Ship in Medieval Economy, 600–1600*. Montreal: McGill-Queen's University Press, 1980.

Questions to Consider:

1. How were Viking ships constructed? What were the economic and cultural ramifications of such shipbuilding?

2. How did Viking ships give Scandinavians advantages in war, overseas settlement, and trade? What were the specific advantages of war and cargo ships?

Lecture Nine—Transcript

A Revolution in Shipbuilding

In this lecture I plan to look at the developments in Scandinavian shipbuilding from really prehistoric times up through the end of the Viking age. This is really a central lecture in understanding the Viking age because without certain breakthroughs in shipbuilding that were achieved at the very end in the 8th century AD and then innovations that occurred in the 10th century, really the Viking age would be impossible. I've alluded to the fact that, for all of the cultural continuity between the age of migrations and the Viking age, the real difference was the fact that the kings and jrals—that would be nobles or earls in English—gained ships that gave them a military advantage for over 300 years.

Between about 790 and 1100, the Scandinavians will dominate the waters of Northern Europe, and that not only includes the seas and the Atlantic Ocean but also the river systems of Western Europe and of Russia because they constructed really spectacular ships, warships, popularly known as the long ship, although many scholars would reserve the term long ship for warships later in the Viking age from the late 10th century, and also cargo vessels, the knarrs—these are ocean-going cargo vessels that could carry settlers to Iceland or the British Isles—and then a whole variety of other ships that we have, including ferries, coastal vessels, fishing ships and the like. The development of Scandinavian shipbuilding is all-important.

I like to look at essentially three issues in this lecture. The first is going to be the evolution of shipbuilding, why the Scandinavians achieved these breakthroughs, and once again we'll see that there are influences from other shipbuilding traditions, notably the Celts of Western Europe as well as the Roman, but again the Scandinavians apply their own genius to create ships that no one else would build. I'd then like to go into a bit about the actual construction of ships in the Viking age, and there are significant points about that because it had major economic and social consequences for Scandinavian communities. And I should stress that the act of building ships, which was an important capital investment in any Norse community, and the sailing of these ships, was a common experience as important as the ancient Germanic gods they worshiped, the common Norse language, the poetry, the legends, the culture of the sea; and going out and either raiding or trading by sea was one of the quintessential elements of Scandinavian civilization. Finally, I'd like to close with a brief example of what this meant in terms of military advantages and we'll use an example coming from the early Viking age, one of the great raids on France as an example of the performance of these Viking warships. So with that in mind, let's take a look at the evolution.

The Viking age ships, the long ships, warships, and cargo ships represent a climax to a very long evolution in shipbuilding. This certainly goes back to the prehistoric age. There are a number of remarkable rock carvings, essentially carvings or painted carvings—sometimes they're just painted; sometimes they're carved with painted highlights—going back to the prehistoric age, the Neolithic age, between 4000 and 2300 B.C., and then there are others coming from the Bronze Age. They show that the Scandinavians, the ancestors of the Scandinavians, the first people in that area, were familiar with constructing ships. These are extremely schematic, and it's difficult to know the precise construction without an archeological find. Nonetheless, they're familiar with building ships that could at least negotiate the coasts. They seem to have been propelled by paddles rather than by actual oars; there are no sails; but from the very start the only way people and goods could have been moved around the core areas of Scandinavia was some type of vessel that could negotiate the rather treacherous seas, such as the Oresund, that is, the narrow strait of water that separates Sjaelland from southern Sweden. You have to have a fairly sophisticated ship in order to do that.

The first major ship that we know of comes from about 300 to 200 B.C., and as it becomes evident in this lecture, most of our information is based on ships that we've recovered in archeological excavation. These are usually burials, that is, ships that have been put in the ground as a funerary monument. It's often been modified in order to carry out the burial. Often sails have been removed. Large numbers of goods are in there. They are either to honor the dead or they might be a votive gift. They might have been given to the gods in recognition for some favor. But nonetheless, these are not working vessels necessarily. They are ships that have been in some cases constructed specifically either for funeral purposes or have been modified for that.

The great exception is the wonderful find of ships made which were sunk in the channel of the Roskilde fjord probably in the early 11th century. There we actually have working Viking ships which we'll get to in this lecture. In any case, our earliest one is a ship known as the Hjortspring ship that comes from Als, an island of Denmark. It's been uncovered in excavation, and it shows some very important features already. As I mentioned, it's propelled by paddles. It certainly confirms what we've suspected from the rock carvings. It's a fairly lengthy vessel. It's about 40 feet in length. It would have had 20 men on the side propelling it.

There are some important provisions on it: one is, there's no evidence there was a sail. It's doubtful it ever had a sail. It seems to be largely a vessel for moving people along coastal waters into the estuaries of rivers. It's not quite like a flatboat or ferry, but it's something more or less in that class. It's certainly not a ship that could go out and handle the North Sea and certainly not the Atlantic. It does not have a keel but it does show certain important innovations, and part of that is the Celtic adaptation of building styles of ships that we know from Roman descriptions, primarily Julius Caesar, as well as the long Celtic tradition of building skin boats, that is, essentially putting down a skeleton construction of ribs and then covering it with skins and caulking the skins. These are known as curraghs. They're used in the British Isles particularly but also on the shores of Northern France, and those skin boats are really quite impressive. Some of them can obtain sizes as much as 40 or 50 feet. They are without keels, and riding those things is like bouncing around on the waters, but, nonetheless, they're really quite durable for doing shipping in rather quiet, enclosed waters such as, say, the Baltic Sea or, in the case of the British Isles, the Irish Sea.

This undecked early ship of about 40 to 50 feet in length was also tied together with planks, and so it shows a mixture of building styles. Part of it is the so-called overlapping clinker or skeleton style. That is a method that's pioneered in northern Europe. The other method of shipbuilding is often called shell construction, and that is building your ships so that the wood fits together airtight. It's essentially the equivalent of building a fine piece of furniture. Viking vessels actually show a combination of these building techniques. The shell construction is usually associated with the Mediterranean, the skeleton construction with Celtic northwest. Both of these constructions will be represented in Viking ships and are indicative of the type of influences getting up to Scandinavia.

Remarkably, the Scandinavians start building their first successful warships and cargo ships probably due to the influence of Roman ship designs. Again, it's often thought in the popular imagination: What do the Romans know about ships? The Roman attitude toward the Mediterranean world was to conquer it over land, corner it, and call it "our sea." But the Romans in the high empire in a sense inherited this whole Celtic shipbuilding tradition, and the Romans had real reason to tap into the trade routes into Northern Europe. In the 1st, 2nd, 3rd century A.D., large numbers of commercial vessels arrive from the Roman world sailed largely by provincials who were mostly of Celtic origin, some of Germanic origins. So the Scandinavians had a chance to see these ships. One of the most important innovations was a sail, and it is still a highly debatable point among scholars: When did sails get put on Scandinavian ships? Some regard the addition of the sail as extremely late, just on the eve of the Viking age, somewhere between maybe 750 and 790, at most a generation before the first raids. Others would argue that the sail was already being in use in the 3rd and 4th century based on comments by Roman authors and also based on the two primary ships we have that we can examine which are clearly the ancestors of Viking ships.

One of those I referred to earlier, and that is the Nydam ship, again a burial ship coming from Denmark, tentatively dated to around 350 or 400 A.D. It's quite a large vessel. It's almost 80 feet in length, and it again is debated whether there was a sail in it. It was a burial ship, and therefore if it did have a sail, a mast, and something to hold it in place, it may have been removed because the grave goods are found in the middle of the ship. The Nydam ship shows a combination of building styles. It shows very much the clinker style of construction. The Scandinavians have now perfected building larger warships. It's still debated whether it was decked or not, but it is propelled by oars, not by paddles; and based on several reconstructions, this ship certainly could negotiate the coastal waters of the North Sea very easily and could move a lot of people and goods around.

The Sutton Hoo ship to which I referred, that ship in Anglo-Saxon England about 625 A.D., is not so useful. The ship itself doesn't survive. It's really an impression in the clay. We have a couple of similar such burials from Norway. One is the Kvalsund ship, and again it's also difficult to make sense out of it because we really don't have that much of the timbered construction. But all three of these vessels, starting with the Nydam ship and ending with this Norwegian ship of about 700, show improved construction of these vessels, especially the side strakes, which are the levels of planking that one constructs. And by the time of somewhere in the early 8th century, the Scandinavians figure out how to put down a keel. Somewhere in the 8th century a keel, that is, a backbone to a ship, becomes a major feature in Scandinavian ship construction, and that is the first important breakthrough, putting in a keel. That keel allows the Scandinavians to begin to construct ships that could really negotiate the sea and the open waters, and once you have a keel, you could set in a foundation on that keel, a keelson, as it's often called, this huge base where you can attach a large mast which will give you an enormous area for sail, and that will give you propulsion, especially out at sea, that previous vessels could not have. And these breakthroughs are made sometime in the 8th century, sometime between 700 and 800 and allow the Scandinavians to build the classic long ships and cargo vessels of the Viking age.

Again, much of the information about these vessels comes from archaeological excavation. There are several excavations that are absolutely important in telling us how these ships were constructed. Two of them were Norwegian burials, to which I've referred earlier. One is the Oseberg ship; that burial is dated to about 834, based on dendrochronology. The vessel itself is probably the equivalent of a royal yacht rather than an actual working warship, and it shows all of the classic features of a Viking age ship: it has a keel; it has a sail set about a third back from the bow of the ship; it also shows a very, very sophisticated construction in which you're building up by levels of strakes on that keel, which is the backbone, and then you put in the ribbing afterwards.

The other important vessel is the Gokstad ship, which is dated to about 900, and it's again a burial ship—it's very closely found in the same area Vest fjord—that is, a warship, and is probably pretty close to the class of warships used in the 9th and 10th century on the first raids. The Gokstad ship for the longest time, and this was a ship that was excavated in the end of the 19th century, was one of our major sources of information. The ship itself is something like 75 feet long and certainly had a keel and keelson capable of carrying a huge mast close to 45 feet in height. There are various reconstructions of the sail, depending on how much height you suspect the ship carried. It could be anywhere from 750 to 825 square feet of sail. That would give you an enormous amount of propulsion. It is absolutely a brilliant piece of work in combining strength and flexibility because in all of these Viking age ships they are built to essentially ride the waters rather than to fight the waves. If they had tried to build ships that were more in the Mediterranean or Roman tradition, those ships probably would have just broken up in the water. They would have been too brittle. Viking age ships, essentially, are able to ride the waves,

There's also a third set of ships that we've excavated, and this was state-of-the-art excavation starting in 1962, and they are now on display in the Roskilde Ship Museum. And those were really six vessels. There's really essentially five they brought up. Two of them were warships that they're making a composite out of. These were ships that were sunk probably to block the bay—it may have been done in the 11th century by Sven Estridsen; it's anyone's guess—so warships couldn't come in and attack the Danish capital of Roskilde. And they think it's perhaps directed at someone like Harald Hardrada, or the King of Norway, who was attacking Denmark at this point. These were working vessels that were sunk to block up a channel. They were able to pump the water out, state-of-the-art archeology, and anyone in Denmark must make a pilgrimage to that ship museum and see it.

In any event, the ships that have been recovered there are usually known as the Skuldelev ships—Skuldelev is the little town near where the ships were found—and they include two important warships which are clearly long ships in the classic sense, perhaps built somewhere between 975 and 1000. An important vessel, a knarr, is our first really good ocean-going vessel, the type of vessel used to settle Iceland, and then there are some smaller vessels, including a coastal vessel, a ship that might have been a fishing ship. All of these ships together show us essentially the culmination of Scandinavian shipbuilding. The warship is about 92 feet in length, a breadth of about 14 to 15 feet. It is the type of ship that would have been used by King Cnut's armies to invade England. There's a somewhat smaller warship that is a class just below it but quite impressive as well. The knarr is a ship that could carry somewhere between 30 and 40 tons worth of cargo, and it also confirms what we're told in the Icelandic sagas of the type of cargo ships that were regularly used in trade between Norway and Iceland, and it's very, very reassuring to have an actual such vessel in the archeological record. All of the ships were clearly working ships. That can be demonstrated in part by the fact that they were repaired, particularly on the bottoms, quite frequently, because Viking ships were beached.

By 790 the Scandinavians have created a remarkable set of war and cargo vessels that no one else has. These ships could be constructed rather readily from the materials at hand and did not require the same kind of specialized labor and facilities as, say, Mediterranean shipbuilding. This is an extremely important point to stress. We can easily follow in the archeological record the increasing experimentation and sophistication and one shudders to think how some of these were actually discovered. You wonder how maybe a Norwegian town launched a vessel with one type of early keel and they never came back, and they eventually concluded, well, that didn't work—let's try something else.

This is all done by trial and error. There are no written manuals, and the shipwrights who constructed these vessels worked largely from memory and experience and would adjust and modify, say, based on the building materials they had at the time. There are undoubtedly variations in caulking material, the proportion of length to breadth of the ship. All of that could be handled based on the materials you had. Whether you had a long ship or knarr these things could be built very, very quickly and easily in a Norse community. You could build them close to the shore. Most of them were probably constructed underneath very simple, temporary structures to protect them. Since Viking ships rode so low in the water, they had a very, very low draught to them; they could be beached anywhere. That's one of the great tactical advantages, both for Viking cargo vessels and warships. You don't need deep-water ports.

These Viking ships can go up rivers very, very far. They are very easy to pick up from rivers and carry from river to river, that is, to make to portage to go from one river system to another. You see this frequently done in France. It's done in England and particularly in Russia, where, in effect, you can move from one river system to another over land rather easily and then go in a totally different direction. That's actually how the Vikings end up on the Volga and then the Caspian Sea.

The other important feature about these ships is that they were built from the existing hardwoods in Scandinavia, particularly oak. That's one reason why Denmark was so important in the Viking age. Denmark had some of the prime oak forests, and the oak was ideal for masts, keels, ribs, and planks. In order to construct this ship though, what the Norse had learned to do was a result of trial and error going all the way back to that Nydam ship. Once you had a keel as a basis of your ship to give it the strength to handle ocean conditions, it also was the basis of constructing. The first thing you laid down was a keel; you found an ideal oak tree of the right length—it could be 90 feet, 60 feet, whatever—and you cut that tree down, and that basic trunk became your keel. Then the large branches were often used as the ribs and the cross sections, and very often they used the grain and the natural curvature of the lumber to build various sections of the ship.

They were very, very cleverly adapting the materials to the construction of the ship. They also built these ships from rather green and unseasoned timber, and that was, again, to retain the flexibility so that the Viking vessels almost bent with the waves. There are reports of this by several reconstructions that have been done. The earliest and most famous is the one done by the Norwegians in 1893 where a replica of the Gokstad ship was constructed and sailed from Bergen to Newfoundland. I think it was about 28 days to do it. The reports very much were the ship rode the waves and there was a certain amount of bending of the ship with the waves; it was very, very flexible.

So the first thing you do is you put down your keel, and then you start building up your strakes, that is, your levels of planking. Once you get those attached to your keel, you put in the various ribbing and crossbeams to reinforce it. This is very, very clever. There's a combination of both shell and clinker construction to build this ship. You caulk it as you go along the way. The boards are nailed into places with washers, iron nails, and then you bend them over with a washer. There is a minimum amount of metal used in this construction.

Furthermore, the ships are remarkably thin in their construction. These are not as heavy and ponderous as you'd think. For instance, the bottom planking of a Viking vessel is essentially one-inch thick. You start with a three-inch oak board, and then you plane it down to essentially one inch. That's just one inch separating you from the Atlantic Ocean. It's a rather terrifying thought. They're fitted into place. We believe that the decks were always movable because there's always the danger of water seeping in, and you have to bail. So once you've got your strakes built up, you then put in your keelson, that is, this construction to hold the mast. Then the mast comes in, and the mast would be another oak tree of appropriate length which has been chopped down and put in place. You can use birch and pine for a lot of the lesser construction. And finally you cut the slots for the oars. You put in the oars—he oars should be prime oak if you can get it—and, presto, you've got a Viking ship. The amount of technical skill is extremely high, that is, the shipwrights directing it really have to understand proportions, which they've all learned through experimentation, but a lot of the work can be done very, very quickly by people who are skilled in wood building, that is, planing the boards, following the grain of the wood and adapting the material that you need. The result is a ship of remarkable flexibility and speed, whether it be a cargo or a warship, and it is a considerable amount of effort to build one of these ships.

To put together a vessel of the Gokstad class, which is a Viking warship about 75-80 feet in length, you need an oak tree just to do the keel and then you need another oak tree for the mast. And you need somewhere between 12 and 13 fully fledged oak trees just to get your basic wood. The construction of these ships involved a great deal of labor in cutting down and preparing the wood. But again you're dealing with a population that is skilled in woodwork. That is the main construction they do, and most Scandinavians communities can do this. They also have now the superior iron tools and nails and clamps necessary to do the construction so you had to have a lot of developments before you got one of these Scandinavian ships.

These vessels are built for speed and efficiency of moving people and goods. They are definitely not built for comfort. Sailing one of these vessels across the North Atlantic is a daunting task in and of itself. You essentially lived on salted and boiled foods. You drank a horrible curdled milk or, to pass the time away, a low-grade mead or beer, probably to pass the time. You didn't build fires. You were open to the elements. You could build a temporary structure perhaps. There are references to that in Icelandic cargo vessels, but you made sure to bring a lot of skins and woolens along with you because you essentially slept on the deck. The conditions were harsh, and you had to be fit in order to handle a ship like this. And that's one reason why the Vikings were such excellent warriors; they were constantly involved in building ships and enduring the conditions necessary to sail these vessels.

The performance of these ships can be deduced by building reconstructions, and again there's a certain amount of debate of how many men would be to an oar. We know how many oars might be in a vessel. Most of these vessels probably could put two or three men to an oar, which would mean a standard long ship of the 9th century carried a crew of at least 50. When you get into the late 10th and 11th century, crews of 100 or even 200 in the great dragon ships is not unusual. So you have a lot of muscle power to move those vessels. In any event, based on these reconstructions, a Viking vessel of the Gokstad ship, a warship sailing an eight-hour day could easily average between three and four knots. And if it's running with the wind and it's got its sail up, there are arguments that it could make anywhere from eight to 12 knots. What does this mean in practical application? An average sailing day is about 40 to 65 nautical miles. A statute mile is about 85 percent of a nautical mile. That means that these vessels gave the Vikings a remarkable tactical advantage.

I want to close the third part of this lecture with just some indication of what this meant. It should explain a great deal of part three, the success of the Viking raids in Western Europe and across Russia. I take as an example a documented case that we know quite well. On March 28, Easter Sunday, a large Danish army occupied the city of Paris in 845. The fleet is reputedly 120 vessels according to some of the accounts. Most of these vessels are apparently arriving from Denmark and Southwestern Norway. And they are, according to some sources, commanded by the legendary hero, Ragnar Lodbrok. Now if you work out the times and distances and when they would have set sail, which would have been maybe at the earliest March 1, and you take the sailing distances that are deduced from these replica ships, that is, easily three to four knots, especially if you have the currents going with you along the North Sea, they could cover somewhere along the order of 900 statute miles from Scandinavia to the mouth of the Seine within about three weeks. They would then sail up the Seine, which is about 150 miles from Paris, and if they were rowing in shifts and even though they were going against the current and dealing with the curves of the river, they could probably reach Paris certainly within a week, certainly within three to four days.

In the process of going to Paris, they ran into two Frankish armies commanded by Charles the Bald. They defeated the smaller one on one side of the Seine. That's where they hanged the 111 prisoners, which panicked the other army, which fled. And that's how they occupied Paris, without resistance. So based on what we know of our sailing distances and based on what we know of this particular campaign, they're quite consistent that a Viking fleet of this size could raid out of Scandinavia, hit a city like Paris within a month, and then get out very quickly. In comparison to the speed of these ships which could cover easily going up river—they're sailing up a river 150 miles—they could do it in four or five days. Most medieval armies by land, assuming they had anything resembling a Roman road, could on average only make 12 or 15 miles a day. Cavalry forces pushing those horses really hard, an elite force, might make 20 miles— that is, Viking fleets which could negotiate along any coast of Europe and could go extremely deep up river systems could move three, four, five times faster than any opponent on land.

Given the fact that the Scandinavians come to have a monopoly of sea power, it is no surprise that the Vikings can raid and attack at will before most of their opponents can even get their forces in the field. This strategic advantage is held by the Vikings for the next 300 years. No one will attempt to contest Scandinavian sea power in northern Europe, and the only major naval battles in the Viking age is Vikings fighting Vikings. And that is one of the most important points that comes out of this lecture, is that by 790 these Scandinavians, propelled with that martial ethos and propelled with that culture to the war gods, now have ships that can get them to go anywhere in Western Europe.

Lecture Ten

Warfare and Society in the Viking Age

Scope:

Viking warriors differed little from their opponents in Western Europe in weapons and tactics, but they waged war far more violently. They were quick to learn from their foes. In the 9th century, Vikings favored heavy Frankish swords and chain mail, and in the next century, they developed the famed double-headed axe. Scandinavian warriors excelled in leaping and running, because rowing their ships put them in first-rate physical condition, and they were expert in foraging, even in winter. Sea kings and jarls assembled their warriors from among kinsmen and neighbors, so that Viking companies were held together by devotion to honor and charismatic leaders. Scandinavians, while appreciating horses for their mobility, fought as infantry drawn up in a shield wall, the tactical gift of the god Odin. Foremost, they waged war by attrition, and fortified their bases with moats and palisades. This construction is evident in the fortified camps and the Danevirke constructed by King Harald Bluetooth of Denmark (r. c. 958–986). The discipline and effectiveness of Viking forces can be seen in the campaigns of the Great Army in 865–878. This Viking army, numbering between 5,000 and 10,000 veteran warriors, by careful logistics and fortified bases, combined with swift strategic strikes, overthrew three of the four Anglo-Saxon kingdoms and brought King Alfred of Wessex to his knees.

Outline

I. In this lecture, we shall look at warfare in the Viking Age, including the Vikings' weapons, training, tactics, and performance as warriors.

    A. The popular image of Vikings as warriors depicts them as quite savage, slashing with their axes and destroying everything in their path.

    B. Of course, in the popular imagination, the Vikings also wore horned helmets, but this perception is false.

II. We will first look at the types of weapons and armament available to the Vikings, which were similar to those used by their opponents in Western Europe. Many of these weapons evolved from a common Roman and Germanic tradition.

A. The primary weapon of attack for the Vikings was a long steel sword. These broadswords evolved from a Roman *spatha* ("saber") and were 2½ to 3 feet long, considerably longer than the Roman *gladius*. Such swords required a good deal of space, skill, and strength to use and were wielded with two hands.

B. By the Viking Age, the Scandinavians were adept in forging iron and steel weapons, but the best swords available and the ones the Scandinavians desired were of Frankish manufacture. Large numbers of Frankish weapons have been found in Scandinavia, despite the Carolingian kings' ban on the export of weapons to that region.

C. The Scandinavians also used the axe as a serious fighting weapon, which had declined in use in Western Europe. A throwing axe might have a range of up to 40 feet, and Scandinavians were deadly in hurling this weapon. Later, in the 10th century, a double-headed axe was developed, which was used by professional warriors in the armies of Cnut and other leaders.

D. The spear also remained important to the Scandinavians. Their spears were quite long, 2 ½ to 4 feet, and fitted with iron heads. Viking warriors were able to catch an opponent's shield with the spear and tear the shield away.

E. Scandinavians had effective defensive armor, and by the late 10th century, many Scandinavian forces sported chain mail. A suit of chain mail consisted of about 35,000 to 40,000 interlocking iron or steel links, covering most of the vital parts of the body and worn over a linen padding.

F. Of course, warriors were also equipped with helmets. These were based on a late Roman design; they were conical and fitted with nose and cheek plates, often made in multiple parts. Such helmets could deflect most blows delivered to the head.

G. This equipment weighed about 30–40 pounds, about the same load that an infantryman today carries into battle. The

Scandinavians, accustomed to rowing in longships and performing other types of hard labor, were conditioned to carry this weight easily.

H. Missile weapons, such as javelins and bows and arrows, had rather limited range. The bow was an adapted hunting weapon, about 4 feet long, and was used effectively in boarding tactics in ship-to-ship combat. Javelins were used similarly and had a range of about 40 yards. Icelandic sagas relate several instances of warriors catching javelins thrown at them, then throwing the weapons back at their opponents.

I. In terms of weapons and armament, when the Vikings launched out on their attacks in 790, they had comparable equipment to the Carolingian armies of northwestern Europe, and they were much better armed than the Celtic peoples of Ireland and northern Britain and the Slavic tribes in Eastern Europe.

J. As soldiers, Vikings appreciated mobility on land as they did at sea; thus, Viking nobles, particularly *jarls* ("earls"), and *lendirmenn* ("leading men") were accomplished horsemen. Viking forces would gather horses after landing their ships and ride inland to the battlefield, but they would then dismount and fight as infantry.

III. If the Vikings' weapons and armament were not too dissimilar from those of their opponents, what gave them the edge in battle?

A. One answer to this question can be found in the bonds of cohesion within these Viking groups. Some scholars have tried to compare the Vikings in this regard to, for example, the pirates of the Spanish Main, but the raiding Vikings were not groups of outsiders like these later pirates.

  1. Viking armies comprised *lendirmenn* and free members of the community and were commanded by sea kings and jarls.

  2. Most Viking fleets had from 3 to 10 ships, all built by members of the same community.

  3. All men of free rank knew how to use weapons, and most were in prime physical condition from rowing and hunting.

4. These groups of warriors were far more coherent than pirate bands.

B. Furthermore, from living in the conditions of Scandinavia, the Vikings had several advantages over their opponents.
1. They were incredibly agile, able to leap to other ships in boarding maneuvers.
2. They had been hardened by Scandinavian winters and had a sound understanding of logistics. Campaigning in winter in France or England would have been easy for the Vikings.
3. Vikings also knew to seize stocks of grain and supplies just after the harvest to stock up to meet future requirements.

C. All free men in Scandinavia were familiar with the use of arms from childhood, and they became expert hunters. This situation stands in strong contrast to what had come about in Western Europe from about 500 on.
1. Most Western European societies were built around a warrior caste, but the majority of the population had come to see military service as a burden. Large numbers of the available forces were essentially militia forces, called out to defend the immediate area. These soldiers lacked the experience and cohesion of Viking warriors.
2. Western European soldiers could be easily ambushed by Viking columns and were often induced to make reckless attacks on Viking shield walls. Western Europeans were not skilled in using edged weapons and were no match for the Scandinavian expertise and determination.

D. The exact numbers of Viking forces are difficult to calculate, and again, there is a tendency by some scholars to minimize the sizes of Viking armies and fleets.
1. The size of individual forces is sometimes estimated at only 1,000–2,000 strong, but in the 9th century, the size and scale of Viking attacks increased significantly.
2. By the end of the 9th century, small contingents of Viking forces, which might represent 10–20 ships, could easily assemble into groups of 100 or more ships. This would bring together 5,000–10,000 seasoned and well-trained warriors.

3. These numbers are the only way to account for the remarkable success of the Vikings, particularly in England in 865–878 or in the siege of Paris.

E. Finally, Vikings applied their skills in woodworking to warfare; they were extremely good at building fortifications, which were often simple earthen ramparts with stockades.

  1. We have two remarkable sets of such fortifications in Denmark. One of them, the Danevirke, was first built in c. 739–740; it runs from the Eider River to the town of Hedeby at the base of the Danish peninsula, essentially sealing off Jutland from Central Europe.

  2. The full system, completed by 960, has an earthen wall about 30 feet wide, a stockade about 6 to 8 feet high, and a huge moat.

  3. From a later building phase, four Viking camps have been excavated that could have housed 2,000–4,000 warriors. The most famous of these is Trelleborg on the island of Sjaelland. These are fortified, circular camps, almost built to Roman specifications, and are associated with King Harald Bluetooth.

  4. In discussing the Vikings' activities overseas, we know that these soldiers understood positional warfare. We have one account of the Battle of the Dyle in 891, in which a Frankish army assaulted a Viking camp, but the fortifications were such that the Vikings were able to reach their ships and escape before the camp was overrun.

IV. To get some sense of the effectiveness of Viking warfare, we'll close with a brief description of a campaign in England that stretched over the years 865–878.

  A. The Anglo-Saxons offer us a detailed account of *micel here* ("the Great Army"). This was an army of Danes and Norwegians who had spent the previous 10 or 15 years ransacking the Carolingian Empire.

  B. The army arrived in East Anglia in the autumn of 865 and intimidated the East Anglian king to allow them to build a base and gather provisions and horses.

  C. In the fall of 866, the army carried out a lightening advance about 180 miles north and seized the city of York, the largest city in northern England and the capital of the kingdom of Northumbria.

D. Northumbria was enmeshed in a civil war, but the two rival Anglo-Saxon kings joined arms and attacked the Vikings in early 867. The Norsemen set themselves up with a shield wall, drove back the English levies, then counterattacked and swept the field, killing both English kings.

E. Then the Vikings moved into Mercia, in the Midlands of England; set up another base at Nottingham; and raided the kingdom of Mercia. The Vikings then relocated back to East Anglia and conquered this kingdom before turning back on Mercia and Wessex.

F. Wessex was only saved when King Alfred took over in 871, rallied the English army, and eventually won a victory that enabled him to negotiate a treaty in 878.

G. All the advantages the Vikings possessed in warfare, that is, their knowledge of logistics, fortifications, political situations, winter campaigning, and so on, are seen in this campaign in microcosm. In 15 years, the Vikings had conquered eastern England and half the Midlands, a feat that had taken the Anglo-Saxons nearly 150 years to achieve.

Further Reading:

G. Halsall. *Warfare and Society in the Barbarian West, 450–900.* London/New York: Routledge, 2002.

P. H. Sawyer. *The Age of the Vikings.* 2nd ed. London: Edward Arnold, Inc., 1971, pp. 127–132.

Questions to Consider:

1. How did Viking armies mirror Scandinavian society? How important were traditions of valor and honor and the devotion to Odin? How did these advantages ensure success on the battlefield?

2. What accounted for Viking skills in logistics and engineering?

3. How did the success of the Great Army in England epitomize the military advantages and skills of the Vikings?

Lecture Ten—Transcript

Warfare and Society in the Viking Age

In this lecture I want to discuss the importance of warfare in the Viking age and particularly look at a number of issues, that is, weapons, training tactics, and the performance of Vikings as warriors. This is an obvious match-up with the lecture dealing with shipbuilding and the nautical skills of the Scandinavians. Very often in popular literature—this would be novels, film—the notion is that the Vikings were a group of savage warriors, homicidal maniacs, had marvelous ships, came dashing into towns cutting and slashing everything in their path. It leads to all sorts of stereotypes; one of the most common is Hagar the Horrible, the comic strip figure running around with the horned helmet. I'm sorry to disappoint a lot of people but the Vikings did not wear horned helmets. The only horned helmets we have come from the early Bronze Age. They may well have been ceremonial helmets. If you think about it for a moment, they're really not very practical in battle. It gives your opponent something to hang on to and yank off. In any event, that image of the horned helmet has not yet died in the popular perception and is going to be long with us.

I think it's important first to look at the types of weapons and armament available to the Vikings, and these were pretty similar to the armaments that would have been used by many of their opponents, especially in Western Europe, and to a lesser extent in the Eastern lands, especially the Byzantine Empire. Many of these weapons come out of a common Roman and Germanic tradition, and the Vikings, in terms of their physical size and overall look, are not too different from most Northwestern Europeans, their opponents, the Franks, the English, Germanic peoples, or the Celts of the British Isles, and had a lot of the same weapons that would have been used on both sides, or variations of them.

Foremost, it's important to note that the primary weapon of attack was going to be the steel sword. The swords that were used in the Viking age were extremely long broad swords, as you would call them, and they come out of a Roman spatha, a saber. They're anywhere from two and a half to three feet in length. They're considerably longer than the classic Roman jabbing weapon, the gladius. Very often swords were required. You needed two hands to wield some of the larger ones, but these swords required a great deal of space and skill and training and strength to use. In the Icelandic sagas, for instance, the ability of men to wield swords in extremely well known, and they're very, very precise in the skills and the types of blows that can be delivered. Someone like Gunnar in the Njals saga, one of the major figures, is reported to be one of the most skilled swordsmen, and he could wield that sword so quickly that it looked like three swords at once in the air. And that gives you some idea of how agile these guys were in using these weapons.

It also required people to be trained in this type of weapon from a very young age; you were going to be trained to use a sword, to handle a shield, spear, whatever the weapons were. Every free Scandinavian, that is, a Scandinavian who was not a trall or a slave, had familiarity in handling these edged weapons. By the Viking age, these Scandinavians were quite adept in forging iron and steel weapons. The sword was the main weapon of attack. Actually the best swords that were used in the Viking age were of Frankish manufacture, especially in the Rhineland, where the best weapons were forged at Cologne. That was a major weapon center, and we are often told, especially by Arab and Western European sources, that the Scandinavians preferred to get Frankish weapons and modified their swords based on Frankish designs. Large numbers of Frankish weapons have been found in Scandinavia, and the depressing fact is that from a Frankish viewpoint the Carolingian kings, starting with Charlemagne, keep banning the export of weapons to Scandinavia. And yet they keep appearing in Scandinavian graves. No one is paying attention to regulations, which is probably true of the arms market of all eras. I think there are 79 swords from Denmark and Sweden from one Frankish manufacturer alone from the 9th century, so, so much for government regulation.

The sword was the primary weapon. The Scandinavians also used the ax as a serious fighting weapon. In much of Western Europe at the time, the ax had essentially gone out of fashion. There were various types of throwing axes. These could have ranges of maybe up to 40 feet. Scandinavians were extremely deadly in hurling this weapon; it usually went about three or four gyrations before it hit its opponent. Later in the 10th century, they developed a long ax that required two hands, perhaps based on models from the Byzantine and Islamic world, and these are the classic axes that are used by the professional warriors in, say, the armies of Cnut. They're actually hired warriors in the Varangian guard of Constantinople or even the English kings. They're depicted on the Bayeux Tapestry, by the way. Those are essentially Danish or Anglo-Danish warriors fighting in the center of the English army for King Harold II against William the Conqueror. The ax was retained as a serious weapon, both as a throwing weapon and then as a primary weapon for close combats. Also, the spear always remained important. Scandinavian spears were particularly long, two and a half to four feet fitted with an iron head, and they're very, very good in catching their opponent on the shield and ripping his shield off his arm, or unbalancing an opponent.

There are a number of descriptions of individual combats in Icelandic saga, and these were usually two families who were feuding with each other. But the audience is extremely keen to know how the weapons were used. How were they wielded? How effectively was the spear used? And we have very, very, precise information on how these weapons were used in combat, and the audience understood and appreciated all of this and expected to be entertained by it. They also had pretty good defensive armor. Again, contrary to popular perceptions where they're clad in all these furs and running around with the various stages of undress in different movies like the Vikings and the long ships, most Scandinavians took the effort to acquire body armor. They were acquiring their first significant amounts of body armor in the Roman age, and as the Viking age progressed and the Vikings raided widely and traded widely, many Scandinavian forces, certainly by the late 10th century, were sporting chain mail. It's not the body armor familiar with many readers, such as what you'd have in the year of the Crusades. Chain mail is a set of interlocking iron link or steel links. It takes about 35,000–40,000 to make a suit, and it would cover most of the vital parts of the body. Usually it was a short sleeved, leaving the arms free. The legs were not actually covered—this was so you could move quickly—but it covered most of your vital parts.

You would wear it over linen padding, and you would also equip yourself with a helmet. And these are helmets that are based on a late Roman design. They're usually known as Spangenhelm, from the German version of it. They're conical helmets. Usually they're multiple parts, although there are some single ones made, and these helmets would sit on your head. And you would be protected with a nose guard, and your eyes were open and there are parts of your neck that are exposed. But it pretty much protected you from most of the types of the blows that you would receive on the head, which would be overhead blows, and usually these helmets were good enough to deflect most sword blows. You had to have a pretty sharp weapon to get through it and it might take two or three blows to damage the helmet so it essentially fell off. And then your victim was exposed to an attack, and there are lots of comments made in all accounts of some king who didn't wear his helmet in combat; ergo, he got killed.

So the body armor that Vikings protected themselves with was pretty comparable to their opponents' shield, chain mail, helmet. They didn't use too much of the so-called lameller armor. That's more common in the Byzantine world. Those are interlocking scales rather than chain mail, but they carried perhaps somewhere between 30 and 40 pounds worth of armor, shield, and helmet for protection, which is about the weight that an infantryman today goes into battle with when you count all of his equipment that he's carrying around. This body armor was articulated so the weight was distributed over your body, and you're dealing with men who are used to hard labor, who are in prime condition from rowing ships, who are skilled in hunting, and therefore wearing this armor in combat is not as arduous as it seems. And it really does give protection. The most exposed areas are the arms and the lower legs, and there you might sustain wounds from arrows or from a well timed-blow. But in close-order fighting, with a large round shield, chain mail armor, and one of these Spangenhelm helmets on, you could go into that combat with a pretty confident sense that unless you really fouled up that you're not going to get too badly damaged. It was a matter of your skill in using the weapon against your opponent.

In terms of missile weapons, which would be javelins and bows and arrows, these had rather limited range. The bow was about four feet in length, and it's essentially an adapted hunting weapon. The Scandinavians are very good at shooting arrows, someone like Harald Hardrada, who is the great Christian Viking warrior. I think if there's a Christian Valhalla, certainly Harald is presiding over it. He's one of the great figures of the 11th century. He ruled Norway from about 1047–1066. He died at the Battle of Stanford Bridge in England. Harald Hardrada was just a superb bowman, and he could hit his enemies. But it required real skill and aim, and it was extremely effective in ship combat where two ships come close together, and it's essentially a boarding tactic, so you can really see your opponent, and you can aim that arrow on someone who's forgotten his helmet. Or you can try to get him in the neck or an exposed arm and then incapacitate him and then board over and finish him off.

Javelins, likewise, relatively limited range, maybe effective 40 yards, and again these weapons were extremely deadly when used by Scandinavians, especially in ship combat, which is essentially ships coming together and fighting, these deadly boarding tactics, and whoever captures, clears the ship of another opponent, takes that ship and wins the battle. We're told that Norwegians were so good at javelins that they could actually catch a javelin thrown at them, deflect it and catch it, and then turn around and throw it back at their opponent. And there are a number of references to this in Icelandic sagas, particularly the *Heimskringla Saga*, which is the history of the kings of Norway, which is one of the many works written by Snorri Sturluson. And we have a number of important combats of great sea battles fought between Norwegians and Danes, and these incidents are reported quite frequently and can't really be discounted as literary creations.

In terms of weapons and armament, when the Vikings launch out on their attacks in 790, they have comparable equipment, say, to the Carolingian armies of Northwestern Europe, their Anglo-Saxon opponents. They are certainly much better armed than the Celtic peoples of Ireland and Northern Britain who do not have nearly the same amount of weapons and equipment. They are better armed than the Slavic tribes in Eastern Europe. The only people who are going to be superior in armament might be Byzantine armies or armies of the Caliphate, which are really on the fringes of the Scandinavian world anyway.

Furthermore, Vikings as soldiers always appreciated mobility just as they did at sea. We are told in sagas and legends that all Viking heroes, people who would be jarls, the nobles, or sea kings, or anyone of substance—the Norwegian term later would be a man who is a member of the *lendirmenn,* that is, the magnates, the squires— they all knew how to ride horses. In any important Viking raid, the first thing that was done, if they were going to penetrate inland in the 9th century, was gather horses. And they would use horses as a form of transportation; that is, they'd ride to the battlefield, but they would dismount and fight essentially as infantry. Part of the speed of

Viking armies operating in Western Europe was their ability to hit areas, acquire horses, move rapidly, dismount, and fight. Unlike many infantry formations of the Middle Ages, Scandinavians were more than determined to meet cavalry charges, particularly in the later 10th and 11th century. We'll discuss one of those, the Battle of Hastings in 1066, which is essentially pitting a feudal cavalry army of knights against the Anglo-Saxon army, which is really a Scandinavian army in many ways—the shield wall; the English army always wins. It's only at the end of the day that it's finally broken by cavalry charges. Most of the time Western European armies, up until the early 11th century, were fighting as infantry. They had a very small cavalry component, and an argument is made that cavalry increased in importance in the later 10th and 11th century in large part to counter Viking raids. There's a legitimate argument to be made for that.

By fighting so many diverse foes, the Vikings gained invaluable lessons in mobility, weapons, and tactics. They were constantly innovating, and if their weapons and armament were not too dissimilar for most of their opponents, well, what gave them the edge in battle? There are certain aspects of fighting that come into this that do not deal with just necessarily the weapons and tactics. One was the incredible bonds of cohesion within these Viking groups. Some scholars have tried to compare the Vikings, for instance, to the pirates of the early Modern age, say, the Spanish Main. A brilliant book on that subject is by Rediker, *Between the Devil and the Deep Blue Sea*, where he really analyzes the different European pirates of the 16th, 17th century as outsiders, and even the privateers. This is not what Viking armies were like. They were not a group of pirate outsiders. They were commanded by sea kings and jarls. They comprised *lendirmenn,* that is, squires, plus the free members of the community. Most Viking fleets comprised anywhere from three to 10 ships. They came from a single area, a community. They had built the ships themselves.

Certainly in the 9th and early 10th century many of them expected to go back home, and so they brought with them the kind of social cohesion that you would expect in a society where all men of free rank know how to use weapons. They're all engaged in hunting. They have the common bond of rowing these ships and being in an absolutely prime, fit condition as a result of that. You're dealing with a far more coherent group of warriors than, say, a pirate band.

Furthermore, in rowing those ships and in living in the conditions of Scandinavia, the Vikings had several advantages over their opponents. One, they were incredibly agile, especially in leaping and jumping. You have to be in order to do the boarding tactics described in the sagas. You could almost think of the Vikings as communities of a whole bunch of crew rowers that you would have in a college team. This is an extremely fit society going out to war.

They also lived in harsh conditions and had to learn to get through Scandinavian winters. Scandinavians were extremely good in determining logistics—what were the food requirements—in foraging, and above all in campaigning in winter. Much of the transportation in Scandinavia in the wintertime is done by skis. It's done over frozen rivers and by sleds. Campaigning in winter in places like France and England was a cakewalk for most of these people, and repeatedly English armies get caught short because the Scandinavians show up in a winter campaign. That's how they surprised Alfred the Great in 878. They hit him at his winter court in January. There wasn't any English army anywhere, and all of a sudden the Danes decide to do a winter campaign. They're very good at seizing stocks of grain and supplies, generally just after a harvest, and then they stock up. And they know exactly how much they need to do to do one of these lightening winter combats. In terms of logistics, in terms of morale, in terms of the bonds of cohesion, in terms of their skill in determining logistics, these people are superb warriors. They are not the stereotypes of a bunch of armed, homicidal maniacs. They wage war violently and effectively. And they have an enormous number of advantages besides just their weapons and those ships.

This is a very important point to stress. The Scandinavians of free rank, and there are not very many slaves in Scandinavian society compared to the overall population, these free men were all familiar in the use of arms from childhood as well as many of them were expert in hunting, and this is in strong contrast to what had evolved in Western Europe from, say, about 500 on. Most Western European societies were built around a warrior caste, and so the warrior caste, that is, the nobility of the Carolingian Empire, their equivalents in Anglo-Saxon England, these men were very, very skilled in weapons, but the majority of the population actually had come to see military service as a burden. Large numbers of forces were nothing more than essentially militia forces that were called out for immediate services in defense of the immediate area. In English that would be the so-called third, and these soldiers lacked that kind of coherence and experience. They could be very, very easily ambushed by Viking columns—there are reports of that—but, above all, they were very often easily induced to make reckless attacks on a Viking shield wall. That attack would be broken, and then the Vikings would counterattack and mop them up.

While the Western European armies did have very fine warriors indeed and some of them were mounted, on the whole you have to keep in mind that the majority of Western European populations just didn't know how to use edged weapons, and when you're fighting in closed combat with edged weapons it's determination and skill and strength that counts, and the Scandinavians had it. Most of the Viking free males knew how to use these weapons very efficiently and in a very deadly fashion. There were some differences when you were dealing with the Celtic populations of Ireland and Scotland, which are much simpler societies, more hunting societies, but there they didn't have the same level of weapons. They were very good at stealth and ambush, but they couldn't stand up to the Vikings in a set piece battle, at least in the 9th century. Irish weapons and equipment would of course improve over time.

Now, with that notion in mind, the exact numbers of these Viking forces are difficult to calculate and there is a tendency by some scholars to minimize the size of Viking armies and fleets. But whatever the numbers are, even if you say a Viking force is only 1,000 or 2,000 strong, and I think those numbers are too low, nonetheless, those 1,000 or 2,000 men have the courage and determination to defeat a foe several times their size if they're made up primarily of militia. According to my reckoning, and I follow a school that is reacting against this revisionist tendency to down date, in the 9th century, especially from 840 on, the size and scale of Viking attacks go up significantly, and certainly by the end of the 9th century the small contingents of Vikings might represent fleets of 10, 15, 20 ships can very easily assemble into larger groups of 100 vessels, 120 vessels, and all of a sudden you have 5,000 or 10,000 very seasoned and well-trained warriors. This is the only way to account for the remarkable success the Vikings had in England, particularly between 865-878, or the kind of attacks they can wage in the Carolingian Empire, where they can put Paris under siege and really bring the Carolingian monarchy to its knees.

One other point that's often overlooked in this, besides having all these skills in actual fighting, most Scandinavians, as I mentioned, are very, very skilled in wood building, woodwork. The Vikings applied this very skillfully to warfare. Contrary again to popular imagination, any Viking force that was going to operate in an area for some length of time—that is, it was not just a hit-and-run attack as some of the initial raids were—was going to fortify its bases.

They are extremely good at building fortifications. These are simple earthen ramparts with stockade, and our best evidence for the type of work they can do comes from Denmark. There are two remarkable sets of construction which most people wouldn't at first associate with Vikings. One of them is the Danevirke which is a set of fortifications that essentially seals off Jutland from Central Europe. Its earliest construction, based on dendrochronology, which is a method of dating construction by tree rings, is dated around 739-740, and it runs from the Eider River to the town of Hedeby, which is at the base of the Danish peninsula. And what it does is act as a barrier for any invading army. There are several later building phases, one in the earlier 9th century, another in the mid- 10th century, clearly to be associated with the kings Gorim the Old and Harald Bluetooth, and the full system by, say, about 960 A.D. is a very, very set of fortifications with an earthen wall about 30 feet wide with a stockade anywhere from six to eight feet high, depending on how you reconstruct it. There is a huge moat in front of it. It is a pretty effective barrier for keeping out an invading army.

At the same time of this last building phase of these defensive works, we have excavated four Viking camps that could house anywhere from 2,000 to 4,000 warriors. The most famous one is on the Island of Sjaelland—that's Trelleborg—which is one of the largest ones. These are fortified camps, circular camps almost built to Roman specification. Again, they are fortifications to be associated with Harald Bluetooth, who ruled from about 958-987, and Harald Bluetooth is probably responsible for the construction of these fortifications. His son Svein actually, I think, abandoned them, and these constructions therefore date from, say, the 960s and 970s. And the camps were clearly used to house professional warriors that were used for securing the kingdom of Denmark by Harald Bluetooth.

In terms of waging wars overseas, you're dealing with a population of warriors who understood essentially positional warfare, taking fortifying bases for their ships, and Viking camps were difficult to assault. And we have report of one assault on one of them, the so-called Battle of the Dyle in 891 where a German army moved up—this would be a Frankish army from what is now Germany—led by Arnulf the Bastard, who is a rather colorful figure. He orders his army to dismount and assault the camp, and though they do carry the camp—they get over the walls—the fortifications are such that the Vikings are able to get to their ships and essentially escape and then head off to England, where they have a happy time plundering England for the next three or four years. The building of bases was just assumed in any of these campaigns.

To get some sense of the effectiveness of Viking warfare let me close with an example, and we'll return to this campaign when we're discussing the Scandinavian impact in England. And this is the campaign that stretches over approximately the years 865-878 in the Anglo-Saxon Chronicle, which is the main record we have—it actually survives in seven different accounts—but the main accounts covering the 9th and 10th century, which are a record of the deeds of the Kings of Wessex, the West Saxons—this the family of Alfred the Great that eventually unifies England—in the Anglo-Saxon Chronicle we have a very detailed account of what they call in Anglo-Saxon *micel here*, the great army. This is an army of Danes and some Norwegians, many of them fighting for 10-15 years in the Carolingian Empire, who in 865 come together in a great force, probably because they've ransacked the Carolingian Empire so much that they cannot get any more booty out of it. So they decide to relocate to England, and this army shows a lot of the qualities of the fighting abilities of the Vikings I've just discussed.

The army arrives in the autumn of 865 in East Anglia, and they literally intimidate the local East Anglian king to allow them to build a base in East Anglia where they gather provisions and horses. Then in the fall of 866, about a year later, they carry out a lightening advance about 180 miles north and seize the city of York, which is the largest city in northern England and the capital of the kingdom of Northumbria. Northumbria at this point is, happily for the Vikings, in the middle of a civil war. The Vikings occupy the Roman city, fortify it. They actually rebuild part of the Roman wall. The two Anglo-Saxon kings decide maybe it's a good idea to take out these invaders. They join arms and attack in early 867, and it's a classic example of the Norse setting themselves up in a defensive position with their shield wall. They drive back the English levies in disorder and then counterattack and mop them up. Both kings are killed. Aella is actually, he's supposedly blood eagle. We'll get into that later on.

Well, then the Vikings, mostly Danes, and the English tend to refer to them as Danes, move into Mercia in the midlands of England, set up another base at Nottingham and eventually raid that kingdom and force to be paid off, relocate back to East Anglia. King Edmund gets a backbone and decides to oppose them. The Vikings wipe them out. They actually martyr King Edmund by tying him to a tree and shooting him with arrows, probably to dedicate him to Odin, and then they turn back on Mercia and the southern kingdom Wessex by seizing control of the Thames valley and waging these essentially positional wars from fortified bases that essentially knock out Mercia, the kingdom of the midlands, and almost brings Wessex to collapse. Wessex is only saved because King Alfred takes over in 871 from his brother and rallies the English army and fights determined battles and eventually wins a victory where he's able to negotiate a treaty in 878. The Viking army withdraws into the midlands in Northern England. It's not really defeated. It withdraws. It's a standoff. That is a stunning piece of campaigning.

Within 15 years this Danish army, which could have numbered between 5,000–10,000 veteran warriors, its composition changes as some of them move off to raid Ireland and newcomers in from Scandinavia. But this Danish army showed a remarkable knowledge of logistics, the political situations, fortified bases, winter campaigns, seizing towns, setting up defensive positions, forcing ill-trained levies to make these attacks, counter-attacking. All the advantages of Viking warfare is seen in this campaign in microcosm. It shows the type of determined and violent foes the Vikings could be. In the end, the only reason they pull out of Wessex is that Alfred is able to make it just costly enough and pay them off with Danegeld that they move into England. But in 15 years they had destroyed three English kingdoms and almost had destroyed a fourth, and they had conquered an area which took 150 years for the Anglo-Saxons to master. No army has done this in Britain since the Roman age.

Lecture Eleven

Merchants and Commerce in the Viking Age

Scope:

The first Vikings raided to seize booty and slaves because of the growth of trade resulting from the economic and demographic recovery of Western Europe during what historians call the *long 8th century* (c. 675–840). Under Charlemagne (r. 768–814), the Frisian port of Dorestad emerged as the leading market town of Northern Europe. Dorestad was the terminus of both the sea routes from Scandinavia and the Mediterranean commerce that arrived at Venice and moved across northern Italy and down the Rhine. European commerce was fueled by the demand for slaves and raw materials in the great cities of the Abbasid caliphate. Scandinavians, too, contributed to commerce in the Viking Age. They extended the range and scale of trade, thereby creating the *northern arc* that stretched from Ireland to the Black and Caspian Seas. Swedes developed the slave trade down the Volga and Dneiper, while their kinsmen in Western Europe traded in Muslim Spain, the British Isles, and the Carolingian Empire. In the early 9th century, market towns first emerged in Scandinavia at Hedeby and Ribe in Denmark, Birka in Sweden, and Kaupang in Norway. Scandinavians then took over the carrying trade across Northern Europe. The profits of commerce, along with the booty and slaves acquired in raids, enriched and transformed Scandinavian society.

Outline

I. In this lecture, we will deal with trade, especially seaborne trade, conducted by Scandinavians and other peoples from the 8th century through the middle of the 12th. The Scandinavians of the Viking Age were just as much engaged in trade as they were in raiding and settling overseas.

   A. The Scandinavians' advances in shipbuilding, so important to their success in warfare, also translated into success in commerce.

   B. The direction and volume of trade and the types of goods that were exchanged all changed significantly in the Viking Age. Many economic historians speak of the Vikings as developing the *northern trade arc*, which eventually extended from Dublin to the mouth of the Volga River and to the shores of the Black Sea.

C. We shall look at two topics in this lecture: first, the forces that drove trade and commerce in the medieval world and, second, the role of the Scandinavians in directing and amplifying this trade.

II. The Viking raids could not have occurred without general prosperity in Western Europe.

A. When the Vikings began to attack Western Europe in 790, they traveled a series of well-established trade routes to hit kingdoms in England and the Carolingian Empire. These areas had been in economic recovery for a period known as the *long 8th century* (675–840). Several important forces were driving this economic development and prosperity.

1. By the mid-7th century, a certain amount of political order had been imposed in Western Europe. The Anglo-Saxon kingdoms had been simplified into Northumbria, Mercia, Wessex, and East Anglia, and Western Europe had been unified by the Frankish kings, first the Merovingians, then the Carolingians. The imposition of this political order allowed for commerce to proceed.

2. Also important were currency reforms instituted by Charlemagne (r. 768–814) and his father, Pepin the Short (r. 751–768). The silver hammered denier was introduced across Western Europe.

B. Starting from 675, the Frisians emerged as the major merchants in the North Sea and beyond. They depended on hulks and cogs, cargo vessels, that were capable of moving large numbers of goods and people. The Frisians moved timber, slaves, furs, and Arctic products from Scandinavia into Western Europe and brought back ceramics, wine, and weapons from the Carolingian Empire.

C. In Frisia, Dorestad emerged as the most important market town in Western Europe.

1. It stands at the base of the Rhine River system and was, thus, linked to Cologne. From Cologne, goods were moved across the Alps to Venice, the prime port for export into the Mediterranean, Byzantine, and Islamic worlds.

2. In this way, the Carolingian Empire linked the northern lands to Western Europe—goods were taken over the river systems of Europe to the port towns in the Mediterranean, where the products were exported south and east.

3. Dorestad also had trading partners in Quentovic, near modern Boulogne, and Hamwic (Southampton).

4. In Scandinavia, the trade routes helped stimulate the development of other market towns, such as Hedeby.

D. The revival of long-distance trade routes was important to the success of the early medieval economy. Scholars debate whether the European economy in general was underdeveloped, essentially little more than a subsistence economy, or whether these economies were more sophisticated, with trade and commerce playing significant roles in medieval life. One major point to note in this debate is that commerce generated income for Carolingian monarchs and Scandinavian sea kings from tolls and taxes levied on trade and collected in silver.

III. It is important to note that the driving force behind this economic development was the Islamic world.

A. Scandinavia and Christian Western Europe were economically quite undeveloped in comparison to the Mediterranean world, the former heartland of the Roman Empire, the southern and eastern portions of which were now part of the Islamic world. The Abbasid caliphs had established the city of Baghdad as the capital of Islam.

B. The cities of the Islamic world, which included Baghdad, the caravan centers of Iran, and the cities of Central Asia, as well as Cairo, Damascus, Tunis, and Cordoba, had an enormous appetite for labor, consumables, and raw materials, and this was fed by European markets.

C. In the generation just before the Viking Age, from about 750–800, the prime commodity exported from Western Europe was slaves, many of them obtained from the peoples of Central Europe who spoke various Slavic languages. The slave market in Western Europe was drying up as a result of both economic and religious factors, so that these Slavic peoples became prime targets of slave raids.

D. The huge demand for slaves can be partly explained by recovery from a demographic collapse in the Islamic and Carolingian empires that had started in the mid-6th century. At that time, a plague had swept across Europe and the Middle East that was probably on the same order of magnitude as the Black Death in the 14th century.

E. When the Vikings launched out on their raids, they found in place a well-established network of trade routes and markets. By 840, with the superiority of the Scandinavian ships, the Vikings captured the carrying trade and developed the northern arc. Starting at this time, the Scandinavians took over Northern European trading activities, many of which led to markets in the Islamic or Byzantine worlds. The Scandinavians succeeded for several reasons.

1. They had built ocean-going cargo vessels that could move products more efficiently than the Frisian vessels.

2. The ability to carry Scandinavian ships from one river system to another gave the Swedes, in particular, the advantage of developing the river routes of Russia. Starting about 750, the Swedes moved into trading posts in Russia and further developed two trade routes, one down the Volga to the Caspian Sea and the other through various river systems that flow into the Black Sea. These became major trade routes in the Middle Ages.

3. The Scandinavians thus were raiding the Slavic populations of Eastern Europe and selling them to the Islamic world. The result was the development of fortified market towns, which became the future Russian cities, as well as sophisticated trading arrangements with the Turkomen khans, who acted as the middlemen between Northern Europe and the Islamic world.

4. In return for their exported goods, the Swedes acquired silver in the form of Muslim coins, as well as silk, spices, and other goods. One of the most remarkable objects acquired was found at Helgö, a bronze statue of a Buddha from the 1st or 2nd century A.D.

F. The Scandinavians also pioneered a western extension of the northern arc, terminating in the cities of York in England and Dublin in Ireland. Dublin, in particular, became the most important market for the export of slaves from Western Europe, again, destined for the Islamic world. By one estimate, somewhere between one-half and two-thirds of all the slaves arriving in the Islamic world for a period of 250 years were sold by Scandinavian merchants.

IV. In addition to the products brought into the Scandinavian world, including silks and wine, trade also led to the development of market towns, concentrations of populations not seen before in Scandinavian history. Three of these are extremely well known from archaeology and from a curious document prepared for King Alfred the Great, probably dating from just before 895.

A. This document is an Anglo-Saxon translation of a 5th-century Spanish bishop's world history written to justify Christianity. Appended to it are accounts of two voyages: First, Oththere (ON: Ottar) reports a voyage from the Arctic circle, along the coast of Norway, to a town believed to be the archaeological site of Kaupang. This was a major market town of more than 100 acres that was clearly a processing center for Arctic goods to be exported east and west.

B. The other voyage is recorded by Wulfstan, who tells of traveling from Hedeby, in southern Denmark, along the southern shores of the Baltic. Wulfstan names several important ports on this route, illustrating the expansion of Scandinavian-style market towns at the mouths of all the great rivers of the Baltic by the end of the 9th century.

C. Hedeby, Birka, and Kaupang have several similarities, including a resident population of more than 1,000 people, specialized areas for manufacturing, and impressive numbers of imported goods. This is the result of wealth coming into these towns from commerce, plunder, and the slave trade.

   1. These towns were also homes to foreigners, including Frisians, English, Saxons, and so on.

   2. The towns played an economic role in Scandinavia that was out of proportion to their size. In these towns, Scandinavians came into contact with other civilizations, discovering new products and learning new skills.

3. Given their economic importance, these towns were also targets for aspiring Scandinavian kings. It is no accident that the three classic Scandinavian monarchies that would emerge at the end of the 10th century were all centered on one of these towns.

4. Finally, these towns would also host the first Christian missionaries, starting in the 9th century with St. Anskar (801–865), and it is through these towns that Christianity would be transmitted to the northern peoples.

Further Reading:

R. Hodges. *Dark Age Economics*. 2nd ed. London: Duckworth, 1969.

Michael McCormick, *Origins of the European Economy: Communications and Commerce, A.D. 300–900*. Cambridge: Cambridge University Press, 2001.

Questions to Consider:

1. What accounted for the success of Scandinavians in developing their northern trade arc? What were the prime goods exchanged?

2. What was the significance of the rise of market towns, such as Hedeby, Birka, and Kaupang? How did trade transform Scandinavian society?

Lecture Eleven—Transcript

Merchants and Commerce in the Viking Age

In this lecture I wish to deal with an important activity of the Viking age, and that is the importance of trade, especially sea-borne trade, commerce, conducted by Scandinavians but also by other peoples from the 8th through the middle of the 12th century even. This is an important point to keep in mind, that the Vikings, the Scandinavians of the Viking age, to be more accurate, were just as much engaged in trade as they were in raiding, attacking, as well as settling overseas. The advantages in shipbuilding so important for their success in war were also the advantages that translated into their success in commerce. It's too often forgotten that many a Scandinavian was far more a merchant in his career than he was a Viking, although there were many individuals who combined both activities, and there were actually individuals who switched their activities in the course of their voyages. Sometimes they might raid, and other times they might trade, depending on circumstance.

Nonetheless, the direction of trade, the volume of trade, the types of goods that were exchanged, all of this changes significantly in the Viking age. Many economic historians actually speak of the Vikings as developing what is known as the Northern Trade Arc, which eventually comes to extend from Dublin in Ireland, and Dublin is essentially a Viking settlement for the period we're discussing, and terminates at the city of Atil which is the capital of the Khazar Khaganate at the mouth of the Volga where the Volga River flows into the Caspian Sea or the shores of the Black Sea that lead to the so-called Rus, that is, the Swedes operating in Russia to the city of Constantinople, today Istanbul. You have this wide trade arc cutting right across Scandinavia in which all sorts of slaves and goods are exchanged, and the Scandinavians become the primary merchants involved in the carrying trade as well as supplying markets with various goods. That important feature of the Viking age, which is easily lost in the annals of campaigns and attacks and raids, really must be stressed because it is a very, very important aspect; it's actually probably almost as important as the raids. It certainly could be argued that trade might have transformed Scandinavian societies in some ways more than the raids and overseas settlements did, but in any case it's important to look at the role of trade in the whole of the Viking age.

In this lecture I plan to look at two aspects of the problem. One is the forces that were driving trade and commerce in the medieval world in the period we're studying, roughly from, say, 700 almost up to 1200 in some cases. The second part of this lecture is to concentrate on the role of Scandinavians in directing this trade, in amplifying it, and extending the range of different types of goods and transactions. That's a pretty impressive order because, as you'll see, the Scandinavians really play an extremely important role in many parts of the world in expanding and even developing trade routes.

First, the Viking raids would not have occurred if there hadn't been prosperity. You don't really attack neighbors who don't have much in the way of plunder, and when the Vikings began to attack Western Europe in 790 they hit a series of well-established trade routes as well as kingdoms in England and the great Carolingian Empire, that was constructed by Charlemagne, who ruled from 768–814, who creates essentially the basis of the political order of medieval Europe. These areas had been under economic recovery for well over a century. In fact, some historians like to speak of what is a period known as the long 8th century, extending from essentially 675 to about 840 A.D. In this long period of 150 or 175 years, however you want to cut up the period, that see significant developments in Western Europe in trade and commerce, the development of towns, monasteries, as major economic centers, that marks a great leap up from where the European economy had been at the time of the collapse of the Roman Empire in the 5th century A.D.

There were several important forces that were driving this economic development and prosperity. One was that by the middle of the 7th century, about 650 A.D., there was a certain amount of political order that was being imposed in Western Europe; that is, the Anglo-Saxon kingdom simplified into the four great kingdoms the Vikings attacked, Northumbria, Mercia, East Anglia—that's more of a courtesy for East Anglia—and Wessex. It also saw the unification of Western Europe under the Frankish kings, first the Merovingian and then starting in 751-754 the Carolingian family that took over, the family of Charlemagne. The imposition of that political order is extremely important. That allowed for commerce to proceed. It gave you the stability and the predictability that is necessary for all types of economic transactions to take place.

There were also important currency reforms issued by Charlemagne and Charlemagne's dad, Pepin the Short, which introduced a new type of silver coin, the so-called hammered denier. That type of coin was adopted in England, and so at least in Christian Europe there was pretty much a standard currency that was used in sophisticated transactions in towns and cities.

That type of political stability, that return of some kind of order of law, was important for the expansion of trade routes in this so-called long 8th century, and in this period the Frisians excelled. They had always played an important intermediary role between Western Europe and Scandinavia in the late Roman age and in the age of Migrations, and starting from 675 A.D. on, the Frisians really emerge as the major merchants in the North Sea and beyond. They had their own shipbuilding tradition, and they did not make the sort of breakthrough the Scandinavians did. They were content to depend on what are known as hulks and cogs, and these are large cargo vessels, not warships, capable of moving large amounts of goods and people. The hulk was essentially a coastal vessel. The cog was a vessel that really operated more on river systems. Nonetheless, the Frisians had the type of ships necessary to move bulk goods, especially from Scandinavia—timber, slaves, furs, arctic products that would be obtained into Western Europe—and vice versa, to bring the ceramics, the wine, weapons, especially iron swords, steel swords, from the Carolingian world into Scandinavia.

This trade was in progress at least a hundred years before the Viking age, so when the Vikings attacked Western Europe they were following very well-known trade routes that had already been pioneered by the Frisians. In Frisia emerged a major market town called Dorestad. Dorestad was the most important market town in Northern Europe. It stands at the base of the Rhine River systems. It's on one of its tributaries and therefore it's linked to Cologne, which was the largest city north of the Alps in the Middle Ages up until the 12th century and from Cologne across the Alps to Venice, which was the prime port for the export of Mediterranean goods.

The Carolingian Empire really led to the reestablishment of trade groups in Western Europe to the Mediterranean ports where various goods were exported out to the Byzantine world, that is, the Byzantine Empire, the eastern Roman Empire in Asia Minor and Greece, or to the Islamic world which was in Spain, North Africa, and today the Middle East. These were the great cities of the Middle Ages. These were the great markets, and what the Carolingian Empire did, compliments of the Frisians, was link the northern lands to the Carolingian Empire. The goods were taken over the river systems of Europe to the port towns in the Mediterranean where the products were exported south and east. This trade network is extremely important, and Dorestad was at the center of all this northern trade. Dorestad also had important trading partners. One was called Quentovic, which is essentially the predecessor of the modern city of Boulogne, and a port in England which was known in Anglo-Saxon as Hamwic, the future city of South Hampton, and so England, Scandinavia, Northern Europe were now linked into this trade route. In Scandinavia, the trade routes helped stimulate the development of market towns already in the 8th century on the eve of the Viking age.

One of them is at Hedeby, which is on the southern side of Schlei fjord [sic firth], which Schlei, or Schleswig, is the modern German city. So Hedeby is actually the predecessor of Schleswig. It's a Danish town, and it's where most of the trade goods I've mentioned before come from Western Europe. They cross the Danish peninsula, they go to Hedeby, and they're exported out to the Baltic, particularly to Birka in Sweden or even to ports up in Norway. The Frisian merchants actually stimulated the first steps to developing these market towns in two generations before the Viking age. Therefore, sailing along these areas and transporting goods had become quite routine.

The revival of long-distance trade routes was really very important to the success of the early medieval economy, and economic historians of the Middle Ages are deeply divided over whether the European economy in general, including Scandinavia in the Viking age was underdeveloped. That's one term that's often used, that it was essentially nothing more than a souped-up subsistence economy and trade. Particularly, long-distance trade played a rather minor role for a society that was essentially a subsistence. That is a minimalist view that has taken off in ancient and economic economies, and I must be quite frank. I tend to err on the other side. I believe that these economies are more sophisticated than just subsistence and that trade and commerce played an extremely important role in medieval life, not only for the Carolingian kings but also for the Scandinavians of the Viking age. Trade, for one important point, generated lots of income and hard cash in the terms of tolls and taxes you could levy on trade, and that would be collected in silver and hard money and that was always appreciated by any monarch, Carolingian king or Scandinavian sea king, as opposed to taking rents and commodities in agricultural products or labor services.

In my estimation, this long-distance trade is extremely important in the revival of prosperity in the Carolingian Empire, the ability of Charlemagne and his successors to tax or to collect money from their subjects and so sustain the royal institutions. What's driving this trade and really ultimately driving this economic development is a point that might seem a bit odd to us at first, and it's the cities of the Islamic world. It is important to keep in mind that not only Scandinavia, but Christian Western Europe, was economically quite undeveloped in comparison to the lands in the Mediterranean world, that is, the old heartland of the Roman Empire, the southern and eastern portions of which were now part of the Islamic Empire, the empire that had been conquered by the successors of Mohammed and, at the start of the Viking age, an empire that was ruled by the Caliph of Baghdad, the so called Abbasid Caliph, who established the great city of Baghdad as the capital of Islam. The cities of the Islamic world, and these were true cities—Baghdad is a city that gets up to a million strong—the great cities, the caravan centers of Iran, the cities of central Asia, Damascus and Syria, Cairo, that emerge in this period in Egypt, Tunis, and Cordova in Spain, the seed of an independent Islamic dynasty there, they had an enormous appetite for labor consumables, raw materials, and this was fed by the European markets.

In the generation just before the Viking age, say, about 750–800, the prime commodity being exported from Western Europe was slaves, many of them obtained from the peoples of central Europe who spoke various Slavic languages. These were Slavic tribes that had moved into central Europe starting in the 7th century who spoke related dialects. That doesn't imply they had any sort of cultural or political unity, but they had a series of related dialects. And they moved in the lands between essentially the Pripet Marshes today in Russia, and the Elba, which used to be essentially the boundary line between East and West Germany and becomes, in effect, the boundary line of the Carolingian Empire of Charlemagne. These numerous tribes that moved in there and spoke languages quite distinct from the Germanic tribes who had migrated into the Roman Empire, they became the prime targets for slave raiding for two reasons: one is that the bishop said it wasn't a good idea to enslave Christians and that kind of cut down on enslaving your fellow English and Frankish neighbors.

But second is that as agriculture develops in both England and the Frankish Empire, you shift over to turning your laborers into serfs, and serfs, while they are tied to the land, have all sorts of rights and no landlord wants to sell his serfs off. He needs the labor services. So for both economic and religious reasons, the slave market in Western Europe was drying up. You didn't have large numbers of captives. What happened is you had extensive raiding in Eastern and Central Europe, and those slaves were then shipped to Venice and other ports and exported to the Islamic world.

It's a significant point by 800 the word slave or *esclave* in French or *slavos* in medieval Latin, is essentially the word Slav being used to designate the captive who's destined for the slave markets, and that means the Islamic world. Now, there's been a very, very clever study done by Michael McCormick recently on this, a really monumental work on the early European economy, and the best guess is that slaves yielded the highest return on any product exported either from Scandinavia or Western Europe to the Islamic world. They were the commodity most in demand, and this meant demand for laborers on plantations, the usual girls that populate the harems, slaves that are enrolled into the slave units of the Islamic world.

There is an appetite for labor to sustain these huge cities of the Islamic world for two reasons: One is, cities consume people; the disease rate, the destruction in cities, you always need to replenish populations. Second, the Islamic world and the Carolingian Empire were recovering from a demographic collapse that had started in the mid-6th century when a plague had swept across Europe and the Middle East, which was probably on the same order of the Black Death of the 14th century, and had major economic and demographic consequences. As a result, when the Vikings launched out on their raids, they found in place well-established trade routes, slave markets in the Islamic world, in Spain, in Baghdad, in the Middle East. They encountered a network of trade routes in Western Europe that were moving bulk goods of the Arctic and the timber products of the forest to the Mediterranean world and to points south. Most of this trade was in the hands of the Frisians. As a result of the Viking raids, as a result of the superior Scandinavian ships, by 840 the Scandinavians captured the carrying trade and developed that Northern Arc of which I spoke at the start of this lecture.

Starting from about 840, the Scandinavians take over many of the trading activities going on in northern Europe, and all those trading activities eventually are going to lead markets in the Islamic or Byzantine world. Here is where they developed the so-called Northern Trade Arc. There are several reasons why the Scandinavians succeeded in this regard. One is those ships, the knarr, the cargo ships. They have built ocean-going cargo vessels that could move products in a way that none of those Frisian vessels could. Second, Scandinavian ships, both warships and cargo ships, can move up rivers and can be carried from portage to portage in a fashion that no other vessel could. That gave the Swedes, particularly, the advantage to develop the river routes of Russia, and we'll discuss in several lectures about the long-term implications of that. But in economic terms, starting from 750, the Swedes move into trading posts in Russia; the most important one is at Holmgard, that is, the future Novgorod. And they develop two trade routes eventually, one down the Volga to the Caspian Sea and the other through various river systems that pick up the Dneiper which flows into the Black Sea. And these trade routes become major trade routes in the Middle Ages. This is a Scandinavian contribution to it, and the biggest commodity is slaves.

The Scandinavians are raiding the Slavic populations of Eastern Europe and selling them to the Islamic world. This results in the development of a number of fortified market towns, which become the future Russian cities. It results in very, very sophisticated trading arrangements with the Turkoman khans who have consolidated kingdoms on the middle and lower Volga and who are the middlemen between Northern Europe and the Islamic world. The Swedes become very, very accustomed to going down the Volga and trading with the so-called Bulgars—these are a Turkish-speaking tribe—and the Khazars, another Turkish-speaking tribe, who have cities that are connected across the Caspian Sea to the great centers of Baghdad and Iran, such as Hamadan. What happens is the Scandinavians bring in large numbers of slaves captured from the Slavic population, furs, timber, Frankish swords. There are at least two independent Arab reports that indicate the Muslims were really impressed by Frankish weapons, and the Scandinavians have them. They're buying them. They're being shipped to Baghdad and in return the Swedes are acquiring an enormous amount of silver, a lot of this in the form of Muslim coins issued in Baghdad and Iran. They're known as a dirham. These are very heavy-weight coins, originally struck at a theoretical weight of 2.79 grams. And they're these flat-hammered silver coins with Islamic script. There are at least 80,000 of them that have been found in hoards and grave deposits in Sweden, primarily around Lake Mälaren and in Gotland. There are also thousands of them found on the Volga trade routes leading from the Caspian Sea. The volume of silver that moved up to Sweden is really quite extraordinary.

In addition, there are fragments of silk, which seems to be one of the most important commodities. Silk production is one of the big features of Baghdad and Iran starting in the 8th century, and some of these silks seem to be from central Asia or the Islamic world. We have fragments from Birka, fragments from Hedeby, one of the market towns in Denmark—this is another commodity that's moving north—various furnished goods, aromatic spices, all moving into Scandinavia to enrich their lives, including scales. Apparently Scandinavians are used to weighing coins and using coins as coins rather than just as bullion or jewelry.

One of the most remarkable objects comes from the town of Helgö, which was found in excavation, and that is this statue of a Buddha from the Gandharan period—I can't remember, the 1st or 2nd century A.D. I just have a vision that some Swedish merchant on the Volga was negotiating with one of the Turks and said, "Here are my Slavic slaves and here are the furs. What am I going to get?" And he's, "Well, I'm little short. Wouldn't you like a statue from…?" "What is it?" "I don't know." It's a novelty and it appears in Helgö as one of these curious trade goods that show up in the type of exchange and the volume of exchange that's going on on the Eastern Trade Route.

The Scandinavians also pioneer a western extension of that Arc and that terminates at the cities of York in England and Dublin in Ireland, both of which are essentially Scandinavian trading towns through this whole period. Dublin, in particular, becomes the most important market for the export of slaves from Western Europe. These would be Irish captives, English captives, Frankish captives, people taken in Viking raids, and in the case of the Irish, it's usually the Irish are enslaving each other and selling them to the Vikings. And the Vikings are arming the Irish with better weapons to incite them to do this. This slave trade is essentially destined to Muslim Spain. By one estimate, somewhere between 50 percent and two-thirds of the slaves arriving into the Islamic world for a period of 250 years is by Scandinavian merchants and carrying trade. They are supplying the bulk of the labor demanded by the Islamic world, which is an interesting point to reflect on. The movement of labor is essentially from Europe to the Islamic world, whereas in our day it's essentially in the reverse: Europe is drawing labor in from the Mediterranean and Islamic world. That's a very important point to keep in mind.

Besides all the products coming into Scandinavia that enriched their lives, including the curious Buddha, there are also silks, which are clearly worn by all the upper classes in Scandinavia by the 10th century. There are references to them all the time in the Icelandic saga. Wine is a commodity that everyone is used to consuming. The trade also led to the development for the first time of market towns, that is, concentrations of populations that we have not seen before in Scandinavian history. There are three of them that are extremely well known by archeology as well as a curious document prepared for King Alfred the Great, probably dating about a little before 895. It's an Anglo-Saxon translation of the Spanish bishop Orosius in the 5th century who wrote this world history to justify Christianity. See how wonderful Christianity is, because life was miserable before Christianity, and he recites every disaster known in classical history. And now things are better.

He didn't encounter the Viking age; he died in 414. In any case, that is updated in Anglo-Saxon tradition and then appended to it are two voyages, one by a man who is identified as Oththere, or Ottar probably in Norwegian. Ottar is his Norwegian name; Oththere is his Anglo-Saxon name. He reports a voyage going from the Arctic Circle along the coast of Norway to a town we believe is the archeological site of Kaupang—today is Vest fjord—which was a major market town of over a hundred acres which was clearly the processing center of all the arctic goods coming in, the timber, which is then being exported east and west where silver and other commodities are coming in. This account is really remarkable. He gives us a very detailed account of how trade is carried out with the Lapps, and Ottar himself is a merchant prince who's made a fortune in trading in sealskins, whalebone. And at the court of King Alfred he's clearly treated as a nobleman of very high rank, and he essentially made his fortune in merchandising. There's no evidence that he was a Viking.

The other voyage is by a fellow named Wulfstan, an Anglo-Saxon name, and he may well have been an Englishman—we're not sure if he was Dane—and he gives an account of the voyage from Hedeby, in southern Denmark, along the southern shores of the Baltic and the trade involved there. That includes slave trade as well, and he names several important ports there. One of them is a port that's been excavated, Wolin or Wolin which may be the site of the later Jomsborg, the Viking encampment. Another one may have been at the mouth of the Vistula. It's called Truso. We're not sure exactly where it is. One guess it's the predecessor of Danzig, or Gdansk. What it shows is the extension of Scandinavian-style market towns at the mouths of all the great rivers of the Baltic, certainly by the end of the 9th century. Hedeby has been excavated. Birka has been excavated. Both of these towns in Denmark and Sweden, respectively, emerge as major market towns, covering maybe 60 acres.

They have together, along with Kaupang in Norway, several important similarities. One is, there was probably a resident population of over 1,000 people. There were specialized areas for manufacturing. The number of imported goods from these towns is impressive—ceramics, glassware from the Rhine, silks from the Near East, perhaps some of them originating from central China—some would even claim from Chinese workshops, or inspired from Chinese workshops. All of this is the wealth pouring into these towns as the result of the commerce as well as the marketing of plunder and slaves, and most of these slaves were taken as captives in raids. Second, the towns clearly are also home to foreigners who are residents there, Frisian, Saxons, English, and Slavs; that is, they have a certain international quality. They are nothing on the order of later medieval towns, and they're not even incipient cities. Nonetheless, they play an economic role in Scandinavia that is all out of proportion to their size.

In these towns is where Scandinavians come into contact with other civilizations. It is here that they learn all sorts of products and skills and make money in a fashion they have never done before. It's through these towns, for instance, that the artistic styles of the

Middle East were transmitted to the Scandinavians and inspired some of the later jewelry styles. It's in these towns where the first coins are minted in Scandinavia, again on a limited number. Furthermore, these towns are important economic centers, which means any aspiring king in Scandinavia is going to want to control them. It's no accident that the three classic Scandinavian monarchies that emerge at the end of the 10th and in the 11th century are all going to center around one of these towns. The Norwegian kingdom is based on Kaupang and its associated towns in the area around Oslo, especially on the Western shore of the Vestford. King Harald Finehair and his successors need those towns. They produce revenue.

At Birka in Lake Mälaren, that city is the nexus of trade routes about to 975–980, when the receding Lake Mälaren causes Birka to lose its port, and what happens is the merchants simply relocate north of Birka on an estuary that connects them to Uppsala and a new town. Sigtuna is founded, and Sigtuna simply takes over where Birka had once been. Sigtuna is not only the new market town connected to the eastern trade, it also doubles as the capital and the mint of the first Swedish kings. Hedeby is perhaps the most important market town in the north. It is clearly the fiscal means whereby the first kings of Denmark, Gorim the Old, Harald Bluetooth, Sven Forkbeard gained the revenues to build the impressive camps of which I spoke, the Dannevirke, the various fortification systems. And it is also the town where again the first coins in Denmark were probably minted. The monarchies that emerge and become eventually the territorial monarchies of Denmark, Norway, and Sweden, very, very much depend on the development of trade and of these new market towns. Finally, the most important point about these market towns, it is here where the first Christian missionaries will arrive, starting with Saint Anskar in the 9th century. And it's through these towns that Christianity is really transmitted to the northern peoples.

Lecture Twelve
Christendom on the Eve of the Viking Age

Scope:

On the eve of the Viking Age, Scandinavians were long familiar with the wider world through commerce, and they had gained invaluable information on currents and winds in the northern waters. The Carolingian Empire, forged by Charlemagne, was the heartland of Western Christendom, but its state lacked the institutions to withstand the stress of civil war and Viking raids after 825. To Scandinavians, the Carolingian world was a source of silver, weapons, textiles, ceramics, and prestige goods. Carolingian kings were also aggressively Christian. In 772–806, Charlemagne conquered and forcibly converted to Christianity the Saxons of northwestern Europe. In southern England, the rival kings of Mercia and Wessex clashed repeatedly, while Northumbria was plagued by civil war. Elsewhere, the Vikings encountered no organized states other than the distant Byzantine Empire. In the Celtic West, monasteries were centers of Christian culture and prosperity, while warlords clashed with local rivals. The Slavic peoples dwelling in the forest zones of Central and Eastern Europe lived in tribal societies. They were ruthlessly raided for slaves by Western Europeans, Turkomen nomads, and Scandinavians. The Vikings, in attacking Christendom, forced their foes to organize into far more effective states.

Outline

I. This lecture serves as a transition between our examination of the development of Scandinavian civilization in the first third of the course and our study of the Scandinavians' impact on the wider medieval world in the Viking Age.

    A. The Scandinavians encountered three medieval civilizations that emerged out of the late Roman world and are now seen as related: Latin Christendom, which would eventually become modern Western Europe; the Byzantine Empire, that is, the eastern portions of the former Roman Empire, centered on the city of Constantinople; and the Islamic caliphate, stretching from Spain across North Africa to its heartland in the Middle East.

B. The greatest interaction between Scandinavia and these civilizations occurs with Western Europe, although the Scandinavians did have a profound influence in Eastern Europe, which is being increasingly documented through archaeology. The Scandinavians' interaction with the Islamic world was primarily through their slave-trading activities.

II. We begin with Latin Christendom at the onset of the Viking Age in the 8th century.

A. The Carolingian Empire stretched from the Pyrenees across Western Europe to the Elba and across most of northern and central Italy. To the Scandinavians, this was an impressive domain. Several important changes had taken place, however, since the last contact of the Scandinavians with the Frankish world in the Age of Migrations.

B. The first of these was a major change of dynasty in the mid-8th century, when a new family, the Carolingians, took over rule of the Frankish heartland from the Merovingian kings. In 751, Pepin the Short, Charlemagne's father, took the crown for himself and was recognized as king of the Franks by the papacy in 754.

1. Pepin and the succeeding Carolingian kings forged medieval Europe. The Carolingian kingdom represented the first synthesis of Roman Christian and Germanic institutions into a major political order since the fall of the western Roman Empire.

2. In many ways, Pepin and Charlemagne saw themselves as the heirs of the Roman tradition. For Charlemagne, this view culminated in his coronation on Christmas Day in the year 800 as Holy Roman Emperor. Henceforth, Carolingian monarchs and their descendants in Western Europe ruled as Roman emperors.

C. By his conquests, Charlemagne greatly extended the range of Frankish political control, which from the Scandinavian viewpoint, was frightening. From 772–804, Charlemagne campaigned repeatedly in northwestern Europe and conquered the region known as Saxony, which is northwest Germany.

1. The Romans had never brought this region under control; it was inhabited by Germanic-speaking peoples who worshiped the ancient gods and maintained close contact with the Danes.
2. The conquest of Saxony was also accompanied by a forced conversion. Those who refused to submit to Christianity were massacred. As a result, many Saxons fled to Denmark, and a resistance movement evolved. We know of one Saxon rebel leader, Widukind, who received aid from Danish kings.
3. When Saxony was finally brought under Frankish control, the Eider River became the northeastern boundary of the Carolingian Empire; the Danish kings saw this as a threat. Many of the early raids carried out against the Frankish Empire might have been in response to threatening moves by Charlemagne.

D. The Carolingian Empire was also the basis for our understanding of the association of political and ecclesiastical institutions in the medieval world.
   1. With this monarchy, the prelates of the Latin Western Church also became secular princes. They administered royal revenues and properties, and they dispensed royal justice. They were members of the same military warrior caste as the nobility.
   2. In the course of the development of Latin Christendom, the Carolingian vision of the episcopacy triumphed, and the hierarchy of the clergy became closely associated with the political order of the monarchy.

E. The Scandinavians also saw Charlemagne's empire as extremely wealthy—a prime target if it could be raided. After 814, such action became much easier.
   1. Charlemagne was succeeded by his son Louis the Pious (r. 814–840), who was politically ineffective. Louis, in turn, tried to transmit power to his oldest son, Lothar (r. 840–855), but his other three sons contested this move. Starting very early in Louis's reign, from the 820s on, the Carolingian Empire saw a number of civil wars over this issue.
   2. In 843, the first significant partition of the kingdom was carried out by the three surviving sons of Louis the

Pious. Lothar received the so-called Middle Kingdom and the imperial title; Charles the Bald received what would evolve into the kingdom of France; and Louis the German received the lands that would evolve into Germany.

3. The civil wars and this partition serve as an ideal entrée for the Viking attacks into Western Europe. The Vikings had begun raiding into Frankish lands in the time of Charlemagne but encountered his naval defenses. After Charlemagne's death, no attempt was made to maintain these naval defenses because the Frankish nobility was too involved in fighting civil wars.

4. The failure, especially of Charles the Bald, to halt Viking attacks would bankrupt the Carolingian monarchy, bring about its demise, and result in the division of the kingdom in the west into feudal states.

F. Finally, there were in Western Europe the various kingdoms and chiefdoms in the British Isles. This region had a mix of Celtic-speaking and Germanic-speaking peoples and no political unity; the only common bond was that all these peoples were members of the Christian Church.

1. By 800, the Anglo-Saxon kingdoms, linguistically and culturally, were part of Western Europe. They were members of the wider Christian community, used Latin as their literary language, and embraced the monastic life, as well as the arts of Western Europe. Many of the monasteries in both Ireland and England were important economic centers, and they were totally undefended.

2. England had politically simplified itself into four leading kingdoms by the time of the Viking Age. Mercia in the Midlands was ruled by Offa (r. 757–796), who imposed his hegemony over the kings of East Anglia and Wessex and held sway in England south of the Humber. North of the Humber was the kingdom of Northumbria, the center of monastic and cultural life associated with early Anglo-Saxon England.

3. On the eve of the Viking Age, Northumbria was in trouble. It essentially consisted of two kingdoms, Bernicia, centered on the port at Bamburgh, and Deira, based on York. These two regions were never well

integrated. When the Vikings began raiding England in the 780s and 790s, not only did they find undefended monasteries along the shores, but they also found little organized opposition.

4. The rest of the British Isles, including Wales, Cornwall, Cumbria, Scotland, and Ireland, were not organized in any fashion as states. Ireland, in particular, was a collection of different tribes and regional kings; it existed only as a geographic expression.

III. In closing, we turn briefly to the other two civilizations that the Scandinavians encountered in the medieval world.

A. The Islamic world was the greatest civilization and the primary economic force driving trade and development in the early Middle Ages. Few Scandinavians ever experienced the cities of Islam; indeed, after 975, the original trade route along the Volga diminished, and the trade route shifted to one along the Dneiper that led Scandinavians into the Byzantine Empire.

B. In Constantinople, the Scandinavians encountered a great bureaucratic state, and in contrast to the Islamic world, they actually visited this capital.

1. Based in the city of Kiev, the Swedish Rus, the Scandinavians who operated in Eastern Europe, brought their ships down the Dneiper, reached the Black Sea, and sailed to Constantinople.

2. Without a doubt, Constantinople was the greatest city in the Christian world. The Byzantine Empire was heir to the Roman political and military traditions; it had an organized trade system and was the source of silk, gold, and spices, acquired through middlemen on the Volga.

3. It is difficult to exaggerate the impact of the experience of Scandinavians upon entering Constantinople. Many Scandinavians traveled to Byzantium to take service as mercenaries, make their fortunes as merchants, and even to settle.

4. In Constantinople, the Scandinavians also encountered Orthodox Christianity, a religion associated with the Macedonian emperors and, in contrast to Christianity in Western Europe, a religion associated with victory.

C. Scandinavian contact with the Byzantine world would have a significant impact. It would lead to the adoption of Orthodox Christianity by the Scandinavians in Russia and have an important influence on state formation in Sweden and Denmark.

Further Reading:

Adriaan Verhulst. *The Carolingian Economy*. Cambridge: Cambridge University Press, 2003.

Mark Whittow. *The Making of Byzantium, 600–1025*. Berkeley: University of California Press, 1996.

Questions to Consider:

1. In what ways was the Carolingian Empire of Charlemagne the most successful state in Latin Christendom? What accounted for the peace and prosperity under Charlemagne? What were the achievements and weaknesses of the later Carolingian empire?

2. What were the achievements and strengths of the Byzantine Empire and the Abbasid caliphate? How did Scandinavians view these distant empires?

Lecture Twelve—Transcript
Christendom on the Eve of the Viking Age

In this lecture I plan to introduce the wider medieval world in order to give an understanding of the extent and range of the Viking impact, and this lecture acts as something of a transition from the first third of the course to the second third of the course. We might take a bit of time to think of where we've been and where we're going. We've looked at developments in Scandinavia going back into the Bronze Age, the influences of outside civilizations, the evolution of a uniquely Scandinavian civilization expressed in its decorative arts and its cults and its martial ethos, the achievements in warfare and shipbuilding that made the Viking age possible and also the rather undervalued and underplayed importance of Scandinavians in medieval commerce.

Starting with this lecture, we're going to expand our view and look at the Scandinavian impact on the wider medieval world in the Viking age from 790-1100. These are the lectures that I believe earned my course at Tulane the name, History 315, better known as Pillage and Plunder 315. We're going to look at the range of Viking attacks and settlements overseas and in some cases even the creation of kingdoms overseas from Ireland all the way through Russia. In the process, the Scandinavians come into contact with three distinct civilizations which are all civilizations that emerge out of essentially the late Roman world. So I think it's important for us to look at those three different civilizations and to try to get an understanding of how the Scandinavians would have viewed them and perhaps also pose some questions even if we really can't answer them. How did the Scandinavians view these worlds? And the people who populated them? who come to be, in many cases, at least in the early stages, foes and captives, and eventually in many cases become neighbors as they settle among them and in even in some cases become assimilated into these civilizations.

The first one we shall look at will be Western Europe, and it's better to use the term Latin Christendom, that is, the kingdoms in Western Europe that acknowledged the spiritual supremacy of the Pope in Rome and will eventually evolve into modern Western Europe of today. The second civilization we'll discuss is the Byzantine world centered on the city of Constantinople, Istanbul in Turkey today, the capital of a great bureaucratic state which is really right in line with the Roman traditions. Constantinople rules over the Aegean world, the lands around the Aegean Sea, primarily the modern land of Greece and also the great peninsula of Asia Minor, or Anatolia, which is the Asiatic heartland of Turkey today. Finally, we'll look also at that Islamic world, and there we'll be a little briefer on it because Scandinavians did not really travel much to the Islamic world. And this is a world that stretches from Spain across North Africa to the heartland in the Middle East, through Iran into Central Asia, clearly the most impressive political and cultural order at the time, the only rival being Tong China at the other end of the Eurasian landmass. Anyone looking at the medieval world in the year, say, 800 at the start of the Viking age would clearly see the Islamic Empire centered at Baghdad and the great Chinese empires as the two greatest civilized orders on the globe. The Scandinavians come into contact with all three of these civilizations, and to different degrees they influence and interact with that.

The greatest interaction is in Western Europe, and our greatest information is about Western Europe. They do have a very, very profound influence in Eastern Europe. It isn't as well documented although archeology now is constantly amplifying that picture, and the Islamic world is much more a case of providing commodities, particularly slaves, to the Islamic world and gaining great wealth. Few Scandinavians ever entered the great cities of Islam. There are some very important Danish and Norwegian raids into Spain in the 840s and 850s. They actually capture the city of Seville very briefly, and Spain at this point is ruled by an independent Muslim ruler, the Emir of Cordova. And these raids, however, never really amount to any kind of significant conquest. And they're pretty much sideshows to the more important attacks going on in the Carolingian Empire. They are quite spectacular, and they're daring and certainly scare the Muslims, actually cause them to send missions off to find out who these strange people are, coming from the North. But in the long run, they don't have nearly the kind of impact that Scandinavian attacks and settlements have in Western Europe, Latin Christendom, or in Eastern Europe.

Let's look at Western Europe, Latin Christendom, at the onset of the Viking age in the 8th century. Clearly, to most Scandinavians the Carolingian Empire, and this is the empire that stretches from the Pyrenees across Western Europe to the Elba, that is, the great river that bisects Germany today, and also across most of Northern and Central Italy, Rome is included within the domains of the Carolingian Empire. It is the seat of the papacy and the popes rule over their own domains, the so-called donation of Pepin, which were lands granted to the papacy by the Carolingian King, Pepin the Short, and the future papal states. So when you speak of the Carolingian Empire, you're essentially talking about most of the core areas of Europe that became the original common market which eventually evolved into the now European Union, that is, the low countries, western Germany, most of Italy except for the far south, France, parts of northern Spain. That constituted most of Latin Christendom. There was a small Spanish kingdom in the northwest, Astorius, which battled the Muslims of Spain. And there were the British Isles which were part of this Christian civilization. But the Carolingian Empire constituted most of Latin Christendom at the start of the Viking age. Certainly by the standards of the Scandinavians, it was an impressive order.

Several important changes, however, had occurred since the last significant contact of Scandinavians with the Frankish world—I discussed in the period of the age of Migrations—and that is, there was a major change of dynasty in the mid 8th century when a new family, the Carolingians, took over ruling the Frankish heartland which had previously been ruled by the Merovingian kings, that is, the descendants of Clovis. In 751 or 754—you can date it either way—Pepin the Short, who had previously been the major domo, that is, the manager, the mayor of the palace of the Merovingian kings, takes the crown for himself. He's eventually recognized as king of the Franks by the papacy, that is, in 754, when he's given a papal coronation. He established a new line of kings, the Carolingians—the son of Pepin will be Charlemagne—and these Carolingian kings really do forge medieval Europe. In some ways the Carolingian order is precocious. It is the first synthesis of Roman Christian and Germanic institutions into a major political order since the fall of the Western Roman Empire.

In many ways, Pepin and Charlemagne saw themselves as the heirs of the Roman tradition. For Charlemagne, this would climax on Christmas day of 800 when he was crowned Holy Roman Emperor, or Emperor of the West, and henceforth Carolingians monarchs and their descendants in Western Europe ruled as Roman Emperors. The

Byzantine Emperor in Constantinople who had a claim to that didn't quite agree with this. It's important point to stress that the Carolingian emperors saw themselves in many ways the heirs to the Roman legacy, and they did inherit a significant number of those Roman institutions that enabled them to build this political order. The fact that the Carolingians, and to a lesser degree the English kings, had those Roman-style institutions, in part explains why they were more successful in fending off Viking attacks than other areas that did not have Roman institutions; that is, there were towns—there was some sort of fiscal basis; there was a population—eventually, once you had intelligent leadership to organize resistance to Scandinavian attacks. Charlemagne also greatly extended the range of Frankish political control. He conquered central Europe. From the Scandinavian viewpoint, this was kind of frightening. Starting in 772 and really extending through a series of campaigns not ending until about 802 or 804, Charlemagne campaigned repeatedly in Northwestern Europe and conquered the region known as Saxony, which is Northwest Germany, a region that the Romans had never brought under control and a region inhabited by Germanic-speaking peoples who worshipped the ancient gods and were in close contact with the Danes. The conquest of Saxony was also accompanied by a forced conversion. There are several reports of massacres of Saxons refusing to submit to Christianity. There are reports of cutting down the sacred trees.

These efforts to convert the Saxons and incorporate them into the Frankish empire resulted in many Saxons fleeing to Denmark. There is a famous resistance leader. His name is Widukind. He carries out a series of rebellions in the 770s and 780s, and he is supported by kings in Denmark. When Saxony was finally brought under Frankish control, the Eider River, that river that cuts Jutland off from central Europe, became the northeastern boundary of the Carolingian Empire and the Danish kings, and there were many kings in Denmark but no king of Denmark. The Danish kings saw the Franks as an aggressive, threatening, Christian power.

One argument can be made that many of the early raids conducted against the Frankish Empire, particularly the first significant attack on Dorestad which occurred in 810 by a very large Danish fleet, commanded by a royal figure who's known as Godfred in the Frankish sources and probably his Norse name is Guthfrith, this attack was probably in retaliation for Frankish violations along the border or threatening moves by Charlemagne. The Carolingian Empire was politically very impressive. Without a doubt it fielded the most impressive army in Western Europe, an army that was extremely large, and at the time of the start of the Viking age a very well- seasoned army that had a tradition of victory behind it with Charlemagne, although, as I stressed in an earlier lecture, fighting was essentially, increasingly becoming the monopoly of the warrior caste and many of the subjects of Charlemagne really knew very little about military service. The other important feature I should stress about the Carolingian Empire, it is the basis for our understanding of the association of political and ecclesiastical institutions in the medieval world. It is with the Carolingian kings that the prelates of Europe, that is, the bishops, the archbishops, the great figures of the Latin Western Church are essentially also secular princes, that they administer royal revenues, properties, they dispense royal justice.

They are members of the same military warrior caste as the nobility, and in the course of the development of Latin Christendom, it is this Carolingian vision of the episcopacy or the prelates, that is, the senior officials, that comes to triumph. So that Christianity in its institutional organization, in its hierarchy of the higher clergy, is closely associated with the political order of the monarchy. These are two aspects of a single political order. It is this Carolingian vision that is eventually carried to England and eventually carried across Western Europe. It is transplanted in the Crusader states. There will be a debate over authority between pope and emperor as to the relationship of the pope and emperor, but no one would disagree that cooperation between the church and the monarchy is expected. Bishops and kings operate in alliance. This is the type of political organization that Scandinavians will learn as a result of the Viking raids and will use to establish the kingdoms of Norway, Sweden, and Denmark.

Finally, as impressive as Charlemagne's empire was, from the Scandinavian viewpoint it was extremely wealthy. It was a wonderful target if you could get to it and fortunately for the Scandinavians after 814 that became much easier. Charlemagne was succeeded by his son Louis the Pious, and as I always mention to my students in class, whenever you encounter a medieval monarch named the Pious, that is an immediate signal to watch out. He's received the title from monks who like him very much because he's endowed a lot of property to the church, but they're generally politically ineffective. And in the case of Louis, he sets new standards on low performance and leadership, especially paying attention to his second wife, Judith of Bavaria, which it was a mistake to marry her in the first place, but, in any case. Louis succeeds to the Carolingian Empire.

And always within the Germanic tradition of kingship, whether it be Christian or pagan, there's a question, Is the kingship a matter of personal property?—that's certainly what Scandinavian sea kings think, that any king in Scandinavia who succeeds to a great hall and has three sons, well, each son has to build his own hall—or, Is the monarchy a unitary state in the Roman sense? This is an issue that will dominate western political thought through the whole Middle Ages, and eventually the Roman notion will win; that is, the monarchy is a single institution and succession should go not only within a family but to a sole member of the family, and this is what immediately comes at issue under the reign of Louis the Pious. He tries to transmit power to his oldest son Lothar to follow as emperor. His other three sons at the time contest this, and starting very early in the reign from the 820s on, there are civil wars that plague the Carolingian Empire over this issue. Is it a single empire or should kingdoms be provided for all of the members of the royal family? In this case, it is the notion of partition that wins.

In 843 the first significant partition is carried out by the three surviving sons of Louis the Pious. Lothar receives the so-called middle kingdom, stretching from the North Sea to Italy with the capitals of Aachen and Rome and the imperial title. That would essentially be represented today by the lands of the low countries, Alsace-Lorraine, Switzerland, and Northern and Central Italy. What will evolve into the kingdom of France goes to Charles the Bald. What will evolve into Germany, the East Frankish lands, goes to another son, Louis the German. Well, this partition and these civil wars are an ideal entrée for the Viking attacks of Western Europe. It's important to stress that many of these Viking raids which started off as raids in the time of Charlemagne and really couldn't do much because Charlemagne had built naval defenses, there is no effort to maintain naval defenses after Charlemagne's death.

The Frankish nobility is too involved in fighting civil wars, and these candidates for the throne, these sons of Louis the Pious, at times even hire Vikings as allies and mercenaries to war against an opponent. The failure, especially of Charles the Bald, the son who received the western portion of the Carolingian Empire, to halt Viking attacks will bankrupt the Carolingian monarchy, end with the demise of that dynasty, and will really end with the kingdom in the West, which will be divided up into feudal states. The Viking attacks have an immediate and dramatic political impact on what is to become France and the core of feudal civilization.

The other elements in Western Europe were the various kingdoms and, in some cases, Iron Age chiefdoms in the British Isles. Here we had a mix of populations, Celtic speaking and Germanic speaking, that is, the future speakers of English. There was no political unity here at all. The only common bond was the fact that they were all members of the Christian church. The Anglo-Saxon kingdoms, and these are the kingdoms created by the descendants of the Germanic peoples who had moved from Scandinavia and Northwest Germany in the age of Migrations by 800 A.D., linguistically and culturally were in many ways part of Western Europe. They used Latin as their literary language. They also used Anglo-Saxon—that is, a form of Old English perhaps is more accurate—which was now heavily influenced by the Latin literary tradition. They were members of the wider Christian community and very, very much embraced the monastic life and the arts of Western Europe, and it's important to stress that while the bishops became, in effect, administrators and advisers to the crown, those who were really engaged in spiritual and cultural activities went into the monastic institutions, which is a separate outfit going back to the traditions of aestheticism of the late Roman world. Britain, England particularly, and Ireland, there monastic institutions flourished. Irish and Anglo-Saxon scholars and monks—they're almost all monks—are regarded as some of the finest in Western Europe. Many of the monasteries in Ireland and on the English shores were important economic centers, as they were in the Carolingian world, and they were totally undefended—the site, Lindisfarne, the greatest monastery in England, beautiful view of the North Sea, an absolute ideal target for Viking attacks.

Second, England had politically simplified itself by the time of the Viking age. There were four leading kingdoms I mentioned earlier.

Mercia and the midlands, which looked like the leading kingdom of England, it was ruled by a king named Offa who at least attempted to style himself as the English equivalent of Charlemagne. He imposed his authority over the English kingdoms south of the Humber, which essentially divides England into two zones. He ruled Mercia; he controlled London and Canterbury, which are the commercial and the religious centers of England. He had subjected the kings of East Anglia and Wessex to his hegemony. North of the Humber was the kingdom of Northumbria, and Northumbria was the center of most of the important monastic and cultural life associated with early Anglo-Saxon England. Northumbria on the eve of the Viking age was in trouble. It essentially consisted of two kingdoms, one north of the Tees, the so called Bernicia, the old core, centering on a port at Bamburgh and embracing what eventually became the Scottish Lowlands and Northern England, and the southern portion of the kingdom, Deira, centered around York and the Yorkshire regions, and these two regions were never particularly well integrated.

When the Vikings started to raid England in the 780s and 790s, not only did they find undefended monasteries along the shores, they really found very, very little organized political and military opposition. Northumbria was in the throes of constant civil war. There were some serious economic problems with the kingdom. In an argument which will come up later on in three or four lectures from now, we will explain how the Vikings in some ways revived Northern England once they settled there, after they trashed the place. The southern kingdoms, it was by no means sure that Mercia was going to end up being the winner. The kings of Mercia were challenged by the kings of Wessex; that's in the southwest of England. So Wessex and Mercia were often fighting among each other when the Vikings started their raids.

As for the rest of the British Isles, those were really not organized in any fashion as states. Wales, Cornwall, and the region known as Cumbria, today Northwestern England and parts of Lowland Scotland, often referred to as Strathclyde, they're Britons, the descendants of the original inhabitants of Britain who had been under Roman rule. There they survived. They had been pushed out of England by the Germanic invaders and became the Welsh, the Cornish men and the so-called Strathclyde Britons who had memories of once ruling over England. This is where the legends of King Arthur emerge among the Welsh, particularly this ancient ancestral battle against the English. There's always a bitter irony to me that they're named Welsh, and often the English refer to the North Welsh, the Welsh of the South, meaning Cornwell, the West Welsh, the real Welsh. Welsh in Anglo-Saxon means foreigner, and only the English can turn people into foreigners in their own homeland. That's just, I think, a significant point in Anglo-Saxon history.

To the north were various peoples dwelling in what would become Scotland, and the Scots were Irish immigrants, Gaelic speakers who had arrived in northwestern Scotland during the time of the age of Migrations, and the Viking attacks on Britain will not only make the kingdom of England but they were also determine that the Scots are going to end up uniting Northern Britain into the Scottish kingdom. Politically, these Viking raids are going to be extremely important in precipitating the consolidation of both Scotland and England. Both of those kingdoms would not have emerged in the way they do without the Viking attacks.

Ireland was a collection of different tribes, regional kings. Monastic life was the key cultural element to Ireland. The monasteries in Ireland not only were cultural centers but they were also important economic centers. Politically, Ireland was divided into essentially Iron Age warlords. The population subsisted on stock raising and hunting and, contrary to many popular notions, there was no Ireland in any sense other than a geographic expression. We're not even sure of the different types of dialects that were spoken there. When the Norwegians begin to attack Ireland at the end of the 8th century and the beginning of the 9th century, they find very, very little organized resistance. In most of the 9th century and a good deal of the 10th century, the Scandinavians will just politically and militarily dominate Ireland with very little difficulty. They find in Ireland actually a society in some ways they can understand and respect because it is a warrior society, and in time there is a great deal of intermarriage between Irish and Scandinavians, and you create a rather distinct Hiberno-Norse, or Irish-Norse, civilization in Ireland. At the start there really isn't anything like an organized state of Ireland. There's a series of competing chieftains for the title of High King of Ireland. One of the reasons for that is Ireland never had a Roman conquest and doesn't have the cities, the roads, and the institutions to build a kingdom the way you do in England and the Carolingian Empire.

Finally, I should mention briefly the other two civilizations. Let's take a look briefly at the Islamic world. Without a doubt, as I mentioned in the previous lecture, this is the greatest civilization, and it is the main economic force driving trade and economic development in the early Middle Ages. This is true up to 1100, about the time of the Crusades. The Crusades actually mark a decisive shift in many ways, and one is in an economic domination on the Eurasian landmass which is shifting increasingly to Western Europe. Few Scandinavians ever encounter the cities of Islam. They did encounter Islam on the banks of the Volga. They trade with various Turkomen tribes who were essentially the peripheral martial lords of the Islamic Empire, the Bulgars, the Khazars, but that trade route diminishes after 975. And that can be documented archeologically, as Muslim coins and products cease to come up the Volga to Sweden and the trade route will shift to the Dneiper, to a western trade route, a trade route that had never been really very important before the Scandinavians and that will lead the Scandinavians into that third civilization, the Byzantine Empire.

In Constantinople in the Byzantine Empire, the Scandinavians encounter a great bureaucratic state, and in contrast to the Islamic world, they actually saw it and visited it. Based on the city of Kiev, which is about 500 miles up the Dneiper from the Black Sea, the Swedish Rus, the Scandinavians who operated in Eastern Europe, managed to bring those ships down the Dneiper and cross some really treacherous rapids and dodge the Turkomen horse archers, who were some of the nastiest people you would ever want to encounter, notably, the Pechinegs. Delightful figures, they're organized into nine

Hordes—that is, they're a basic social institution—and get to the Black Sea and eventually sail to Constantinople. Constantinople at the time is without a doubt the greatest city in the Christian world, in Western Europe or in Eastern Europe. It may have been a population of close to a million. Perhaps it was 500,000, but it's on an order of magnitude between five and ten times greater than the largest city in Western Europe, which was Cologne, which was about 50,000.

In Constantinople, Scandinavians encountered an empire that was heir to the Roman political and military traditions, that had an organized trade system and was also the fount of silks, gold, and spices that they were acquiring through middlemen on the Volga. One of the reasons why, in the 9th century, they shifted their activity to Constantinople is they could get directly to the access of all those goodies they wanted on the Northern Trade Arc. They could get to Constantinople and trade in a great city. It is difficult to really exaggerate the impact of that experience of Scandinavians entering the one city they saw in the Middle Ages, and, as I mentioned, in Norse text it's often known as Miklagard, that is, great city. You say the great city or the city, they mean Constantinople.

Many Scandinavians, not only from Sweden but from Norway, Denmark, from distant Iceland, will take the road to Byzantium, or Constantinople—Byzantium is the early Greek name for the city—and there will take service as mercenaries. They will make fortunes as merchants. Some will settle in the Byzantine Empire, and it is in Constantinople they encounter it at the time under the great Macedonian Emperors who are responsible for the political revival of the Byzantine world. And they also encounter an Orthodox Christianity that is very rich in its iconography, its icons, and its traditions, and is a religion now associated with victory, with the victory of the Macedonian emperors, quite in contrast to the way Christianity was doing in Western Europe.

The Viking attacks on Western Europe in the 9th and 10th century, in my opinion, probably led many Scandinavians to consider Christianity a religion of slaves and the defeated. In Constantinople, it was quite different. And some of the earliest conversions occur among Scandinavians who've been in Constantinople, particularly Queen Olga ,or, as she's known in her Swedish name, Helga, who is reported to have attended a church service at Hagia Sophia and converted on the spot. "God has got to dwell in a church like this. Anyone who can build something 17 stories high with a great dome has got to have God on their side." So the contact with the Byzantine world will have a very, very profound influence. It will lead to the adoption of Orthodox Christianity by the Scandinavians in Russia, who will then go on to create Orthodox Russia. It also has an important influence in state formation in both Sweden and Denmark. Both the kings of Denmark and Sweden looked east. They looked to the principality of Kiev and ultimately to Constantinople as models for their own political organization of kingdoms as well as to

Western Europe. This is the world as it was seen from Scandinavian eyes, Western Europe, the Islamic World, and the Byzantine Empire, and this is the world that is soon to be attacked in the upcoming lectures by the Scandinavians. And in all of these regions they will have a very profound and immediate impact.

Timeline

4000–2300 B.C.	Neolithic Age: beginning of agriculture and stock-raising
2300–1950 B.C.	Chalcolithic Age Arrival of Indo-European speakers into southern Scandinavia Evolution of Finns (Suomi) and Lapps (Sami)
2300–450 B.C.	Bronze Age
1550–1100 B.C.	Apex of the Northern Bronze Age in Scandinavia Expansion of settlements in central Sweden and western Norway Amber route between the Baltic and Mediterranean worlds
1100 B.C.	Solar chariot at Trundholm (Denmark)
1100–500 B.C.	Collapse of long-distance trade and decline of prosperity Spread of cremation as a burial practice
800–500 B.C.	Emergence of Halstatt Celtic Iron Age civilization in Central Europe
500–100 B.C.	La Tène Celtic civilization: Rise of towns (*oppida*) and iron technology
450 B.C.	Rise of trade between Scandinavia and Celtic Europe (450–50 B.C.) Formation of Germanic languages
c. 325–310 B.C.	Visit of Thule (Norway) by Pytheas of Massilia
c. 200–100 B.C.	Creation of runes based on north Italic scripts
125–120 B.C.	Migration of Cimbri and Teutones from Jutland into Central Europe

	Decline of Celtic towns in southern Germany (c. 125–75 B.C.)
c. 100 B.C.	Gundestrup cauldron
58–49 B.C.	Julius Caesar conquers Gaul
c. 50–1 B.C.	Germanic tribes settle Central Europe between the Rhine and the Vistula
27 B.C.– A.D.14	Reign of Augustus: foundation of the Roman Empire Expansion of trade between Scandinavia and Western Europe
16–9 B.C.	Roman conquest of the Germanic tribes between the Rhine and the Elbe
A.D. 5	Tiberius's naval expedition to Jutland
A.D. 9	Arminius destroys Roman legions in Teutoburg Forest Romans withdraw to the Rhine and Danube frontiers
c. A.D. 50–200	Revival of the Amber route Rising prosperity in bog deposits in Denmark Shift to wealthy barrow tombs in Denmark and Sweden
98	Cornelius Tacitus writes *Germania*
c. 150–200	Goths cross from Sweden to the southern Baltic shores
235–285	Civil war and frontier wars in the Roman Empire Consolidation of West Germanic confederations of Franks, Saxons, Alemanni, and Sueves
c. 245–280	Goths and East Germanic tribes raid the upper and lower Danube frontier
c. 260–285	Frankish and Saxon pirates raid the shores of Britain and Gaul

284–305	Reign of Diocletian: establishment of the dominate (Roman autocracy)
306–337	Reign of Constantine: creation of Christian monarchy (312–337)
c. 350	Nydam ship burial, Denmark Gallehus horns of Jutland
378	Battle of Adrianople: Goths defeat and slay Emperor Valens Renewed Germanic migrations into the Roman Empire (378–476)
395	Division of eastern (Byzantine) and western Roman Empires Collapse of the western Roman Empire (395–476)
432	St. Patrick (389–461) consecrated apostle to the Irish Conversion of Ulidia (eastern Ulster) by Patrick (432–461)
433–452	Reign of Attila the Hun
c. 450–650	Migration of Jutes, Angles, Saxons, and Frisians from Jutland and northwestern Germany to England
481–511	Clovis, king of the Franks, founds Merovingian kingdom in Gaul
494	Clovis and the Franks convert to Catholic Christianity
c. 523–528	Raid of Hygelac (ON: Hugelik), king of Gotar, on Frisia
c. 530–550	Reign of Beowulf over Gotar
c. 550–575	Reign of Hrolf Kraki, Skjoldung king of Hleidr Reign of Adils, Yngling king of Uppsala
597	Mission of St. Augustine to England: conversion of the English

600–800	Vendel period in Scandinavia: royal Swedish burials
	Helgo, leading port of Lake Mälaren
c. 625	Ship burial of Sutton Hoo, East Anglia
627	Conversion of King Edwin of Bernicia (r. 616–633) to Christianity
634–642	King Oswald unites Bernicia and Deira into the kingdom of Northumbria
	Cultural flowering of northern England (650–800)
675	Foundation of Dorestad: rise of Frisian trade (675–840)
c. 675–700	Composition of *Beowulf*: rise of a Christian literature in Old English
c. 700	Ship burial at Kvalsund, Norway
	Construction of port town Birka, Sweden
	Emergence of Scandinavian languages (700–800)
c. 700–710	St. Willibrod's mission to Ongendus (Angantyr), king in Jutland
c. 737–740	First construction of the Danevirke and Haeveg ("army route") in Jutland
	Development of Danish port at Ribe
c. 750–790	Breakthroughs in Scandinavian shipbuilding (keel, sails, and rigging)
	Swedes open eastern routes along the Volga River to Atil on the Caspian Sea
c. 750–775	Battle of Bravellir: Harald the Wartooth, last of the Skjöldung kings, defeated by Sigurd Hring, ruler of the Gautar.
	Oseberg/Borre decorative styles in Scandinavia (c. 750–975)
751	Pepin the Short seizes the Frankish throne and founds the Carolingian dynasty

757 ....Accession of King Offa of Mercia (r. 757–796)

768 ....Accession of Charlemagne (r. 768–814), king of the Franks

772 ....Charlemagne initiates Frankish conquest of Saxony (772–804)
Destruction of the Sacred Tree (Irmiusul) at Erseburg

778–785 ....Rebellion of the Saxons under Widukind

789 ....Danish Vikings raid the shores of Portland, Wessex

793 ....Three Norwegian ships sack the monastery of Lindisfarne, Northumbria

794 ....Norwegian Vikings sack the monastery of Jarrow, Northumbria

795 ....Norwegian Vikings sack the monastery of Iona, Scotland
Norwegian Vikings sack the monastery Rechru on the island of Lambay
Vikings raid the shores of Ireland and the Shannon Valley (795–840)
Viking base camps at Dublin, Wexford, Waterford, Cork, and Limerick

800 ....Coronation of Charlemagne as Emperor of the Romans
Charlemagne constructs naval defenses along the Scheldt and lower Rhine
King Guthfrith (also known as Godfred; ON: Guthfrid) secures Jutland and Hedeby (c. 800–810)
Second phase of construction at Danevirke
Norse settle Shetlands, Orkney, and Hebrides (800–825)

802 ....Accession of King Ecgbert of Wessex (r. 802–839)
Rivalry between Wessex and Mercia

839 ....Louis the Pious receives Rus envoys along with Byzantine mission

840 ....Thorgils captures Armagh and performs rites of Thor
Thorgils's wife, Aud (Ota), acts as seer (*völva*) at the monastery of Clonmacnoise
Gaill Gaidaill, Irish apostates, ally with the Vikings (840–870)

841 ....Harald Klak receives island of Walcheren
Danish Vikings sack Rouen and raid the lower Seine valley

842 ....Vikings sack Hamwic (Southampton) and Quentovic (Boulogne)

843 ....Treaty of Verdun: partition of the Carolingian Empire

844 ....Vikings ravage Garonne valley, shores of Asturias, and sack Seville, Spain

845 ....Mission of al-Ghazal from Muslim Cordoba to the Vikings of Dublin
Horik, "king in Denmark," sacks Hamburg
Vikings under Ragnar Lodbrok defeat Charles the Bald and sack Paris
Charles the Bald pays Ragnar *danegeld* of 7,000 pounds of silver

846 or 847 ....Defeat and death of Thorgils in Meath

847 ....St. Anskar succeeds to joint archbishopric of Hamburg-Bremen

848–850 ....Danish Vikings ("Black Foreigners") challenge Norwegians for Ireland

850 ....Danish Viking establish base on Sheppey, England
Death of Harald Klak, Viking lord in Frisia
Emergence of skaldic poetry in Scandinavia (c. 850–900)

Christian mission of Ardgar to Birka (850–852)

| 851 | Battle of Carlingford Lough: Danes and Irish allies defeat Norwegians |
| | Danes occupy Dublin |

852 ....Arrival of Olaf and second great fleet from Norway
Submission of Vikings to Olaf at Dublin (c. 852–871)
Development of slave trade in Ireland

855–857 ....Bjorn Ironside fortifies Viking base on Oissel at the mouth of the Seine

859 ....Danish sea kings Hastein and Bjorn Ironside raid Spain

860 ....Gardar Svavarrsson discovers Iceland
Hastein and Bjorn Ironside enter Mediterranean, raid shores of southern France, and sack Luna (860–861)
Rurik (ON: Erik) invited to rule the Slavs from Holmgard (Novgorod)
Foundation of Kiev as Rus market town
First Rus naval attack on Constantinople

861 ....Weland and Danish Vikings ravage the Seine and Somme valleys

863 ....Dorestad abandoned

864 ....King Charles the Bald issues the Edicts of Pîtres

865 ....Great Army arrives in East Anglia under Halfdane and Ivar the Boneless
Voyage of Floki Vilgerdarson to Iceland (875)

866 ....Great Army captures York

867 ....Battle of York: Vikings defeat and slay Northumbrian Kings Osbert and Aelle:

Danish conquest of southern Northumbria (Deira)

Collapse of first English kingdom; English earls rule at Bamburgh

868 ....Great Army ravages northern Mercia from base at Nottingham

King Burgred (r. 852–874) pays *danegeld* for the Great Army to retire into East Anglia

869 ....Battle of Hoxne: defeat and martyrdom of King Edmund (r. 855–869)

Great Army overruns East Anglia: collapse of the second English kingdom

Ivar the Boneless departs for Ireland (869–873)

870 ....Halfdane and the Great Army seize Wallingford, ravaging Mercia and Wessex

Arrival of reinforcements from Scandinavia and the Carolingian Empire

Great Army seizes and fortifies Reading

871 ....Battle of Ashdown: Halfdane defeats King Aethelred I of Wessex (r. 865–871)

Death of Aethelred I and accession of Alfred the Great (r. 871–899)

Battle of Wilton: Alfred defeated by the Great Army Alfred pays *danegeld* for withdrawal of the Great Army

Ingolf Arnarson settles Iceland (871–873)

Norwegian emigration to Iceland (c. 870–930)

872 ....Rebellion in York against the Viking client king Ecgbert

Halfdane and the Great Army move north against the rebels in York

873 ....Great Army seizes Repton: Burgred abdicates and makes a pilgrimage to Rome; Halfdane proclaims Ceowulf II (r. 874–879) king of Mercia

	Vikings fortify the Five Boroughs in northern Mercia (Nottingham, Derby, Stamford, Lincoln, and Leicester)
874	With reinforcements from Scandinavia, Guthrum pacifies East Anglia Halfdane and veterans of the Great Army secure Yorkshire (874–975)
c. 875	Emergence of Jellinge decorative style (c. 875–975) Battle of Hafsfjord: Harald Finehair defeats *jarls* and kings of Vestlandet
875	Halfdane partitions the lands of Yorkshire among veterans of the Great Army Creation of Viking Kingdom of York Guthrum and the Great Army invade and ravage Wessex (874–877) Alfred the Great assumes a defensive positional war
876	Accession of Charles the Fat (r. 876–888) as king of East Francia (Germany)
877	Death of Charles the Bald, king of West Francia (France) Accession of Louis II (r. 877–879): civil war in the Frankish world
877–879	Partition of lands in East Anglia to veterans of the Great Army Second Danish settlement in England
878	Guthrum and the Great Army capture Chippenham (January 8) Alfred and his *thegns* driven into exile; Alfred rallies his army Battle of Eddington: Alfred defeats Guthrum Treaty of Wedmore: Vikings withdraw north of the Thames Guthrum, baptized as Aethelstan, rules in East Anglia (r. 878–890)

879 ....Danish Vikings cross from England to seize base at Ghent

Vikings raid Lowlands, Rhineland, and western Saxony (879–881)

c. 880............................King Harald Finehair unites Norway (r. 880–930)

Prince Oleg (r. 879–913) relocates Rus capital from Holmgard to Kiev

881 ....Election of Charles the Fat as Holy Roman Emperor (r. 881–887)

King Louis III of France (r. 879–881) defeats Vikings at Sancourt

882 ....Vikings sack Trier and Cologne

Charles the Fat fails to contain Danes in the Lowlands

885 ....Siegfried (ON: Sigurd) and Danish Vikings besiege Paris (885–886)

886 ....Charles the Fat pays Vikings 7,000 pounds of silver to raise the siege of Paris

Alfred occupies London and the lower Thames

Alfred reforms army, constructs burghs and fleet, and improves coinage

887 ....Charles the Fat deposed by Frankish nobility

Arnulf the Bastard (r. 887–899) elected king of East Francia

Eudes (Odo; r. 888–897) elected king of West Francia

890 ....Battle of the Dyle: King Arnulf storms Viking base camp

891..............................Vikings strike first silver pennies in East Anglia and York

Trade and prosperity rise in the Danelaw (890–1000)

891–894 ....Viking attacks on Wessex by Haesten (ON: Hadding)
Inconclusive fighting: Vikings retire to France or settle in England

895 ....Arrival of sea king Hrolf (Rollo) in the lower Seine valley

897 ....Accession of Charles the Simple (r. 897–922) as king of France

899 ....Accession of Edward the Elder as king of Wessex (r. 899–924)

c. 900–905.....................Gokstad ship burial, Norway

902 ....King Cearbhall of Leinster occupies Dublin (r. 902–914)

907 ....Prince Oleg (ON: Helgi) leads second Rus naval attack on Constantinople

911 ....Charles the Simple invests Hrolf (Rollo) with fief in Rouen, Normandy
First Byzantine-Rus commercial treaty

914 ....Arrival of Sigtrygg and the third great Norwegian fleet
Norwegian sea kings seize the Hiberno-Norse ports (914–920)
Second Norwegian immigration to Ireland (914–950)

917–918 ....Edward the Elder subjects the Danes of East Anglia

919 ....German nobility elects Henry the Fowler (r. 919–936) king of Germany
End of Carolingian Dynasty in East Francia (Germany)
Vikings under Rognvald seize Nantes and raid Brittany (919–937)
The Five Boroughs submit to the authority of Edward the Elder

920	Hiberno-Norse of York acknowledge Edward the Elder as their lord
	Unification of England under Edward the Elder
	Sigtrygg , exiled Hiberno-Norse king of Dublin, seizes and rules York (920–927)
921–922	Ibn Fadhlan, Abbasid envoy to Bulgars, describes the Rus on the Volga
924	Accession of Aethelstan, king of Wessex (r. 924–939)
925	William Longsword (r. 925–942) succeeds as count of Rouen
	Normans adopt French language and perfect heavy cavalry (c. 925–1000)
927	Death of Sigtrygg I; Olaf Kvaran Sigtryggson succeeds at York
	Aethelstan occupies York, expelling Olaf Kvaran
930	Ulfljot establishes the *Althing* of Iceland
	Erik the Bloodax succeeds as king of Norway (r. 930–936)
934	Accession of Olaf Guthfrithson as king of Dublin (r. 934–941)
	Imposition of Norse power over the lands of the Irish Sea
	Norwegian settlements of Galloway and Wales
	German King Henry I invades Jutland
936	Battle of St. Brieuc: Duke Alain of Brittany defeats Viking raiders
	Gorm the Old secures Jutland as his kingdom (r. 936–958)
	Hakon the Good received as king of Norway (r. 936–960)

937	Battle of Brunanburh: Aethelstan defeats coalition of Hiberno-Norse, Scots, and Britons and recaptures York
	Duke Alain captures Nantes, ending the Viking state in the lower Loire valley
939	Death of Aethelstan; accession of Edmund (r. 939–946) as king of Wessex
	Olaf Guthfrithson (r. 939–941) and Hiberno-Norse reoccupy York
940	King Edmund cedes the Five Boroughs to Olaf Guthfrithson
941	Death of Olaf Guthfrithson; Hiberno-Norse army proclaims Olaf Kvaran king of York
942	Edmund retakes the Five Boroughs
943	Expulsion of Olaf Kvaran from York by his Danish subjects
	Dispute over leadership in the Hiberno-Norse army at York (943–947)
	Igor (ON: Ingvar) leads third Rus naval attack on Constantinople
944	Igor leads fourth Rus naval attack on Constantinople
945	Olaf Kvaran seizes Dublin (r. 945–980): apex of Hiberno-Norse power
	Second Byzantine-Rus commercial treaty
	Queen Olga (Helga) assumes regency of Kiev (r. 945–964)
948–952	Olaf Kvaran fails to secure York and the northern Danelaw
	Erik the Bloodax, exiled king of Norway, intervenes in York
954	The Danes of York drive out Eric the Bloodax and accept as their lord King Edwig of Wessex (r. 946–959)
958	Accession of Harald Bluetooth as king of Denmark (r. 958–986)

c. 975–1050...................... Emergence of Mammen decorative style (c. 975–1065)

976 .... Accession of Brian Bóruma (r. 976–1014) as king of Munster, Ireland

978 .... Accession of Aethelred II (r. 978–1016), the Unready, as king of England

980 .... Battle of Tara: Olaf Kvaran defeated by Mael Sechlainn II of Meath (r. 980–1022): end of Hiberno-Norse military power
Construction of market town Sigtuna, Sweden
Accession of Prince Vladimir (ON: Valdemar) as prince of Kiev (r. 980–1015)
Accession of Erik the Victorious as king of Sweden (r. 980–995)

980–1200 .... Emergence of the Urnes decorative style

983–984 .... Erik the Red explores Greenland

985 .... Erik the Red founds the Greenland colonies

986 .... Svein Forkbeard (r. 986–1014) expels his father, Harald Bluetooth
Bjarni Herjulfsson first reaches North America

987 .... French nobility elect Hugh Capet (r. 987–996) as king of France
End of the Carolingian Dynasty in West Francia (France)

c. 988............................ Battle of Hjorungavag: Jarl Hakon defeats Danish-Jomsviking fleet

989 .... Accession of Sigtrygg III Silkbeard as Hiberno-Norse king of Dublin
Christianization of Dublin and rise of trade
Conversion of Vladimir to Orthodox Christianity
Emperor Basil II forms Varangian Guard

991 ....Renewed Viking attacks on England (r. 991–1002)
Svein Forkbeard consolidates his control over Denmark

995 ....Olaf Tryggvason acclaimed king of Norway
Promotion of Christianity in Norway
Accession of Olof Skötkonung as king of Sweden (r. 995–1022)

997 ....Bishop Thrangbrand preaches Christianity in Iceland (997–1000)

1000 ....Brian Bóruma recognized as high king of Ireland
Althing in Iceland officially converts to Christianity
Battle of Svold: death of Olaf Tryggvason
Svein Forkbeard imposes overlordship on Norway

1001 ....Voyage of Leif Eriksson to Vinland

1002 ....St. Brice's Day Massacre: Svein Forkbeard declares war on England

1003 ....Svein Forkbeard invades England

1004–1005 ....Voyage of Thorvald Eriksson to North America

1006–1007 ....Jarl Tore directs Danish attacks on England

1009 ....Jarl Thorkell the Tall commands Danish forces in England (1009–1011)
Thorfinn Karlsefni leads first settlement in Vinland (1009–1012)

1013 ....Svein Forkbeard and Cnut invade England
Freydis and Thorvald lead second settlement in Vinland (1013–1014)

1014 ....Death of Svein Forkbeard: Cnut hailed as king by the Danish army

1015 ....St. Olaf acclaimed king in Norway

Edmund Ironside recovers Wessex (1015–1016)

1016 .... Battle of Nesjar: St. Olaf secures Norway
Deaths of Aethelred II and Edmund Ironside
Cnut hailed as king of England and appoints earls

1019 .... Accession of Prince Yaroslav the Wise of Kiev (r. 1019–1054)
Emergence of Slavic Orthodox civilization
Cnut accepted as sole king of Denmark; institutes royal reforms

1022 .... Accession of Anund Jakob as king of Sweden (r. 1022–1050)

1026 .... Battle of the Holy River: strategic check of St. Olaf

1028 .... St. Olaf driven out of Norway
Cnut the Great hailed as king of Norway

1030 .... Battle of Stiklestad: defeat and death of St. Olaf
Svein Alfivason (r. 1030–1035) alienates his Norwegian subjects

1034 .... Harald Hardardi enters the Varangian Guard (1034–1043)

1035 .... Magnus the Good received as king of Norway
Death of Cnut the Great: succession crisis
Harthacnut recognized as king of Denmark and England

1037 .... Harold I Harefoot usurps the throne of England (r. 1037–1040)

1038 .... Treaty of succession between Harthacnut and Magnus the Good

1040 .... Death of Harold II; Harthacnut received as king of England

1042 ....Death of Harthacnut: succession crisis in Denmark

Edward the Confessor acclaimed king of England

1043 ....Magnus the Good received as king of Denmark

Magnus wages war against Wends and Jomsborg

1044 ....Svein Estrithson (r. 1042–1044) raises revolt in Denmark

Danish-Norwegian War (1044–1064)

1045 ....Harald Hardardi and Svein Estrithson ally against Magnus the Good

Sinking of ships in Limsfjord, near Skuldelev (c. 1045–1050)

1046 ....Harald Hardardi and Magnus the Good share the Norwegian kingdom

1047 ....Death of Magnus the Good

1062 ....Battle of Nissa River: Harald Hardardi defeats Svein Estrithson

1064 ....Treaty between Harald Hardardi and Svein Estrithson

1066 ....Death of Edward the Confessor; Harold II hailed as king of England

Harald Hardardi invades England and wins the Battle of Fulford

Battle of Stamford Bridge: defeat and death of Harald Hardardi

Battle of Hastings: defeat and death of Harold II

William I, the Conqueror, king of England (r. 1066–1087)

1067 ....Accession of Harald Kyrii as king of Norway (r. 1067–1093)

Founding of German port Lübeck

1164 ....Uppsala elevated to archbishopric and primate of Sweden

1169 ....Valdemar leads Wendish crusade and conquers Rügen
Danish expansion along the southern Baltic littoral (1169–1180)

1170 ....Arrival of Richard de Clare, "Strongbow," earl of Pembroke
English conquest of Dublin and the Pale
End of Hiberno-Norse civilization

1182 ....Accession of Cnut VI as king of Denmark (r. 1182–1202)

1202 ....Accession of Valdemar II as king of Denmark (r. 1202–1241)
Extension of Danish power in northern Germany (1202–1227)

1210 ....Valdemar II leads Danish crusades into Estonia (1210–1219)
First Swedish crusade against the Finns (1210–1216)

1217 ....Accession of Hakon IV as king of Norway (r. 1217–1263)
Centralization of royal power and prosperity in Norway

1220 ....Snorri Sturluson composes the *Prose Edda*
Composition of the *King's Mirror*

1225 ....Snorri Sturluson composes *Heimskringla*
Hanseatic *kontor* ("community") founded on Visby, Gotland

1227 ....Battle of Bornhöved: defeat of Valdemar II by German vassals
End of Danish domination in the Baltic
German ports and Teutonic Order colonize Baltic lands

This page left intentionally blank

Guide to the Scandinavian Landscape

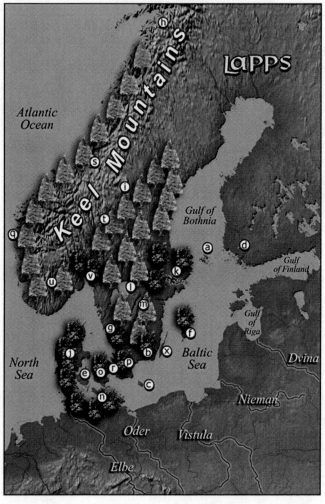

Key

Aland Islands	a
Blekinge	b
Bornholm	c
Finland	d
Fyn	e
Gotland	f
Halland	g
Halogaland	h
Jamtland	i
Jutland	j
Lake Malaren	k
Lake Vanern	l
Lake Vattern	m
Lolland & Falster	n
Oland	x
Sjaelland	o
Skane	p
Sogne Fjord	q
Sund	r
Trondelag	s
Upplands	t
Vestfold	u
Viken & Oslo Fjord area	v

coniferous forest, e.g. pine

deciduous forest, e.g. oak

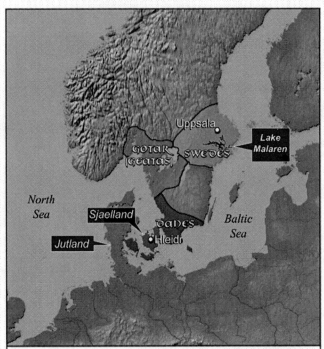

Heroic Scandinavia, 475-600

The Heroic Age in Scandinavia precedes the period of true territorial states. The boundaries shown here reflect not political borders, but areas inhabited by the peoples (Danes, Gotar, Swedes) that would form the basis for the kingdoms that emerged by 1100. Kingdoms in this period centered around great halls such as Hleidr, the home of the legendary figure Hrolf Kraki, and Uppsala, the seat of his Swedish rival Adils. Note also that in this period, Danish power was concentrated on the island of Sjaelland, not the Jutland peninsula.

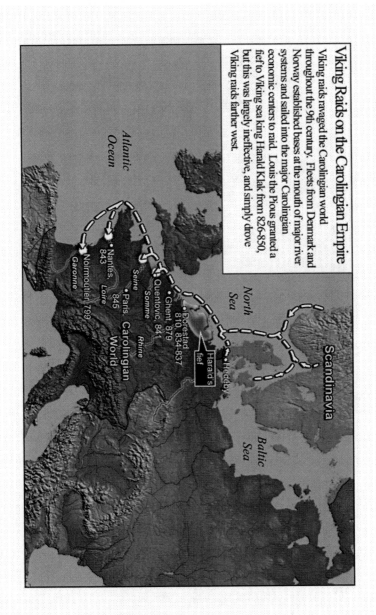

Viking Raids on the Carolingian Empire

Viking raids ravaged the Carolingian world throughout the 9th century. Fleets from Denmark and Norway established bases at the mouth of major river systems and sailed into the major Carolingian economic centers to raid. Louis the Pious granted a fief to Viking sea king Harald Klak from 826-850, but this was largely ineffective, and simply drove Viking raids farther west.

Atlantic Ocean

Nantes, 843
Noirmoutier, 799
Garonne
Loire
Paris, 845
Seine
Quentovic, 841
Somme
Ghent, 879
Rhine
Dorestad 810, 834-837
Harald's fief
Hedeby

Carolingian World

North Sea

Baltic Sea

Scandinavia

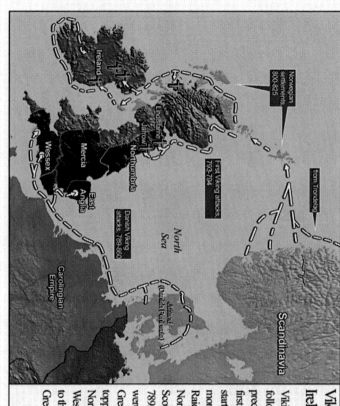

Viking Raids on England and Ireland

Viking raids into England and Ireland followed familiar trade routes that preceded the Viking Age. The very first attacks came out of Norway, starting in 793 and centering on the monasteries of Northern England. Raids on Ireland were facilitated by Norwegian settlement in northern Scotland and the Scottish islands. In 789, the Danish attacks began, and these were a preview of the campaign of the Great Army from 865-878 which toppled the English kingdoms of Northumbria, Mercia, and East Anglia. Wessex, of course, would hold out due to the leadership of King Alfred the Great.

Scandinavian Kingdoms, 1100-1300

Shown here are the three kingdoms of Sweden, Denmark, and Norway as they existed from 1100-1300. These newly Christianized kingdoms established primates in Uppsala, Lund, and Nidaros, and became integrated into Europe. Their primacy receded during this period, however, as Denmark's influence was checked by the Holy Roman Empire to the south, and Sweden was challenged by Russia to the east.

237

Glossary

Specialized Terms:

Althing: The national assembly of Iceland founded in 930 and reformed to include a higher court of appeals in 965. The *Althing* convened each summer at Thingvellir.

andri: The title of high king of Ireland; awarded to the leading ruler, who was crowned at the ancient capital of Tara.

Bayeux Tapestry: Commissioned by Bishop Odo of Bayeux, half-brother of William I, circa 1066–1076; it depicts the Norman conquest of England.

berserker: "Bear shirts," frenzied warriors of Odin who attacked in a rage. In later sagas composed in the Christian era, berserkers were cast as supernatural figures, but all legendary heroes were regarded as berserkers. See *comitatus*.

Birchlegs (ON: Birkibeinar): A Norwegian party opposed to the descendants of King Inge (1135–1161) in the civil wars down to 1217.

Bjarkamal: A famous skaldic poem (known today in fragments) in which the heroes Bjarki and Hjalti defiantly exchange remarks of their doom and defeat at the hall of Hrolf Kraki.

blood eagle: This sacrificial rite to Odin was performed by cutting the victim's ribs by the spine so that they resembled an eagle's wings; the lungs were then pulled out. The rite, while doubted by some modern scholars, is reported in sagas.

boruma: The tribute exacted by a victorious Irish king to denote submission of his rivals.

boyar: Slavic nobleman, used to translate Norse *jarl*.

bracteate: A silver coin minted from a single die so that the image of the reverse is the mirror of that on the obverse.

Bretwalda: "Britain ruler," an Anglo-Saxon honorific title for an English king who achieved primacy in the island.

burgh: A fortified Anglo-Saxon town. A network of such positions was constructed by Alfred the Great and Edward the Elder.

chain mail (ON: *brynja*): Armor made of interlocking steel chains.

comitatus: Latin for "retinue of ruler." Cornelius Tacitus in *Germania* uses the term to describe professional warriors attached to a Germanic lord. See **berserker**.

Croziers (ON: Baglar): A Norwegian party supporting the descendants of King Inge (r. 1135–1161) in the civil wars down to 1217.

curragh: A Celtic coastal skin boat, without keel, constructed with a rib frame.

danegeld: The payment of silver by English or Frankish monarchs to Vikings.

Danelaw (OE: Denelagu): The Danish settlement in England during the 9th and 10th centuries.

Danevirke: A wooden palisade with fossa first constructed circa 737, which stretched from the market town Hedeby west toward the Eider River. There were three building phases in about 739, 808–810, and 968. Valdemar I (r. 1157–1182) replaced the system with a brick and mortar wall.

dendrochronology: The scientific method of dating by tree-ring patterns.

denier: Silver coin of the Carolingian Empire fixed at 1.65 gr and 20 mm by Charlemagne in 800–814.

dirhem (2.97 grs.): Silver coin of the Islamic world carrying Kufic inscriptions.

Domesday Book (1086): A census of England complied on orders of King William I.

dreng: "Brave man"; designated the Anglo-Danish landowner in the Danelaw. See *thegn*.

druzhina: Company of armed retainers of Russian princes from the 11th century.

Dubhgaill: "Black Foreigners," the Irish designation for Danish Vikings.

Edda: Denotes collections of poems and stories of the Norse gods. The *Poetic Edda* is a collection of poems composed between the 9th and 11th centuries. In about 1220, Snorri Sturluson composed his *Prose Edda* based on the Eddaic poems.

ell: A measurement of cloth (between 37 and 45 inches in length) used as a means of reckoning wealth in Scandinavia.

Finngaill: "White Foreigners," the Irish name for Norwegian Vikings.

Flateyjarbok: The Norse chronicle of the monastery of Flatey, Iceland, which records myths and legends of early Scandinavia.

flokkar ("flocks"): Professional companies of armed retainers during the Norwegian civil wars in 1130–1217.

Futhark: See **runes**.

fyrd: The Anglo-Saxon levy of the 9th through 11th centuries; an armed warrior was maintained for royal service by ever five units of hides in a shire.

Gaell-Gaidaill: "Foreign Gaels," apostate Irish who allied with Norse Vikings in the ninth century.

Gardariki: "Kingdom of fortified towns"; Norse for Russia in the 9th and 10th centuries.

godi (gothi; pl. *godar*): "Chieftain"; a figure skilled in law and negotiation who assumed a leading position in Icelandic society. The position (*godarod*) could be held jointly, transferred, or sold.

Gotar or Gautar (OE: Geatas): The "Goths" dwelling in southern Sweden.

Gragas: "Grey Goose Laws"; the first written compilation of Icelandic law, circa 1115.

Haerveg: "Army route"; the principal north-south wooden corduroy highway of Jutland first constructed in the early 8th century.

hagiography: The genre of saints' lives.

Hanseatic League or Hansa: This German consortium of cities comprised two groups, the Wendish towns headed by Lübeck and the towns of the Rhineland and Westphalia. In the 13th century, Lübeck and her trading partners took over the shipbuilding and carrying trade in the Baltic Sea. In the 14th century, Hanseatic communities (*kontor*) enjoyed privileges and fiscal exemptions in leading Scandinavian ports and dominated banking.

Havamal: "Sayings of Har"; an Eddaic wisdom poem, in which Odin names his titles and gives aphorisms.

Heimskringlasaga: Written by Snorri Sturluson circa 1225, this saga records the history of the kings of Norway from earliest times to 1177. One-third of the work is devoted to St. Olaf (1015–1030).

hide: This fiscal unit of land (120 acres) was the basis for military service and taxation in Anglo-Saxon England.

housecarl: A professional Scandinavian warrior maintained by the English monarchy from the reign of Cnut the Great (r. 1014–1035).

Hrafsmal (*Speech of the Raven*): A skaldic poem celebrating the victory of Harald Finehair at Hafrsfjord circa 875–880.

hundred: The division of a shire.

Islendingabok (*Book of Icelanders*): Written by Ari the Learned (1067–1148) to record the descent of Icelandic families from the original settlers.

jarl: Norse for nobleman, "earl."

Jomsvikings: A company of professional Vikings who had their base at Jomsborg (Wolin) at the mouth of the Oder and were allied to the Jelling kings of Denmark. Their exploits were celebrated in a saga of the 13th century.

kenning: A metaphorical phrase adapted to skaldic meter.

Kensington Stone: A hoax perpetrated in 1898 by Olaf Ohman in Minnesota. The stone was purported to be a rune stone erected by Swedish Vikings.

King's Mirror: Composed in Latin as an exhortation to ideal kingship for Norway in about 1220. The values were based on St. Augustine's views of a just king (*rex iustus*).

knarr: A Scandinavian ocean-going cargo ship.

lamellar armor: Composed of overlapping steel or leather scales.

Landnamabok (*Book of Settlements*): Written by Ari the Learned (1067–1148); reports the settlement of 430 individuals in Iceland in 879–930.

law rock (ON: *logberg*): The location where cases in the *Althing* were announced.

law-speaker (ON: *logosumadr*): Elected to a three-year term to preside over the *Althing* and to recite the laws.

leding (Danish), **leidang** (Norwegian), or **ledung** (Swedish), from Old Norse **leidang**: The ship levy was an obligation of free men to serve in the fleet at royal command. Under King Valdemar I of Denmark (r. 1157–1182), the ship levy totaled 1,400 ships manned by 160,000 men. Service was often commuted into cash payments.

lendirmenn: Norse landed notables, "squires," who controlled local justice and *things*.

lens: A fief awarded to a vassal by the crown from the 12th century on.

Miklagard: "Great City"; the Norse name for Constantinople.

motte and bailey castle: An earthen mound with palisade and moat constructed in early medieval Europe.

Norman: Frankish term for Scandinavian Vikings; it was derived from medieval Latin *Normanni*, "Northmen."

Old Church Slavonic: The literary language created by St. Cyril (827–869) for the translation of the Bible.

oppidum (pl. *oppida*): A Celtic fortified town of the La Tène civilization (500–50 B.C.)

Ostmen: "Easterners"; Norse settled in the Irish ports from the late 10th century on. In Anglo-Irish law of the 12th and 13th centuries, Ostmen were still recognized as a privileged legal class with a distinct Norse language.

Pale: The area of English settlement in Ireland after 1170.

pandemic: A cycle of plagues, such as those in 542–750 and those following the Black Death (1347–1351), that lead to demographic collapse.

Papar: Old Norse term for Irish anchorites encountered in Iceland and the Western Isles.

peers of France: The leading feudal lords who owed direct homage to the king of France. The secular peers were the count of Flanders, duke of Normandy, duke of Burgundy, duke of Aquitaine, count of Champagne, and count of Toulouse. The ecclesiastical peers were the archbishop of Rheims, and the bishops of Langres, Beauvais, Chalons, Noyon, and Laon.

penny (1.10–1.35 grs.): Silver coin of Anglo-Saxon England, minted on varying weight standards. The Anglo-Saxon penny inspired the first Scandinavian coinages.

portage: The conveying of ships overland between river systems.

Ragnarsdrapna: The earliest surviving poem written by Bragi the Old, c. 850–900.

ridings (ON: *thridjungr*): "Thirds"; divisions of Yorkshire.

Rigsthula: The Eddaic poem in which Heimdall, watchman of the gods, uses the guise of Rig to father the classes of mortals.

runes: The early Germanic alphabet devised from north Italic script in about 300–100 B.C. The original long Futhark comprised 24 runes, whereas the short Futhark of the Viking Age had only 16 runes. Runes had magical and numerical value and, thus, were sacred to Odin.

Rus: The term is of uncertain origin; it may be derived from Finnish *Ruotsi*, the name for Swedes. The term designated those Swedes who settled in what became Russia between the 8th and 10th centuries.

Russian Primary Chronicle: A monk of the Cave Monastery, outside of Kiev, composed this narrative of early Russian history in about 1115. The chronicle was based on oral traditions and includes many early documents.

seithr: The ritual of summoning spirits by a *volva* dedicated to Freya.

sept: The extended clan in Ireland by which descent and inheritance was determined.

shire: Anglo-Saxon term for "county."

skald: A Norse poet between the late 9th and 14th centuries who employed the complicated skaldic meters and kennings. Skalds at the Danish and Norwegian courts devised a wide range of laudatory and narrative skaldic poems.

Skjoldungar (OE: Scyldingas): "Shield-bearers"; the legendary Danish kings of Sjaelland descended from Skjoldr.

Skraelingar: "Screechers"; Old Norse name for indigenous peoples of North America and Greenland.

spangelhelm: A class of early medieval conical helmets based on late Roman prototypes.

Stave church: An early medieval wooden-frame church.

Svear: Old Norse for Swedes, who occupied the regions around Lake Mälaren.

syncope: The linguistic process of a language reducing the syllables in words.

thegn: An Old English landowner whose lordship entailed royal military service. See *dreng*.

thing: The assembly of free men in Germanic society that passed laws and settled legal disputes. In 930, Iceland was divided into four quarters, each with its own regional *thing*.

Thule: In the Classical Age, this term designated the shores of Norway above the Arctic Circle. From the 9th century, Christian authors used it to designate Iceland. The term also designated the farthermost, unexplored regions of the world.

Union of Kalmar (1397): The formal act of uniting the three crowns of Denmark, Sweden, and Norway under Erik of Pomerania.

Varangian Guard: The elite regiment of Scandinavians formed by Byzantine emperor Basil II in 988–989.

Varangians: "Men of the pledge"; Vikings recently arrived from Scandinavia either in Russia or the Byzantine Empire during the 10th and 11th centuries.

Vinland: The region discovered by Leif Eriksson in 1001; it originally designated Newfoundland, but it was extended to include regions of the Lower Saint Lawrence and Nova Scotia, where Norse attempted settlement in 1001–1014.

Vinland Map: Purportedly dating to circa 1440, the map was acquired by Yale University in1965 and declared a fraud in 1974. In the upper left corner, Vinland and Greenland were forged. The map was bound with a genuine manuscript reporting the papal mission of Giovanni Caprini to the Mongol court in 1245–1246.

Voluspa: "Sayings of the prophetess"; the first poem of the *Prose Edda*, in which a *volva* recites the story of the creation and destruction of the world.

wapentake (ON: *vapnatak*): "Brandishing arms"; the division of shire in the Danelaw.

Ynglingar: The legendary kings of Uppsala who claimed descent from Yng ("Ing"); a title for the god Frey.

Norse Gods and Mythology:

Aesir: Gods of the principal family headed by Odin who dwell in Asgard.

Asgard, Asgarth: The home of the halls of the gods.

Baldr: The blameless god and son of Odin, slain by blind Hodr at the connivance of Loki. The act led to the binding of Loki.

Fafnir: The dragon slain by Sigurd in the legend of the Volsungs.

Fenrir: A gigantic wolf, an offspring of Loki and Angrboda, that is bound by deception; the god Tyr loses his right hand in the process. The wolf will swallow Odin at Ragnarök.

Frey: Son of Njord and god of fertility who surrendered his sword to woe, the giantess Gerd. At Ragnarök, he is slain by Surt, the fire giant. The Yngling kings of Sweden claimed descent from Frey.

Freya: The fertility goddess, daughter of Njord. She possesses many of the same powers as Odin, and she was identified with many lesser goddesses.

Heimdall: The watchman of Bifrost, the rainbow bridge and entrance to Asgard. In the guise of Rig, he fathers the classes of mankind. At Ragnarök, he and Loki will slay each other.

Hel: The daughter of Loki and Angrboda who is assigned by Odin to the realm Niflheim.

Loki: The god of mischief, he fathered, with the giantess Angrboda, the wolf Fenrir, the Midgard serpent (*Midgardsormr*), and the goddess Hel. A god of guile, Loki often accompanies Thor in his adventurers. His instigation of Baldr's death leads to Loki's binding until Ragnarök when he and Heimdall will slay each other.

Midgard, Midgarth: "Middle Earth"; the land of mortals.

Midgard Serpent: The offspring of Loki and Angrboda, the giant serpent encircles the Earth. At Ragnarök, Thor will slay the monsters, but he himself will die from the venom spewed over him by the dying beast.

Nerthus: A fertility goddess revered by the tribes of Jutland and described by Cornelius Tacitus. She was paraded in a sacred cart. She was likely a namesake and female consort to Njord of the Viking Age.

Niflheim: The cold realm of the underworld presided over by Hel.

Niflungs: The dwarves of the Rhine who had guarded the gold treasure cursed by Loki. The treasure is acquired by Sigurd upon slaying Fafnir. Gunnar, in turn, acquires the hoard after arranging Sigurd's death. Atli of the Huns, lusting for the hoard, lures Gunnar and the Burgundians to their death.

Njord: The god of fertility and associated with the sea travel. He was father of Frey and Freya, and the three joined the Aesir in Asgard to reconcile an ancient war between the two families of gods. See **Nerthus**.

Norns: The three sisters and fates: Urd (past), Verdandi (present), and Skuld (future).

Odin (OE: Woden): The supreme god of the Aesir, noted for his ecstatic powers in battle and poetry. He slays Ymir and creates the universe. He hangs himself on Yggdrasill to release the power of runes and gives up his eye for a drink at the well of Urd. He patronizes and collects the greatest heroes for Valhalla for the combat of Ragnarök.

Ragnarök: The final doom, when the gods and monsters are destroyed in a great combat. The event is preceded by a triple winter, and final destruction will result from fire and water. A new world will be reborn under Baldr.

Thor (OE: Thunor): The red-haired sky god of Odin and Jord who was the friend of mankind and subject of myths. He drives a goat-drawn chariot and smashes giants with his hammer, Mjollnir. His adventures include travels to the realm of Utgard-Loki and fishing for the Midgard serpent.

Tyr (OE: Tiu or Tew): The original Germanic sky and war god (Tiwaz); he lost his hand as a pledge in the binding of Fenrir. In the Viking Age, Odin had assumed many of the qualities and powers of Tyr.

Utgard-Loki: The giant rival of Thor. By a series of trials, he deceives and bests Thor, Loki, and Thor's companion, Thjalfi

Valhalla: The hall of Odin in Asgard, where heroes feast until Ragnarök.

Valkyries ("choosers of the slain"): Female spirits who select the fallen for Valhalla; they also direct the course of battle.

Vanir: The gods of fertility, foremost Njord and his children, Frey and Freya.

Volsungs: The legendary Frankish kings favored by Odin, of whom Sigmund and Sigurd were the greatest heroes.

Yggdrasil: The world tree at the center of the universe; its branches hold the nine realms. At the three great roots are the wells of the three Norns.

Battles:

Carlington Lough, 851: Naval victory of the Danish Vikings over the Norwegian Vikings. The Danes, on advice of their Irish allies, invoked St. Patrick.

Clontarf, April 23, 1014: Brian Bóruma defeated a Viking-Norse coalition raised by Sigtrygg III Silkbeard of Dublin. Brian, while victorious, was slain. Mael Sechlainn II of Meath thus regained the high kingship of Ireland.

Dyle River, 891: The tactical victory of King Arnulf the Bastard over the Vikings. The Franks stormed the Viking camp, but the Vikings withdrew into England.

Edington (or Eddington), May 878: Decisive victory of Alfred the Great over Guthrum and the Great Army. The Danes thereafter agreed to the Treaty of Wedmore.

Fulford, September 20, 1066: King Harald Hardardi of Norway and Earl Tostig defeated Earls Morcar and Edwin outside of York.

Hafrsfjord, c. 880: The decisive naval victory of King Harald Finehair over the *jarls* and kings of Vestlandet.

Hastings, October 14, 1066: The victory of William I, the Conqueror, over Harald II, king of England. The victory gained William the English throne.

Hjörungavág, c. 988: The naval victory of Jarl Hakon the Great over the Danes and Jomsvikings commanded by Thorkell the Tall and Sigvaldi.

Nesjar. April 1016: Decisive naval victory of St. Olaf over his Norwegian foes, led by Svein Hakonsson; the victory secured for Olaf the crown of Norway.

Nissa River, August 9, 1062: The naval victory of King Harald Hardardi over Svein Estrithson off the western shores of Sweden. Svein had to abandon his flagship, but the victory brought Harald no strategic gains.

Sancourt, 881: The victory of King Louis III of France over a Viking column. The victory was celebrated in the Old High German epic *Ludwigslied*.

Stamford Bridge, September 25, 1066: The victory of Harald II, king of England, over King Harald Hardardi and Earl Tostig.

Stiklestad, July 29. 1030: The Norwegians defeated and slew St. Olaf, who had sought to regain his throne with Swedish allies.

Svold, 1000: The naval victory of King Svein Forkbeard of Denmark over King Olaf Tryggvason of Norway. Olaf leaped into the sea from his flagship, *Long Serpent*. The battle was most likely fought off the southern shores of Skane.

Tara, 980: The decisive victory of King Mael Sechlainn II of Meath over Olaf Kvaran of Dublin. The Irish victory ended the military domination of the Hiberno-Norse.

Biographical Notes

Absalon, born c. 1128; bishop of Roskilde, 1158–1178; archbishop of Lund, 1178–1201. Cousin and counselor to King Valdemar I of Denmark, Abaslon directed the conquest and conversion of the Wends in 1158–1170 and advanced ecclesiastical and royal institutions.

Adam of Bremen, fl. c. 1070–1080. A German cleric, Adam composed in Latin the *History of the Archbishops of Hamburg-Bremen*; he obtained his information on Scandinavia at the court of King Svein Estrithson of Denmark.

Adils (OE: Eadgils), Yngling king of Uppsala, r. c. 550–575. Adils was the rival of Danish king Hrolf Kraki (OE: Hrothluf) and married to Hrolf's mother, Yrsa. In *Beowulf*, Eadgils regained the throne of Uppsala and slew his uncle Onela (ON: Ali) with the aid of Beowulf.

Aelfgifu (ON: Alfifa) of Northampton. King Cnut married her as his first wife around 1015. She was mother to Cnut's sons, Svein, king of Norway (r. 1030–1035), and Harold I Harefoot, king of England (r. 1037–1040).

Aelle II, king of Northumbria, r. 862–867. Aelle usurped the throne and, thus, ignited a civil war. He, along with rival Osbert, was defeated and slain by the Great Army at York in 867. In Norse legend, Alle captured and threw Ragnar Lodbrok into a snake pit. Ragnar's sons, Halfdane and Ivar, avenged Ragnar by carving a blood eagle on the back of Aelle.

Aethelred I, king of Wessex, r. 865–871. Aethelred was the son of King Aethewulf (r. 839–858), and he supported his brother-in-law, King Burgred of Mercia, against the Great Army. In 870–871, he campaigned against the Great Army based at Reading, but he died prematurely and was succeeded by his brother Alfred the Great.

Aethelred II the Unready, born c. 968, r. 978–1016. Son of King Edgar (r. 974–978), who was nicknamed "*unraed,*" that is, lacking in counsel. Aethelred II failed to control Viking raids from 991. In 1002, he provoked the Danish invasions by ordering the St. Brice's Day Massacre. He was driven from England by Svein Forkbeard in 1013–1014 and returned with his son Edmund Ironside but died in

1016. In 1002, he married as his second wife, Emma, sister of Duke Richard II of Normandy and mother of Edward the Confessor.

Aethelstan, king of England, r. 924–939. Aethelstan imposed direct rule over Viking York after the death of Sigtrygg in 927 and defeated a Scottish-Norse army at Brunanburh in 937; thus, he was hailed king of all Britain. He issued law codes and advanced royal administration. He was godfather to the future King Hakon the Good of Norway.

Alcuin of York (OE: Ealhwine), 735–804. Of a distinguished Northumbrian family, this monk and scholar revived learning at the court of Charlemagne from 781.

Alfred the Great, king of Wessex, born c. 849, r. c. 871–899. Alfred succeeded his brother Aethelred I and secured the withdrawal of Guthrum and the Great Army by payment of *danegeld*. In 878, after the victory of Eddington, Alfred imposed a treaty on the Danes and secured the future of Wessex. By his reforms, he turned Wessex into an effective kingdom and revived spiritual and intellectual life.

Ammianus Marcellinus, c. A.D. 330–395 Roman soldier and historian, Ammianus wrote a Roman history from Trajan (98–117) to Valens (364–378) that contains information on the Germans and Huns.

Anskar, St. (or Ansgar), 801–865. Apostle to the north, Anskar was trained at the monastery of Corbie and led the first missions to Denmark (826–828) and Sweden (829–831). He led a second mission to Hedeby and Birka in 850–852. Anskar, archbishop of Hamburg in 831, was granted the joint see of Hamburg-Bremen in 845, which he made the primate of Scandinavia.

Anund Jakob, king of Sweden, r. 1022–1050. Anund was the second Christian king to rule from Sigtuna, and he intrigued to end Danish overlordship. In 1030, he backed St. Olaf's desperate return, then supported Svein Estrithson against Magnus the Good and Harald Hardardi.

Ari Thorgilsson the Learned, 1067–1148. Based on oral accounts, Ari, a *godi* and scholar, composed the *Islendingabok* (*Book of Icelanders*) and *Landnamabok* (*Book of Settlements*) on the discovery and settlement of Iceland

Arnulf the Bastard, king of Germany, born 850, r. 887–899. Arnulf was elected by the Eastern Frankish nobility to succeed his uncle Charles the Fat. In 891, he defeated a Viking force at the Battle of the Dyle, but the Vikings withdrew the England.

Attila (ON: Atli), king of the Huns, born c. 406, r. 433–452. Attila forged a great barbarian empire in Central and Eastern Europe and invaded the western Roman Empire in 451 and 452. His empire collapsed upon his death. In the Volsung legend, Attila was remembered as Atli, an avaricious king who lures Gunnar and his kin to their destruction.

Basil II Bulgaroctenus, Byzantine emperor, born 958, r. 978–1025. The greatest warrior emperor of the Macedonian dynasty, Basil II conquered Bulgaria and crushed rebel Anatolian families. In 988–989, he formed the Varangian Guard and cemented a matrimonial alliance with Prince Vladimir of Kiev.

Bede the Venerable, 673–735. Northumbrian monk and scholar at Jarrow, he penned the *Ecclesiastical History of the English People*— the first English history.

Beowulf, legendary king of Gotar (OE: Geatas), r. c. 535–550. The hero celebrated in the Old English epic, composed c. 675–700.

Bjarki, Bodvar. A Norwegian hero, he fought in the shape of a bear and was the greatest champion of Danish king Hrolf Kraki. Bjarki is considered a Norse recasting of Beowulf. The *Bjarkamal* ("lay of Bjarki") is an exchange between Bjarki and his companion Hjalti at the final battle of Hleidr. The lay was sung by warriors of St. Olaf at Stiklestad in 1030.

Bjarni Herjulfsson. In 986, this Icelandic merchant, en route to join the Greenland colony, was driven off course and arrived off the coasts of Markland (Labrador). He sailed northeast to Greenland, also discovering Helluland (Baffin Island). His report inspired the voyage by Leif Eriksson in 1001.

Bjorn, king of Birka, c. 825–850. Bjorn, likely a vassal to the Swedish king of Uppsala, received St. Anskar in 829–831.

Bjorn Ironside, Viking sea king, c. 850–862. Bjorn, operating from a base on the island of Oissel at the mouth of the Somme, raided the Carolingian Empire. Charles the Bald engaged the Viking Weland to eliminate Bjorn. Bjorn, however, paid off Weland and joined the Viking expedition into the Mediterranean in 859–862.

Bragi Boddason the Old, Norwegian skald, c. A.D. 850–900 Bragi composed the first known skaldic poem, *Ragnarsdrapa*, in which he describes the images on the shield of Ragnar Lodbrok.

Brian Bóruma, mac Cennetig, king in Munster, born c. 941, r. 976–1014. Brian turned his ancestral marcher lordship of Thomond into the leading Irish kingdom. In 1002, he was recognized as high king (*andri*). In 1014, he fell in his victory over Norse and Irish foes at the Battle of Clontarf, and thereafter, his kingdom fragmented.

Brodir, Viking sea king of the Isle of Man, died 1014. Summoned by Sigtrygg III Silkbeard, Brodir fell at the Battle of Clontarf after he had cut down Brian Bóruma.

Brynhild. Sister of Atli in the Volsung legend, Brynhild was punished by Odin, who put her into a sleep ringed by a wall of fire Sigurd awakened her and pledged his love. But Sigurd was later bewitched into marrying Gudrun, sister of Gunnar, and then, by deception, Sigurd won Brynhild for Gunnar. The clash of Brynhild and Gudrun led to Sigurd's death. Brynhild joined Sigurd on his funeral pyre and entered Valhalla as a Valkyrie. Brynhild is loosely based on Bruechildis (died 613), wife of Sigeibert I, Frankish king of Austrasia (r. 561–575).

Burgred, king of Mercia, r. 852–874. Burgred was the ally and brother-in-law of Aethelred I of Wessex. In 868, he paid *danegeld* to the Great Army. Failing to check the Danes in 873–874, Burgred abdicated and retired to Rome.

Charlemagne, **Charles the Great**, king of the Franks, r. 768–814. This Carolingian ruler was crowned Roman emperor in 800, thus founding the Holy Roman Empire. He built the first effective state in Western Europe since the end of Roman power. By his conquest and conversion of the Saxons in 772–806, Charlemagne provoked Danish raids along the shores of Frisia.

Charles the Bald, king of the Western Franks, r. 840–877. The youngest son of Louis the Pious, Charles obtained France as his realm at the Treaty of Verdun (843). He failed to check Viking attacks and, thus, undermined royal finances and credibility.

Charles the Fat, Holy Roman Emperor, r. 881–888. The son of Louis the German, Charles ruled as king of Italy from 879 and was crowned Holy Roman Emperor in 881. He reunited the Carolingian Empire in 884. His indifferent leadership led to his deposition and retirement into a monastery.

Charles III the Simple, king of France, r. 897–922. Charles, posthumous son of Louis II, was twice passed over for the succession and came to the throne in a weak position. In 911, he invested Hrolf (Rollo) with the fief of Normandy. In 922–923, Charles was overthrown in a baronial revolt and died imprisoned in 929.

Clovis, king of the Franks, born c. 466, r. 481–511. Clovis made the Franks and his family, the Merovingians, the paramount power in Gaul and southern Germany. Around 496, he converted to Catholic Christianity and assured Frankish political dominance in Western Christendom.

Cnut (or Canute or Knut), king of Denmark, born c. 995, r. 1014–1035. The son of Svein Forkbeard and Queen Gunnhild, Cnut was hailed king by the Danish army in England upon his father's death. In 1014–1016, Cnut conquered England, and in 1019, he was hailed as sole king in Denmark. In 1028, he was acclaimed king of Norway at the Trondelag *thing*. Cnut ruled as a great Christian king, but he drew on Scandinavian traditions to maintain his far-flung realm.

Cnut IV, St., king of Denmark, r. 1080–1086. The second son of Svein Estrithson, Cnut was murdered at Odense by rebellious crews who refused to sail against England. In 1101, Cnut was canonized as a royal saint.

Cnut VI, king of Denmark, r. 1182–1202. The elder son of Valdemar I, Cnut VI imposed Danish hegemony over the pagan Pomeranians and subjected Holstein.

Columba, St., 521–597. A scion of the Hy Neil, Columba (Irish: Comcille) organized Irish monastic life and, in 563, founded Iona, the greatest Celtic monastery in the British Isles.

Constantine VII Porphyrogenitus, Byzantine emperor, r. 913–957. This scholar-emperor wrote *De Administrando Imperio* (*"On the Government of the Empire"*), which contains a wealth of information on the Rus, Slavs, and Turkomen tribes.

Cyril, St. (Constantine), 827–869, and **St. Methodius**, 826–886. The Greek brothers were hailed as the apostles to the Slavs for their efforts to convert the Czechs, Serbs, and Bulgarians. Cyril devised the "Cyrillic" alphabet for the translation of the Bible into Slavic.

Dunstan, St., archbishop of Canterbury, born 909, r. 961–978. Dunstan reformed English monastic and cultural life, disrupted by the Viking attacks, and worked for the conversion of all Danes in England.

Eadred, king of England, born 923, r. 946–954. The son of Edward the Elder, Eadred exploited the turbulent wars between the Hiberno-Norse and Danes to impose English control over York.

Edgar, king of England, born c. 942, r. 959–975. The son of King Edmund, Edgar effected the formal unification of England at his accession. He sponsored administrative, legal, and monetary reforms and assisted St. Dunstan in spiritual reforms.

Edmund, king of East Anglia, r. 855–869. Edmund was coerced to grant the Great Army a base at Thetford in 865. In 869, he fell fighting the Danes. Edmund was captured and martyred, and the Danes of East Anglia minted memorial pennies in his name circa 900–915.

Edmund, king of England, born c. 921, r. 946–954. Edmund succeeded his brother Eadred and battled the Hiberno-Norse kings of York.

Edmund Ironside, king of England, born c. 990, r. 1016. The son of Aethelred II and Aelfgifu, Edmund mounted a recovery of southern England from Cnut in 1015–1016. His sudden death on November 30, 1016, left Cnut sole king of England.

Edward the Confessor, king of England, born c. 1004, r. 1042–1066. The son of Aethelred II and Emma, Edward was reared as an exile at the Norman court until invited to ascend the English throne in 1042. A Norman in speech and outlook, Edward clashed with Earl Godwin and his sons. Edward's death precipitated a succession crisis in 1066.

Edward the Elder, king of Wessex, born c. 871, r. 899–924. The son and heir of Alfred the Great, he consolidated his father's reforms, conquered East Anglia and the Five Boroughs, and imposed his hegemony on Danish York.

Edward the Martyr, king of England, born 962, r. 975–978. The elder son of King Edgar, the young king was a protégé of St. Dunstan. His murder, on orders of his stepmother, Aelfrida, resulted in the accession of the infant Aethelred II.

Emma, queen of England, c. 986–1052. The daughter of Richard I of Normandy, Emma married King Aethelred II in 1002; then, in 1017, she married Cnut. Her son by Cnut, Harthacnut, succeeded as king of Denmark and England in 1035. In 1037, Emma was exiled by her stepson, Harold I Harefoot when he seized the throne. She was restored to favor and returned to England, when her son Edward the Confessor was acclaimed king in 1042.

Emund the Old, king of Sweden, r. 1050–1060. The half-brother of Anund Jakob, he was the last king of the family of Erik the Victorious. With his death, the Svear and Gotar elected kings from among leading families.

Erik of Pomerania, king of Norway, r. 1389–1442; king of Denmark and Sweden, r. 1396–1439; died 1459. Erik was the great-nephew and adopted son of Queen Margaret, who succeeded to all three kingdoms under the Union of Kalmar. His favoritism to German and Danish courtiers lost him support, and he was ultimately deposed and succeeded by his nephew Christopher of Bavaria.

Erik the Bloodax, king of Norway, r. 930–936. He succeeded to his father, Harald Finehair, who retired, and pursued ruthless blood feuds against his kin that earned him his nickname. Driven from Norway by his half-brother Hakon, Erik was twice hailed as king of York (r. 948; 952–954). He was expelled by his Danish subjects and fell at the Battle of Stainmore in 954. His wife, Gunnhild, "mother of kings," and their sons pursued a feud against King Hakon of Norway.

Erik the Red, c. 950–1002. A restless Viking who was outlawed first from Norway, then from Iceland in 982. In 983–985, Erik explored and founded the Norse colony in Greenland.

Erik the Victorious, king of Sweden, r. 980–995. With the favor of Odin, Erik ruled from Sigtuna and battled and drove into exile his rival king, Svein Forkbeard of Denmark.

Erik IX, St., king of Sweden, born c. 1120, r. 1156–1160. A Swedish nobleman, he had been a rival to King Sverker I. He was elected by the Swedish *thing*, but he was murdered at Uppsala. He was canonized a royal saint, and his Finnish expedition of 1156 was later presented as a crusade.

Estrith. Daughter of King Svein Forkbeard and an uncertain wife. In about 1015, she married Jarl Ulf, and she was the mother of King Svein Estrithson.

Floki Vilgerdarson, Raven Floki. In c. 875, this Norwegian Viking explored southern Iceland and attempted a settlement on Vatnsfjord. He departed after the first winter, naming the island Iceland.

Freydis. Illegitimate daughter of Erik the Red. She and her husband, Thorvald, participated in the settlement of Vinland led by Thorfinn Karlsefni in 1009–1012. The couple led their own abortive settlement in 1013–1014

Gardar Svavarrsson. A Swedish merchant who was blown off course and discovered Iceland in c. 870.

Gizur Isleifsson, bishop of Iceland, r. 1082–1106. In 1096, he levied the first tithe in Iceland and, thus, recorded the first census of households.

Guthfrith (also known as Godfred; ON Guthfrid), king of Jutland, r. c. 800–810. Guthfrith clashed with Charlemagne along the Eider frontier, attacked Frankish Slavic allies, and raided Frisia. He was murdered and succeeded by Hemming (r. 810–812).

Godwin, earl of Wessex, c. 1016–1053. The leading English earl of royal descent, Godwin accepted Cnut in 1016 and was rewarded with the earldom of Wessex. He acted as the king-maker in the succession crises of 1035–1042, and in 1042, he secured the accession of Edward the Confessor. In 1051–1052, he was driven into exile by Edward, but he was restored to favor. In 1018, he married Gyda, daughter of Jarl Thorkell the Tall.

Gorm the Old, king of Denmark, born c. 910, r. 936–958. A Viking sea king, Gorm united Jutland into a Danish kingdom and ended German influence. A staunch pagan, Gorm built a great hall at Jelling and raised two tumuli and memorial rune stones for himself and his wife, Queen Thyri.

Gudrun. Sister of Gunnar and wife of Sigurd in the cycle of the Volsung. Her quarrel with Brynhild led to the treacherous death of Sigurd. Gudrun, who was then married to Atli, king of the Huns, avenged the deaths of her kinsmen by burning Atli in his hall. She egged on her sons Hamdir and Sorli (by her third marriage to Jonak) to avenge their sister by slaying the tyrant Jormunrek, king of the Goths.

Gunnar, king of the Burgundians in the Volsung cycle. Gunnar marries Brynhild with the aid of Sigurd. He is convinced to have Sigurd slain by Hogni and the spiteful Brynhild and, thus, acquires the Niflung treasure. He and his brothers are lured to their deaths at the hall of Atli, king of the Huns, and are avenged by their sister Gudrun.

Gunnhild, daughter of Gorm of the Old and wife of Erik the Bloodax, (r. 930–936). Dubbed the "mother of kings," Gunnhild is portrayed by hostile sources as a sorceress and schemer who intrigued to overthrow Hakon the Good and restore her sons to Norway.

Guthfrith, king of Dublin, r. 921–934; king of York, r. 927. Guthfrith expelled his brother Sigtrygg II from Dublin and briefly asserted his domination over York.

Guthrum, Viking sea king, c. 870–890. Guthrum commanded the campaign of the Great Army to conquer Wessex in 874–878. Defeated at Eddington by Alfred the Great, Guthrum submitted to baptism, agreed to the treaty of Wedmore, and withdrew to rule in East Anglia.

Hakon the Good, king of Norway, r. c. 936–960. The son of Harald Finehair, Hakon was fostered by King Aethelstan of England. He expelled his unpopular half-brother Erik the Bloodax and ruled according to customary law. A Christian, Hakon also paid respects to the ancestral gods. He was mortally wounded in the naval Battle of Srorth and succeeded by his nephew Harald Greycloak.

Hakon IV, king of Norway, born 1204, r. 1217–1263. Hakon was one of Norway's greatest kings, securing a hereditary monarchy and advancing royal justice. Hakon restored Norway after a ruinous civil war between Birkebeiner (Birchlegs) and Baglar (Croziers). Hakon initiated the incorporation of Iceland and died while on expedition to the Hebrides.

Hakon Sigurdsson the Great, jarl of Trondelag, r. 970–995. A staunch pagan, Hakon was exiled by Harald Greycloak and later assisted in Greycloak's murder. Hakon ruled over northern Norway as a Danish vassal, and in about 988, he defeated the Danes and Jomsviking at Hjorungavag. In 995, the unpopular jarl was overthrown by the sea king Olaf Tryggvason.

Halfdane Ragnarsson, r. 865–877. With his brother Ivar, Halfdane commanded the Great Army in England in 985–872. He conducted the partition of lands among Vikings in Yorkshire, and in 877, he fell in a Scottish campaign.

Harald Bluetooth, king of Denmark, r. 958–986. The second Jelling king, Harald converted to Christianity in 960–965. He secured the Danish islands and Skane, built a new capital at Roskilde, extended the Danevirke, constructed military camps, and raised his own memorial rune stone and church at Jelling.

Harald Finehair, king of Norway, born c. 845, r. c. 880–930. A petty king in Uppland, Harald mobilized Viking fleets to royal service. At the Battle of Hafrsfjord (c. 875–880), he defeated the kings of Vestlandet and henceforth reigned as king of Norway. Harald ruled by customary law, matrimonial alliances, and personal loyalty of jarls and *lendirmenn*. Later authors anachronistically attributed many royal institutions to Harald. In about 930, he retired in favor of his son Erik the Bloodax and died about 933.

Harald Greycloak, king of Norway, r. 960–970. The son of Erik the Bloodax and Queen Gunnhild, Harald Greycloak succeeded Hakon the Good. He and his brothers, the Erikssons, proved tyrannical Christian lords. Harald was lured to his death at Roskilde by Harald Bluetooth and Jarl Hakon the Great.

Harald Klak, Viking sea king, r. 826–850. Exiled from Denmark by rivals, Harald Klak submitted to baptism and received a fief in Frisia from Louis the Pious. In 841, Harald received the island of Walachern.

Harald Kyrri the Quiet, king of Norway, r. 1066–1093. He restored peace and prosperity to Norway, founding the port of Bergen and promoting episcopal organization.

Harald Sigurdsson Hardardi the Ruthless, king of Norway, born c. 1015, r. 1046–1066. The half-brother of St. Olaf, Harald escaped from Stiklestad to the court of Kiev. In 1034–1043, Harald distinguished himself in the Varangian Guard so that he returned to Scandinavia with veterans and wealth. He allied first with Svein Estrithson in 1045, then agreed to share the Norwegian kingship with his nephew Magnus the Good. In 1047–1064, as sole Norwegian king, he failed to conquer Denmark. He fell at the Battle of Stamford Bridge in a bid to conquer England in 1066.

Harold II Godwinson, king of England, born 1022, r. 1066. The son of Godwin, Harold succeeded to the earldom of Wessex in 1053. He claimed the right of succession by virtue of a final wish of his failing brother-in-law Edward the Confessor. He was defeated and slain by William I at the Battle of Hastings.

Harold I Harefoot, king of England, r. 1037–1040. The younger son of Cnut and Aelfgifu, he resented his half-brother King Harthacnut. Harold usurped the English throne in 1037. Because Harold died prematurely, Harthacnut was received as king in England.

Harthacnut (Cnut III), king of Denmark and England, r. 1035–1042. The son of Cnut and Emma, Harthacnut succeeded as king in Denmark and England, but in 1037, Harold I usurped the throne of England. In 1038, Harthacnut concluded a fateful agreement with rival Magnus the Good so that he was free to invade England. In 1040, Harthacnut was received in England after Harold's death. Harthacnut died without heirs.

Hastein (ON: Hadding), Viking sea king, c. 855–895. He raided the Carolingian Empire and, in 859–862, commanded with Bjorn Ironside the raid into the Mediterranean. In 882–894, he led the Viking attacks into Wessex.

Helgi the Lean, Norwegian Viking of Hordaland. Around 915–930, Helgi departed Norway and settled in Iceland, reputedly in protest of the tyranny of King Harald Finehair. He invoked Christ as a personal protector, but he also worshiped the ancestral Norse gods.

Henry I the Fowler, king of Germany, r. 919–936. Duke of Saxony, Henry was elected king of Germany by the nobility and founded the Saxon Dynasty. In 934, he campaigned in Jutland, thus provoking the emergence of a Danish kingdom.

Herigar (ON: Hergeir), c. 800–845. The "prefect," perhaps a jarl, of King Bjorn of Birka, he was patron to St. Anskar in 829–831 and built the first church in Sweden.

Hogni. Half-brother of Gunnar in the Volsung cycle. He is depicted as a suspicious advisor to his brother, but he endured a heroic death at the hall of Atli.

Horic (ON: Erik) **the Elder**, king in Denmark, r. 813–854. The Danish king of Hedeby and southern Jutland who received St. Anskar, and permitted the construction of the first church. He was a rival to Harald Klak, the vassal of Louis the Pious.

Hrolf (Rollo), count of Rouen, r. 911–925. Hrolf was a Danish sea king who operated along the Seine from 895. In 911, he received the fief of Normandy from Charles the Simple and transformed his Vikings into landed Christian knights.

Hrolf Kraki (OE: Hrothluf), Skjöldung king of Sjaelland, c. A.D. 550–580 Hrolf ruled from Hleidr as the favorite of Odin and was served by the greatest warriors of Scandinavia. He clashed with rival king Adils of Uppsala. On his famous ride to Uppsala, Hrolf lost Odin's favor, and he and his champions fell in an epic battle at the hall of Adils.

Hugh Capet, king of France, r. 987–996. He was elected king by the Frankish nobility and, thus, established the Capetian dynasty with his capital at Paris.

Hygelac (ON: Hugleik), king of West Gautar (OE: Geatas), c. 490–528. Hygelac was the lord of *Beowulf* and fell in a raid on Frisia. His kingdom included the coastal lands of Sweden north of the Gota River (Västergötland) and around Lake Vaenir.

Ibn Fadlan, Ahmad ibn al-Abbas Rashid ibn Hammad, Arabic geographer. Sent as envoy of the Abbasid Caliph al-Muqtadir to the Bulgars in 921–922. He gave an eyewitness account of the Rus on the Volga.

Igor (ON: Ingvar), prince of Kiev, r. 913–945. The son of Rurik, he launched two naval attacks against Constantinople in 943 and 944 and, thus, obtained a favorable commercial treaty from Byzantine emperor Constantine VII.

Ivar, Viking sea king, c. 914–968. In 914, Ivar arrived in Ireland from Norway and reoccupied Limerick in 919–920. His raids along the Shannon provoked Cennetig (r. 938–954) of the Dal cais family and ruler of Thomond to destroy the Viking base and expel Ivar.

Ivar Ragnarsson the Boneless, Viking sea king, c. 795–873. He and his brother Halfdane, sons of Ragnar, commanded the Great Army that invaded England in 865. Ivar has been identified by some scholars with his namesake, the Norse king of Dublin.

John I Tzimisces, Byzantine emperor, r. 969–976. John overthrew his uncle Nicephorus II for mishandling the invasion of Prince Sviatoslav. In 971, John defeated Sviatoslav at Durostorum and compelled the withdrawal of the Rus from the Balkans.

Julius Caesar, Gaius, 101–44 B.C. Roman senator, dictator, and author. In his commentaries on the conquest of Gaul (*De Bello Gallico*), Caesar provides the earliest description of Germanic society.

Leif Eriksson the Lucky, 982–1025. On orders of Olaf Tryggvason, Leif brought Christianity to the Greenland colonies. In c. 1001, he sailed west along the North American shores, discovering Vinland (Newfoundland). When he succeeded to the leadership of Greenland, his brothers took the initiative of settling Vinland.

Leofric, earl of Mercia, born 968, r. 1016–1057. A leading English noble, Leofric took service with Cnut and gained an earldom. An opponent of Earl Godwin, Leofric is best remembered as the husband of Godgifu, Lady Godiva.

Lothar, Holy Roman Emperor, r. 840–855. Lothar, the eldest son of Louis the Pious, was crowned joint emperor in 817. From 829, he warred with his father and brothers over the succession. At the Treaty of Verdun, he received the Middle Kingdom, the imperial title, and the capitals Aachen and Rome.

Louis III the Stammerer, king of France r. 879–882. This Carolingian king intercepted and defeated a Viking raiding column at the Battle of Sancourt in 881. The event was celebrated in the Old High German epic *Ludwigsleid*.

Louis the German, r. 840–876. The third son of Louis the Pious, he received Eastern Francia by the Treaty of Verdun. He acted as the patron of St. Anskar.

Louis the Pious, Holy Roman Emperor, r. 814–840. The son of Charlemagne, Louis the Pious proved unequal to the task of ruling the Carolingian Empire. From 829, his sons warred over the succession, and Louis proved unable to check Viking attacks.

Mael Sechlainn II, king of Meath, r. 980–1022. He ended Norse military power by defeating Olaf Kvaran at the Battle of Tara (980) and was hailed high king (*andri*) of Ireland. He battled Brian Bóruma successfully in 982–997 and, in 1002, was forced to recognize Brian as high king. In 1014, after Brian's death at the Battle of Clontarf, Mael Sechlainn regained the high kingship and political domination in Ireland.

Magnus the Good, king of Norway, born 1024, r. 1035–1047. The son of St. Olaf, Magnus was received as king after the Norwegians expelled Svein Alfivason. In 1043, he was elected king of Denmark, but he was soon opposed by Svein Estrithson. Magnus accepted as his co-king his uncle Harald Hardardi in 1046, but Magnus died soon afterward.

Magnus III, Barelegs, king of Norway, r. 1093–1103. The son of Harald Kyrri, Magnus revived royal expansion in the British Isles. He led three expeditions to secure the Orkney isles, the Hebrides, and the Isle of Man in 1098 and 1102–1103.

Magnus VI, king of Norway, r. 1263–1280. The son of Hakon IV, Magnus is hailed as the law-mender (*lagabote*), because he codified law in Norway and Iceland. By the Treaty of Perth, he relinquished Norwegian claims to the Isle Man and the Hebrides.

Margaret, queen of Denmark and Norway, born 1353, r. 1375–1412. The daughter of King Valdemar IV, she was married to King Hakon VII of Norway in 1363. By the accidents of dynastic marriages and deaths, she had claims to all three Scandinavian kingdoms. She secured Norway for her great-nephew Eric of Pomerania in 1389. By the Union of Kalmar (1397), Eric succeeded to Margaret in Denmark and Sweden.

Naddod, Viking sea king. In about 865–870, he was credited with discovering Iceland when his ship was blown off course.

Nicephorus II Phocas, Byzantine emperor, r. 963–969. As Domestic of the East, he employed Varangian mercenaries in his reconquest of Crete in 957. As emperor, he precipitated the Rus invasion of the Balkans by directing Prince Sviatoslav to attack Bulgaria. The diplomatic fiasco led to the murder of Nicephorus by his nephew John Tzimisces.

Njal Thorgeirsson, 935–1010. The *godi* and protagonist of *Njal's Saga*, he is depicted as sagacious. He and his friend Gunnar Hamundarson (945–992) negotiated repeatedly out of blood feuds provoked by their wives, Bergthora and Hallgerd. Njal and his family were burned in their farmstead by rivals led by Flosi Thoradsson.

Odo (Eudes), count of Paris, r. 860–888; king of France, r. 888–897. Odo defended Paris against the Vikings in 885–886 and, thus, was elected by the West Frankish nobility as the first king not of the Carolingian house.

Offa, king of Mercia, r. 757–796. A brilliant king, Offa imposed Mercian hegemony over the English kingdoms south of the Humber and fostered religious and cultural life. He constructed Offa's Dyke, an earth wall to mark off the Welsh frontier. He introduced penny coinage to England.

Ohthere (ON: Ottar), c. 890–894. A Norwegian merchant prince, he reported to the court of King Alfred his trading activities and voyage from the Arctic Circle to Kaupang. The account was included in the Old English translation of Orosius.

Olaf, Norse king of Dublin, r. 852–871. He is often identified with his namesake, Olaf the White, in Icelandic saga. In 852, Olaf arrived with a Norwegian fleet and ended Danish rule over Dublin. He and his brother Ivar (r. 871–873) founded the Hiberno-Norse kingdom.

Olaf Guthfrithson, king of Dublin, r. 934–941; king of York, r. 939–941. In 937, Olaf was defeated in his first bid for the throne of York by King Aethelstan at Brunanburh. In 939, Olaf seized York and, in 940, secured the Five Boroughs. His premature death led to the collapse of a Viking kingdom of Dublin and York.

Olaf Haraldsson the Stout, St. Olaf, king of Norway, born c. 995, r. 1015–1030, A Viking sea king, Olaf raided in the Baltic and served under Thorkell the Tall in 1009–1013. In 1013, he entered the service of Aethelred II and embraced Christianity. In 1015, he sailed to Norway. By his victory at Nesjar (1016), he ended the regime of jarls Svein and Erik (sons of Hakon the Great) and was proclaimed king. Olaf alienated his pagan subjects by his assault on the cults, and he clashed with King Cnut. In 1026, he suffered a strategic defeat at the Battle of the Holy Rive, and in 1028, he was driven from Norway. His desperate gamble to retake Norway ended in his defeat and death at the Battle of Stiklestad. Within a year of his death, miracles were proclaimed at his tomb, and Olaf was hailed as the national saint of Norway.

Olaf Hoskuldsson the Peacock, c. 938–1006. The model *godi* in *Laxdaela Saga*, who refused to avenge the death of his son Kjartan at the hands of Kjartan's foster brother Bolli. He could not prevent the blood feud promoted by Gudrun, wife of Bolli and jilted fiancé of Kjartan, and Olaf's wife, Thorgerd.

Olaf Kvaran Sigtyrggson, king of York, r. 941–943, 949–952; king of Dublin, r. 945–980. Twice hailed as Norse king of Dublin, Olaf retired to Dublin. He based his power on his navy, the revenues of the slave trade, and alliances with Irish rulers. He was decisively defeated by Mael Sechlainn at the Battle of Tara in 980.

Olaf Tryggvason, king of Norway, born c. 970, r. 995–1000. A sea king, Olaf raided in the Baltic and the British Isles, where he converted to Christianity. He married Gyda, sister of Olaf Kvaran. In 995, he arrived with a veteran fleet to overthrow Jarl Hakon the Great and was acclaimed king of Norway. Olaf violated customary laws and imposed Christianity on his subjects. At the Battle of Svold (1000), Svein Forkbeard the Norwegian exiles defeated Olaf, who leaped from his flagship, *Long Serpent*, into the sea.

Olof Skötkonung, king of Sweden, r. 995–1022. The son of Erik the Victorious, Olof embraced and ruled from Sigtuna. He was compelled to recognize a Danish overlordship, but he adapted royal institutions of King Cnut the Great.

Oleg (ON: Helgi), prince of Kiev, r. 879–913. Successor to Rurik, Oleg relocated his capital from Novgorod to Kiev. In 907, he launched the second Rus attack on Constantinople and, thus, negotiated a favorable commercial treaty with the emperor Leo VI.

Olga (ON: Helga), queen of Kiev. The wife of Igor, she acted as regent for her son Sviatoslav in 945–964. According to Constantine VII, Olga converted to Christianity upon a state visit to Constantinople (dated to either c. 945 or 957).

Ongendus (ON: Angantyr). A Danish king in Jutland, he rejected the missionary efforts of St. Willibrord in about 700–710. This ruler might have ordered the first phase of construction of the Danevirke.

Ota (ON: Aud; Arabic: Nodd), Norse queen of Dublin, c. 838–847. Wife of Turgeis, Ota acted as *völva* and received al-Ghazal, Umyyad envoy to Majus (Vikings) in 845.

Otto I, king of Germany and Holy Roman Emperor, r. 936–973. The second Saxon king, Otto was crowned Holy Roman Emperor in 962. In about 965, Otto I invaded Jutland to extend Christianity and German influence. Harald Bluetooth, however, converted to Christianity and sought to create his own national church.

Patrick, St., 389–461. The son of a Roman decurion, he was enslaved by Irish pirates at age 16, but he escaped to Gaul and entered the monastery of Lerins. Commissioned apostle to the Irish, Patrick sailed to Ireland circa 432–433 and preached in Ulster, establishing a church at Armagh.

Pepin the Short, king of the Franks, r. 751–768. Pepin founded the Carolingian dynasty. In 756, he endowed the papacy with lands in central Italy (the *Donation of Pepin*), thereby founding the Papal States.

Pytheas of Massilia, Greek explorer and scholar, c. 380–310 B.C. Around 325–315 B.C., Pytheas traveled to Britain and Thule, the latter likely northern Norway. In *On Oceans*, he first described the aurora borealis, the midnight sun, and living conditions north of the Arctic Circle.

Ragnar Lodbrok, Viking sea king, c. 845–865. A legendary Danish Viking, Ragnar was credited with many adventures in the Carolingian world and the attack on Paris in 845. In about 865, he was perhaps captured and executed by King Aelle II of Northumbria.

Richard II, duke of Normandy, r. 996–1026. Richard pursued an alliance with the Capetian monarchy and Aethelred II of England. In 1006, he was elevated to duke and a peer of France. An energetic ruler, Richard dominated northern France and promoted monastic reform.

Rimbert, archbishop of Hamburg-Bremen, r. 865–888. A disciple of St. Anskar, Rimbert penned the *Vita Anskarii* to celebrate his master and advance the see's claims as primate of Scandinavia.

Rognvald, Viking sea king, c. 919–937. Rognvald seized Nantes as a Viking base and raided the lower Loire and Brittany. Rognvald and his Vikings were decisively defeated by Count Alain Barbetorte of Brittany (r. 936–952), who captured Nantes and ended the Viking menace.

Rurik (ON: Erik), Rus prince of Novgorod, c. 860–879. A Viking sea king, Rurik was invited by the warring Slavic tribes to rule over them. Rurik refounded the Rus town Holmgard (Novgorod), and his jarls Dir (ON: Dyr) and Askold (ON: Hoskuld) established another settlement at Kiev. His descendants ruled in Russia down to 1612.

Saxo Grammaticus, 1150–1216. Danish cleric and protégé of Archbishop Absalon, he wrote in Latin *Gesta Danorum*, a history of the Danish kings in 16 books from the legendary Skjold to Valdemar II.

Siegfried (ON: Sigurd), Viking sea king, c. 880–891. This sea king besieged Paris in 885–886 and extorted *danegeld* from Charles the Fat. He was slain at the Battle of the Dyle.

Sigtrygg II, king of Dublin, r. 917–921; king of York, r. 921–927. In 914, this Viking sea king arrived off Ireland and secured Dublin; he defeated high king Niall Glundub in 919. Sigtrygg was driven out of Dublin by his brother Guthfrid and seized Danish York, where he ruled as a vassal of King Aethelstan.

Sigtrygg III Silkbeard, king of Dublin, r. 989–1036. Sigtyrgg, son of Olaf Kvaran and Princess Gormflaith of Leinster, forged the alliance against Brian Bóruma at Clontarf. Sigtrygg maintained a brilliant court, minted the first coins in Ireland, and promoted Christianity.

Sigurd. The son of Sigmund, Sigurd was the hero of the epic cycle of the Volsungs and the favorite of Odin. He slew the dragon Fafnir and gained the treasure of the Niflungs. He burst through the ring of fire to awaken and win Brynhild, but he was duped into marrying Gudrud. He then won, by deception, Brynhild for Gunnar. The wronged Brynhild connived in Sigurd's death, but she joined him on his pyre to enter Valhalla. Sigurd is loosely based on Sigebert, a Frankish king of Austrasia (r. 561–575).

Sigurd Jorsafar, king of Norway, r. 1103–1130. The son of Magnus Barelegs, Sigurd ruled jointly with his brothers Olaf and Eystein. In 1107–1110, Sigurd went on crusade and, in this way, raised the international standing of the Norwegian crown.

Sigurd the Stout, jarl of Orkney, r. 985–1014. A restless Viking sea king, this Sigurd built a powerful jarldom in the British Isles. He fell fighting against Brian Bóruma at the Battle of Clontarf.

Snorri Sturluson, Icelandic writer, poet, and politician, 1179–1242. Snorri composed the *Prose Edda* and the *Heimskringlasaga* and is considered the author of *Egil's Saga*. Twice law-speaker of the *Althing*, he dominated Icelandic politics and gained powerful patrons at the Norwegian court during his visit in 1217–1218. He was murdered by rivals on grounds of treason to King Hakon IV.

Svein Alfivason, king of Norway, r. 1030–1035. The elder son of King Cnut and Aelfgifu (ON: Alfifa), Svein alienated his Norwegian subjects, who drove him into exile and invited Magnus the Good to assume the Norwegian throne. Svein died an exile at Roskilde.

Svein Estrithson, king of Denmark, born c. 1018, r. 1046–1074. The son of Jarl Ulf and Estrith, half-sister of Cnut, Svein warred for Denmark with Magnus the Good and Harald Hardardi (r. 1044–1064). In 1066, he was undisputed king in Denmark, and he consolidated the royal institutions of his uncle, King Cnut.

Svein Forkbeard, king of Denmark, r. 986–1014. The illegitimate son of Harald Bluetooth, Svein overthrew his father. Around 988, his Danish and Jomsviking allies were defeated at Hjorungavag so that Svein faced attacks by his rivals Erik the Victorious and Olaf Tryggvason. From 1003 on, Svein directed attacks on England, and in 1013–1014, he campaigned for the conquest of the island. After his sudden death in 1014, his son Cnut was hailed as king by the Danish army.

Sverker I, king of Sweden, r. 1130–1150. Sverker seized power in a civil war and founded the rival royal line to the family of St. Erik IX. His troubled reign was contested from 1150, and ended completely with his murder in 1156.

Sviatoslav (ON: Sveinheld), prince of Kiev, r. 964–972. The son of Prince Igor, Sviatoslav smashed the Khazar kaganate in about 965. He was defeated by Byzantine emperor John I in an effort to conquer the Balkans (967–971). His death at the hands of the Pechenegs plunged the Rus state into civil war.

Tacitus, Cornelius, c. A.D. 56–115 Roman senator and historian. He composed *Germania* (c. A.D. 98), which is an invaluable source, despite its moralizing bias, for early Germanic society

Thorfinn Karlsefni. He and his wife, Gudrid (widow of Thorvald Eriksson), led Norse settlers who sought to colonize Vinland in 1009–1012.

Thorkell the Tall, Jomsviking and jarl. In about 988, Thorkell commanded the Danish-Jomsviking fleet at Hjorungvag. He led the forces of Svein Forkbeard against England in 1009–1011, but he defected to Aethelred II in 1012–1014. Reconciled to Cnut, he received an earldom in East Anglia in 1017. His sister Gyda married Earl Godwin. Thorkell acted as regent in England from 1019–1020. He was banished by Cnut in 1021 but was restored to favor in Denmark in 1027.

Thorvald Eriksson, died 1005. Younger brother of Leif the Lucky, Thorvald led an expedition to Vinland in 1004–1005. He was mortally wounded in a clash with the Skraelingar.

Thyri, queen of Denmark; see **Gorm the Old**.

Tostig, earl of Northumbria, r. 1055–1065. Son of Earl Godwin, Tostig was expelled from York by his outraged subjects. Morcar, brother of Earl Edwin of Mercia, succeeded in Northumbria. When his brother Harold II refused to restore his earldom, Tostig turned to King Harald Hardardi of Norway. Tostig fell at the Battle of Stamford Bridge.

Turgeis (ON: Thorgils), Norse king of Dublin, r. 838–847. A Viking sea king, Turgeis organized the Norse companies and sacked Armagh, where he performed rites to Thor. He was captured and drowned by King Mael Sechlainn I of Meath.

Ulf Thorkilsson, born c. 995, jarl in Denmark, 1019–1026. Ulf married Estrith, half-sister of Cnut. He ruled Denmark as the deputy of Cnut, but he was executed on grounds of treason at Christmas 1026. His son was King Svein Estrithson.

Unn (or Aud) **the Deep-Minded**. Norwegian lady of Hordaland, she emigrated to Iceland around 915–930, reputedly to escape the rule of Harald Finehair. Unn was remembered in saga as a formidable ancestress of leading families.

Valdemar, king of Sweden, r. 1250–1275. The adolescent son of Earl Birger and Princess Ingeborg, Valdemar was elected king and, thus, founded the Folkung dynasty (1250–1363).

Valdemar I the Great, king of Denmark, r. 1157–1182. Valdemar and his counselor, Absalon, restored royal authority and waged crusades against the Wends. Valdemar forged royal fiscal and legal institutions and patronized arts and letters; thus, his reign is considered the zenith of medieval Denmark.

Valdemar II, king of Denmark, r. 1202–1241. The younger son of Valdemar I, he succeeded his brother, Cnut; continued expansion in the Baltic; and advanced royal justice. He led three crusades against the Estonians in 1210–1219, but he was forced to relinquish all Danish conquests, save Rugen and Estonia, after his defeat at the hands of his German vassals at the Battle of Bornhöved in 1227.

Valdemar IV, king of Denmark, r. 1340–1375. He restored royal power within Denmark and recaptured Scania and Gotland in 1361, but he failed to curb the privileges of the Hanseatic League. His daughter Queen Margaret realized Valdemar's plans of uniting the three Scandinavian realms under one crown.

Vladimir (ON: Valdemar), prince of Kiev, r. 980–1015. The son of Sviatoslav, Vladimir reunited the Rus principalities and converted to Orthodox Christianity in 988 or 989. He laid the foundations of the Slavic Russian state.

Weland (ON: Volund), Viking sea king, c. 858–862. Weland raided along the Somme Valley. In 858, Charles the Bald contracted with Weland to attack the Viking base at Oissel. Weland, who embraced Christianity, permitted the Vikings of Oissel to depart on payment of ransom. He was killed in a private quarrel with a pagan follower.

Widukind, died c. 808. Widukind led the Saxon rebellion against Charlemagne in 777–778 and received assistance from the Danes. In 785, he submitted to Charlemagne and received baptism and a fief.

William I the Conqueror, king of England, born c. 1028, r. 1066–1087. The illegitimate son of Duke Robert I and Herleva, William was acclaimed duke in 1035. He matured into a brilliant ruler. In 1066, he conquered England and forged an Anglo-Norman monarchy.

Willibrord, St., c. 657–738. A Northumbrian monk, Willibrord was commissioned apostle to the Frisians in 695 and ordained as the first bishop of Utrech. In around 700–710, he led the first mission to Jutland but failed to convert King Onegendus.

Yaroslav the Wise, prince of Kiev, r. 1019–1054. A son of Vladimir, Yaroslav defeated his rival brother, Svyatopolk (r. 1015–1019), and united the Russian principalities. He forged an Orthodox Slavic kingdom, but he also hosted Scandinavian visitors and exiles and maintained his own Varangian Guard.

Bibliography

General Studies:

Abrams, Holger. *The Vikings*. Translated by A. Binns. New York: Frederick A. Praeger, 1961. A survey with emphasis on archaeology and material life in Scandinavia.

Brondsted, J. *The Vikings*. Translated by K. Skov. Baltimore: Penguin Books, 1960. Replaced by Roesdahl but still excellent on archaeology

Christiansen, Eric. *The Norsemen in the Viking Age*. London: Blackwell's Publishers, 2002. Emphasizes material life and society in Scandinavia.

Foote, Peter, and David M. Wilson. *The Viking Achievement: The Society and Culture of Early Medieval Scandinavia*. London: Sidgwick and Jackson, 1970. Classic study with excellent discussion of arts and literature.

Graham-Campbell, J. *The Viking World*. New Haven: Ticknor and Fields, 1980. Lavishly illustrated, oversized book with fine discussions on arts, sites, and shipbuilding.

Jones, Gwyn. *A History of the Vikings*. Oxford: Oxford University Press, 1968. Classic political and military narrative of Vikings at home and overseas to 1066.

Logan, F. Donald. *The Vikings in History*. London: Hutchinson and Company Publishers, 1983. Strong on western Viking voyages.

Oxenstierna, Eric. *The Norsemen*. Translated by C. Hutter. Greenwich: New York Graphics Society, 1959. Recommended for discussion of trade routes and goods.

Roesdahl, Else. *The Vikings*. Translated by S. M. Margeson and K. Williams. 2nd ed. Baltimore: Penguin Books, 1998. Recommended introduction to be used in tandem with the Penguin atlas of John Haywood.

Sawyer, Birgit, and Peter Sawyer. *Medieval Scandinavia from Conversion to the Reformation, c. 800–1500*. Minneapolis: University of Minnesota Press, 1993. Excellent on social history and Scandinavia in the later Middle Ages.

Sawyer, Peter H. *The Age of the Vikings*. London: Edward Arnold, 1971. Seminal revisionist study on the Vikings.

———, ed. *The Oxford Illustrated History of the Vikings*. Oxford: Oxford University Press, 1997. Collection of articles on specific topics.

Reference Works:

Haywood, John. *The Penguin Atlas of the Vikings*. New York: Penguin Books, 1995. Excellent selection of maps best used in tandem with Rosedahl's survey

Lindow, John. *Norse Mythology: A Guide to Gods, Heroes, Rituals, and Beliefs*. Oxford: Oxford University Press, 2001. A useful reference work.

Pulsiano, P., and K. Wolf, eds. *Medieval Scandinavia: An Encyclopedia*. New York: Garland Publishing, 1993. Strong on literature and social history.

Sources in Translation:

Adam of Bremen. *History of the Archbishops of Hamburg-Bremen*. Translated by F. J. Tschan. New York: Columbia University Press, 1993. Indispensable source for Christianity in Scandinavia.

Alexander, M., trans. *The Earliest English Poems*. Baltimore: Penguin Books, 1966. Selection includes Old English heroic literature other than *Beowulf*.

Byock, Jesse, trans. *The Saga of King Hrolf Kraki*. New York: Penguin Books, 1998. Readable modern translation with excellent notes. Recommended for the heroic temper of the Viking Age.

———, trans. *The Saga of the Volsungs*. New York: Penguin Books, 1990. Readable modern translation with excellent notes.

Cook, R., trans. *Njal's Saga*. New York: Penguin Books, 1997. Readable modern translation with excellent notes on the longest and most celebrated family saga.

Douglas, David C. *English Historical Documents*. Vol. 1, 2nd ed. London: Methuen, 1979. Translation of all essential sources for English history during the period 500–1042.

Fell, C. E., and N. Lund, trans. *Two Voyagers at the Court of King Alfred: The Ventures of Ohthere and Wulfstan Together with the Description of Northern Europe from the Old English Orosius*. York: William Sessions, 1984. Crucial sources for trade and geography of Viking Age Scandinavia.

Fox, D., and H. Palsson, trans. *Grettir's Saga*. Toronto: University of Toronto Press, 1964. Recommended saga for the adventure of the Viking Age.

Gantz, Jeffrey, trans. *Early Irish Myths and Sagas*. New York: Penguin Books, 1981. Recommended start for comparative Celtic literature.

Helmold. *The Chronicle of the Slavs*. Translated by F. J. Tschan. New York: Columbia University Press, 1935. An important source on German-Danish relations.

Hollander, Lee M., trans. *The Poetic Edda*. Austin: University of Texas Press, 1962. The best modern translation of the poems.

———, trans. *The Saga of the Jomsviking*. Austin: University of Texas Press, 1955. Exciting saga of late Viking Age Scandinavia.

Jones, Gwyn., trans. *Erik the Red and Other Icelandic Sagas*. Oxford: Oxford University Press, 1961. Recommended for short family sagas.

Keynes, S., and M. Lapidge, trans. *Asser's Life of Alfred and Other Contemporary Sources*. New York: Penguin Books, 1983. Recommended collection of sources on King Alfred the Great.

Magnusson, M., and H. Palsson, trans. *Laxdaela Saga*. New York: Penguin Books, 1969. The most romantic and appealing of the family sagas.

———, trans. *The Vinland Sagas: The Norse Discovery of Americ.* Baltimore: Penguin Books, 1965. The two sources on the Norse settlement of Vinland.

Nelson, J. L., trans. *The Annals of St-Bertin*. Manchester: Manchester University Press, 1991. The main Carolingian chronicle on Viking raids.

Page, R. I. *Chronicles of the Vikings: Records, Memorials and Myths*. Toronto: University of Toronto Press, 1995. Useful collection of diverse sources.

Palsson H., trans. *Hrafnkel's Saga and Other Stories*. Baltimore: Penguin Books, 1971. A collection of delightful family sagas.

Palsson, H., and P. Edwards, trans. *Eyrbyggja Saga*. Rev. ed. New York: Penguin Books, 1989. Recommended saga on Icelandic blood feud and family.

————, trans. *Egil's Saga*. New York: Penguin Books, 1976. Saga of the swashbuckling Viking Egil.

————, trans. *Knytlinga Saga: The History of the Kings of Denmark*. Odense: Odense University Press, 1986. Older, dated translation of Cnut and the Danish kings.

————, trans. *Orkneyinga Saga: The History of the Earls of Orkney*. New York: Penguin Books, 1978. The heroicized settlement of the western islands.

————, trans. *Seven Viking Romances*. New York: Penguin Books, 1986. Highly recommended selection.

Saxo Grammaticus. *The History of the Danes, Books I–IX*. Edited and translated by H. E. Davidson and Peter Fisher. Woodbridge: Boyell and Brewer, 1998: Translation of only the legendary books.

Smiley, J., and R. Kellogg, eds. *The Sagas of the Icelanders: A Selection*. New York: Penguin Books, 1997: A recommended introduction to the range of family sagas.

Sturluson, Snorri. *Edda*. Translated by A. Faulkes. London: Everyman, 1987. Currently the only complete translation in English but in a stilted style.

————. *King Harald's Saga*. Translated by M. Magnusson and H. Palsson. Baltimore: Penguin Books, 1966. A modern translation of the saga of King Harald Hardardi taken from *Hemiskringla*; recommended.

————. *Heimskringla: History of the Kings of Norway*. Translated by Lee M. Hollander. Austin: University of Texas Press, 1964. Highly recommended source for the Viking Age.

————. *The Prose Edda: Tales from Norse Mythology*. Translated by J. I. Young. Berkeley: University of California Press, 1965. Readable selections of parts 1 and 2 of Snorri's handbook.

Truso, J. F., ed. *Beowulf: The Donaldson Translation, Backgrounds and Sources, Criticism*. New York: W. W. Norton and Company, 1975. Recommended translation with excellent articles and notes putting the poem in a Scandinavian context.

Whaley, D., trans. *Sagas of Warrior-Poets*. New York: Penguin Books, 1997. Recommended selection.

Whitelock, Dorothy, ed. and trans. *The Anglo-Saxon Chronicle: A Revised Translation*. London: Eyre and Spottiswoode, 1965. An indispensable source.

Monographs:

Abels, Richard. *Alfred the Great: War, Kingship and Culture in Anglo-Saxon England*. London: Longman, 1998. Recommended biography

Bagge, Sverre. *Society and Politics in Snorri Sturluson's Heimskringla*. Berkeley: University of California Press, 1991. A fine scholarly study on medieval Norway and Snorri.

Bates, David. *Normandy before 1066*. London: Longman, 1982. Recommended modern study.

Blackburn, M. A. S., ed. *Anglo-Saxon Monetary History: Essays in Memory of Michael Dolley*. Leicester: Leicester University Press, 1986. Selection of learned essays but premised on Dolley's implausible reconstruction of Anglo-Saxon coinage and royal finances.

———, and D. N. Dumville. *Kings, Currency, and Alliances: History and Coinage of Southern England in the Ninth Century*. Woodbridge: Boydell Press, 1998. Includes scholarly articles on coinage to elucidate the Vikings in England.

Blair, P. H. *An Introduction to Anglo-Saxon England*. 3rd ed. Cambridge: Cambridge University Press, 2003. Best introduction to Anglo-Saxon England.

———. *The World of Bede*. Cambridge: Cambridge University Press, 1970. Recommended study for early Anglo-Saxon intellectual life.

Blondal, Sifgus. *The Varangians of Byzantium: An Aspect of Byzantine Military History*. Translated and revised by B. S. Benedikz. Cambridge: Cambridge University Press, 1978. Recommended introduction.

Blunt, C. E., B. H. I. Stewart, and C. S. S. Lyon. *Coinage in Tenth-Century England from Edward the Elder to Edgar's Reform*. Oxford: Oxford University Press, 1989. A collection of studies also premised on the implausible Dolley thesis.

Brogger, A. W., and H. Shetelig. *The Viking Ships*. New York: Twayne Publishers, 1971. A classic study.

Bruce-Mitford, R., ed. *Recent Archaeological Reports in Europe*. London: Routledge and Keegan, 1975. A collection of scholarly articles on northern Europe in the Celtic, Roman, and Viking Ages.

Byock, Jesse. *Viking Age Iceland*. New York: Penguin Books, 2001. A brilliant work on society and sagas; a model study.

Chadwick, Nora. *The Celts*. Baltimore: Penguin Books, 1970. A survey of literary sources and archaeology of the Celts of the British Isles before the Viking Age.

Christiansen, Eric. *The Northern Crusades*. 2nd ed. New York: Penguin Books, 1997: Excellent study on Scandinavia and the Baltic in the later Middle Ages.

Clarke, H., and B. Ambrosiani. *Towns in the Viking Age*. Leicester: Leicester University Press, 1991. An important scholarly study.

Crumlin-Pedersen, Ole, ed. *The Skuldelev Ships I: Topography, Archaeology, History, Conservation, and Display*. Roskilde/Oxford: Oxbow Books, 2004. Study and analysis of the important finds of Viking ships.

Davidson, H. R. Ellis. *Gods and Myths of Northern Europe*. Baltimore: Penguin Books, 1964. Recommended study.

———. *Myths and Symbols in Pagan Europe: Early Scandinavian and Celtic Religions*. Syracuse: Syracuse University Press, 1988. Judicious comparison of Germanic and Celtic cults; fine use of archaeology and classical literary texts.

De Vries, J. *Heroic Song and Heroic Legend*. Translated by B. J. Timmer. Oxford: Oxford University Press, 1963. Older but recommended introduction.

De Vries, Kelly. *The Norwegian Invasion of England in 1066*. Woodbridge: Boydell Press, 1999. Detailed military study of the invasion of Harald Hardardi.

Dolley, Michael. *Viking Coins of the Danelaw and of Dublin*. London: British Museum, 1965. Illustrated handbook.

Duffy, Sean. *Ireland in the Middle Ages*. New York: St. Martin's Press, 1987. Standard political and genealogical narrative of Celtic Ireland with little attention to the Norse.

Dumezil, Georges. *Gods of the Ancient Northmen*. Translated and edited by H. Haugar. Berkeley: University of California Press, 1973. Provocative and controversial anthropological analysis.

Forte, A., R. Gram, and F. Pedersen. *Viking Empires*. Cambridge: Cambridge University Press, 2005. New study of the Viking impact in the British Isles with an up-to-date bibliography.

Geary, Patrick J. *Before France and Germany: The Creation and Transformation of the Merovingian World*. Oxford: Oxford University Press, 1988. Best introduction for the Age of Migrations.

Grierson, Philip, and Mark Blackburn. *Medieval European Coinage I: The Early Middle Ages (5th–10th Centuries)*. Cambridge: Cambridge University Press, 1986. Superb study on coinage and history in the early medieval West.

Halsall, Guy. *Warfare and Society in the Barbarian West, 450–900*. New York: Routledge, 2003. Recommended introduction with a fine bibliography of older literature.

Hansen, I. L., and C. Wickham, eds. *The Long Eighth Century: Production, Distribution and Demand*. Leiden: Brill, 2000: Seminal scholarly articles on economic history.

Haskins, Charles H. *The Normans in European History*. New York: Houghton Mifflin Company, 1915. Classic study.

Hodges, Richard. *Dark Age Economics: The Origins of Towns and Trade, A.D. 600–1000*. 2nd ed. London: Duckworth, 1989. Analysis based on new archaeology.

———. *Towns and Trade in the Age of Charlemagne*. London: Duckworth, 2003. Fine study of the strength of the Carolingian economy.

———, and David Whitehouse. *Mohammed, Charlemagne and the Origins of Europe*. Ithaca: Cornell University Press, 1983. Recommended introduction to early medieval trade.

Howard, Ian. *Swein Forkbeard's Invasions and the Danish Conquest of England, 991–1017*. Woodbridge: Boydell Press, 2003. Recommended study, with an excellent discussion on the formation of the Danish kingdom.

Ingstad, H., and A. S. Ingstad. *The Viking Discovery of America: The Excavations of the Norse Settlement in L'Anse aux Meadows, Newfoundland*. New York: Checkmark Books, 2001. Definitive study of the site in Newfoundland and evaluation of the sagas.

Klindt-Jensen, Ole. *Denmark before the Vikings*. London: Thames and Hudson, 1957. A sound archaeological study.

Lawson, M. K. *Cnut: The Danes in England in the Eleventh Century*. London: Longman, 1993. Recommended modern biography; strong on the institutions in England.

Lyon, H. R. *The Vikings in Britain*. New York: St. Martin's Press, 1977. Recommended survey of legal sources, archaeology, and place names, especially important for Vikings in Scotland..

McCormick, Michael. *Origins of the European Economy: Communications and Commerce, A.D 300–900*. Cambridge: Cambridge University Press, 2002. Major study on the European economy.

Nelson, J. L. *Charles the Bald*. London: Longman, 1992. Recommended biography.

Petersson, H. B. A. *Anglo-Saxon Currency: King Edgar's Reform to the Norman Conquest*. Lund: Berlingska Boktryckeriet, 1969. Important collection on the coin hoards in Scandinavia but flawed in its interpretation of the production and distribution of Anglo-Saxon coins.

Randsborg, K. *The Viking Age in Denmark: The Formation of a State*. New York: St. Martin's Press, 1980. Recommended study that makes fine use of rune stones as a source of social history.

Riché, Pierre. The *Carolingians: A Family Who Forged Europe*. Translated by M. I. Allen. Philadelphia: University of Pennsylvania Press, 1993. Recommended introduction.

Rollason, David. *Northumbria, 500–1100: Creation and Destruction of a Kingdom*. Cambridge: Cambridge University Press, 2003. Wide-ranging scholarly study on northern England.

Russell, J. C. *The Germanization of Early Medieval Christianity: A Sociohistorical Approach to Religious Transformation*. Oxford: Oxford University Press, 1994. A ponderously written analysis of Christianizing but a useful collection of sources and bibliography.

Sawyer, Birgit. *The Viking-Age Rune-Stones: Custom and Commemoration in Early Medieval Scandinavia*. Oxford: Oxford University Press, 2000. Sophisticated use of rune stones as sources of social history.

Sawyer, Peter H. *Kings and Vikings*. London: Methuen, 1982. Recommended survey.

Smith, B., ed. *Britain and Ireland, 900–1300: Insular Responses to Medieval European Change*. Cambridge: Cambridge University Press, 1999. A collection of provocative articles on the Viking impact.

Smyth, Alfred P. *King Alfred the Great*. Oxford: Oxford University Press, 1995. Major bibliography, but speculative and based on a questionable interpretation of sources.

———. *Scandinavian Kings in the British Isles, 850–880*. Oxford: Oxford University Press, 1977. Controversial study on political history.

———. *Scandinavian York and Dublin: The History and Archaeology of Two Related Viking Kingdoms*. New Jersey: Templekeiran Press, 1979. A telling comparison of two Viking societies but controversial in its political history.

Spufford, Peter. *Money and Its Use in Medieval Europe*. Cambridge: Cambridge University Press, 1988. Recommended study on the role of medieval coinage.

Turville-Petre, G. *The Heroic Age of Scandinavia*. London: Hutchinson's University Library, 1951. A thoughtful study of the period from the Age of Migrations through the Viking Age by a great literary scholar.

Unger, R. W. *The Ship in the Medieval Economy, 600–1600*. London/Montreal, 1980. An excellent study.

Verhulst, A. *The Carolingian Economy*. Cambridge: Cambridge University Press, 2002. Fine use of archaeology and text to demonstrate economic growth and trade.

Williams, Ann. *Aethelred the Unready*. London: Hambledon and London, 2003. The newest study with a bibliography that includes older literature.

Wilson, David M., and O. Klindt-Jensen. *Viking Art*. 2nd ed. London: George Allen and Unwin, 1986. The standard study.

Internet Resources:

http://www.anth.ucsb.edu/faculty/walker/Iceland/mosfell.html. The website of Professor Jesse Byock, University of California, Los Angeles, leading authority on Viking Age Iceland, with information on his archaeological project in the Mosfell Valley.

http://www.gettysburg.edu/~cfee/courses/English4012001/English40 12001.html. The website of Professor Christopher Fee, University of Gettysburg, with emphasis on Viking settlement in the British Isles.

http://www.vikings.ucla.edu. An additional website from Jesse Byock.

http://viking.hgo.se/. The website of the popular *Viking Heritage* publication.

http://www.bbc.co.uk/history/programmes/bloodofthevikings/. The website of the BBC documentary.

http://www.vikinganswerlady.com/varangians.htm. A popular summary of Vikings in the East, with a useful introductory bibliography.

http://ww.vikingart.com/VikingArt.htm. A useful website, with an introduction and illustrations of the main Viking decorative styles.

http://www.worldofthvikings.com/. Guide to Viking sources on the Internet.